Networking China

THE GEOPOLITICS OF INFORMATION

Edited by Dan Schiller, Pradip Thomas, and Yuezhi Zhao

A list of books in the series appears at the end of this book.

Networking China

The Digital Transformation of the Chinese Economy

YU HONG

Urbana, Chicago, and Springfield

© 2017 by the Board of Trustees
of the University of Illinois
All rights reserved
1 2 3 4 5 C P 5 4 3 2 1
♾ This book is printed on acid-free paper.

Cataloging-in-Publication Data is available on the Library
of Congress Website.
ISBN 978-0-252-04091-7 (cloth: alk.)
ISBN 978-0-252-08239-9 (paper: alk.)
ISBN 978-0-252-09943-4 (ebook)

Contents

Introduction: China, Crisis, and Communications   1

1. Driving Capitalism to Western China:
   IT and the Unwieldy Export-Processing Regime   14

2. Repurposing Telecoms for Capital:
   Networking and Inequality   35

3. Forging Broadband for the Commanding-Heights Economy:
   State-Business Relations in Networking   51

4. Making a Home-Base Strategy: 3G and 4G Mobile Communications
   and Industrial Policy   79

5. Recasting the Media System: Network Convergence
   and Digital TV   101

6. Building Network Nation: Domestic Thrusts
   and Global Impacts   123

   Conclusion: Communications and China's Political Economy   147

   Appendix   155

   Notes   157

   Index   211

Networking China

Introduction
China, Crisis, and Communications

On January 21, 2015, Chinese Premier Li Keqiang delivered a most anticipated speech at the World Economic Forum's annual meeting in Davos, Switzerland. After reviewing the worrisome situation of worldwide deflation and slow recovery ever since the 2008 economic crisis, he assured the global audience of an optimistic outlook for the Chinese economy. In his speech, the premier called for fostering new growth engines in China and expressed his determination to push forward a restructuring plan. In Davos and on many other occasions, Premier Li and his new administration indicated that communications, across its entire range from telecommunications to broadband and from wireless networks to digital media, is a key pivot of making a sustainable economic recovery. Later in 2015, this optimism for communications culminated in the domestic policy Internet Plus intended for economic restructuring. Internet-related business is seen as a boon to the nation, and networking and computing technologies are expected to retool traditional industry and commerce.

The premier's speech, lauded by foreign observers for its reassuring message, and the media attention it received illuminate several current encompassing themes. Crisis and restructuring are the first and foremost keywords for the post-2008 global economy, and China and the communications industry are two leading engines. *Networking China: The Digital Transformation of the Chinese Economy* examines the genesis, mechanisms, and dynamics of forging a network-based economy in China during the crisis and the restructuring act that followed.

This volume focuses on policy and political-economic transformations accompanying the formation of an encompassing, ubiquitous, and strategic sector. Traversing hardware manufacturing, network operation and management, and digital media, this book investigates major pressure points where sector-specific transformations interact with the broader context of crisis and rebalancing. It explicates why and how communications has become a pillar industry the Chinese state designated to power China's political economy forward out of the stagnation that still afflicts the greater capitalist world economy. This book also delineates some leading internal contradictions and international constraints that accompany the central position assigned to communications in the economic restructuring plan and, paradoxically, limit and hinder this networking-for-restructuring program even as it gathers momentum.

Contexts: Crisis, Communications, and Restructuring

The global economic crisis that the 2008 US housing bubble triggered defines today's world. China has not been immune from the aftermath. What is less evident is that the country itself was also part of the historical buildup to the 2008 crisis. In the 1980s, China's reentry into global capitalism coincided with the neoliberal policy–accelerated expansion of transnational capital. At the behest of foreign capital, the state poured resources into an export-processing sector in the name of industrialization and modernization. For the following decades, China derived its phenomenal growth from the low-wage mode of accumulation and from heavy investment in production facilities, basic infrastructure, and real estate.

China's economic miracle, however, is part of a global scale of imbalances. In the run-up to the 2008 crisis, unsustainable economic dynamics prevailed: as the downstream processing-and-assembly hub in the Asia-based production network, China produces the world's largest volumes of consumer goods for export, its export hinging on leveraged spending in the global north, especially the United States. Despite stagnation in wages and in private-sector job growth, US household consumption as a share of the gross domestic product (GDP) still moved up from 66 percent in the late 1990s to over 70 percent in 2007, contributing approximately 16 percent of world output and making the United States the leader. As economist Martin Hart-Landsberg notes, no country is ready to replace the United States as the global pole of consumption that sustains the engine of globalized production.[1]

The highly leveraged spending created a broken balance sheet for the United States, helping to lead to the housing bubble's sudden explosion and the financial meltdown on Wall Street. On the other side of the Pacific Ocean, China faced a different set of serious problems, including downstream positions in the global division of labor, uneven regional development, and the rise of social and labor tensions. All of these compounded the global crises. In the ensuing rally at the 2009 G20 Leaders' Summit for economic rebalancing, the goal of changing the status quo called for intervention with power relations at home and abroad.[2] The Chinese state, however, had partially lost authority over its export economy to transnational capital. Thus, prior to the 2008 economic crisis, the state's efforts to rebalance the Chinese economy had been little more than rhetoric.

The sudden decline of global export markets forced the Chinese state to take increasingly decisive and systematic actions to diversify the economy in a way never seen before. The state defines economic restructuring as a purposeful transition from the export- and investment-driven growth to a consumption-based and innovation-driven economy. The state pledges to cultivate more-sophisticated divisions of labor, foster domestic-consumption capacity, and encourage innovation and entrepreneurship. As imbalances exploded in the liberalized global sector of the economy, major restructuring measures had to pivot on the state-controlled sector "inside the system."[3] In this context, the state declared communications, preferably the state-controlled division, would be its next pillar industry, using it as a lever to achieve restructuring goals, such as reversing domestic residential underconsumption, correcting innovation deficits in manufacturing, and ameliorating social and regional inequalities.

Global capitalism and its crises have had intricate relationships with communications. In *Digital Depression* (2014), Dan Schiller unravels the ways in which communications becomes "an emerging pivot of the ever-mutating capitalist political economy" and how market-oriented deployment of communications is responsible for exacerbating some unresolved structural contradictions. In transnational production and the accompanying program of market coordination, corporate power has systematically utilized information and communications technology (ICT). Productivity and efficiency, as a result, reached unprecedented heights, albeit reinforcing chronic overcapacity, corporate consolidation, and labor exploitation. In the realm of finance, "network-enabled financialization" accelerates capital's circulation but worsens the debt-driven imbalance and adds further volatility and risk to the system.[4] Indeed, communications affects the political economy of global capitalism and plays a substantive role in capitalist crises.

An overview clarifies the central position China assigned to the communications industry in the economic restructuring plan: Telecommunications operators are competing to expand their wired and wireless broadband networks under the state's new national broadband strategy. Broadband is already expected to become the platform for twenty-first-century trade in a new breed of software and information technology (IT) services, such as logistics, e-commerce, and consulting. Cloud computing and the internet of things, two most promising ICT applications, are seen as new, trillion-dollar information-service industries, capable of transforming the wider economy and social life. By modernizing the network infrastructure, state planners also hope to build more-competitive ICT manufacturing industries, ending China's overdependence upon foreign corporations for industrial and technological capacities and possibly turning the country into a global ICT leader. Finally, distribution networks are becoming more mobile, digital, and ubiquitous—and this is accompanying an astronomical expansion of production and consumption of content, applications, and services, all required for a new information economy.

Although promising as an abstract idea, actual restructuring processes are rife with contradictions and surprises, and the promise of communications for general economic recovery and development should not be taken for granted. On China's domestic front, globalization, decentralization, and marketization have made conceptualizing one coherent "national" plan increasingly difficult. Fragmented class interests, incompatible regional experiments, self-serving bureaucratic interests, and competing developmental visions are pulling the rebalancing in different directions. In view of the tensioned influences of global and domestic dynamics, between state socialist principles and capitalist fundamentals and between elitist modernization drives and grassroots demands for equity, this book investigates their expressions in the field of communications and addresses how they limit the economic restructuring when communications takes up a pivotal role.

The process of constructing an encompassing sector of the communications industries is not a simple matter, either, and is contingent upon the forces and actors driving the process. To understand the nature of China's restructuring process in the realm of communications, its key players, and their respective strategies and interests, this book examines the political economy of communications, focusing on how the state, in conjunction with market forces and class interests, constructs and realigns this designated pillar sector and on how these processes affect the accompanying power dynamics. This book asks the following questions: What verifiable policy and political-economy transformations accompany the realignment and construction of a strategic sector? Do state policies improve China's ability on both the domestic and international fronts to control, influence, and profit from information, communications, and culture—and why? How does the state harness the capital to create new spaces of production and consumption?[5] To what extent are state mandates carried out? How are competing interests expressed in policy implementation and with what implications?

The crisis in the Chinese economy is a result not only of capitalist dynamics but also of social relations and class politics. Achieving the goal of restructuring, thus, requires challenging certain power interests, including a fundamental change in the old practices of sacrificing labor rights, social needs, and domestic capacity for sustaining an export-processing economy. In what ways, if any, does China's political-economic restructuring redistribute power and resources to disadvantaged social groups and regions? Or is restructuring merely a pragmatic compromise to maintain economic growth? And have the normative views on the proper relationship of the state, the market, and the society undergone a significant paradigm shift? Premised on Philip Huang's conceptualization about the dominant purpose of state intervention in the economy, this book asks an additional question: is China going further down the path of "state capitalism" or adjusting its course to give "real substance to the official rhetoric of socialist market economy," emphasizing equity and common prosperity?[6]

The stakes are high. Transnational corporate capital has controlled global production and exploited global labor and, thus, caused incessant stagnation.[7] The question, will China's actions of further embracing communications, to rejuvenate the economic system and renegotiate the country's relationship with global capitalism, provide relief or drag the world further into crisis, has impact on the global capitalist system as a whole. One proposition of the current volume is that instead of challenging head-on the low-wage mode of capital accumulation, the state and Chinese ruling elites have prioritized communications industries and policies as technological fixes. That is, the crux of the restructuring measures is to subject the realm of communications to an intensified, sweeping corporate transformation, resulting in investment drives and profit-making industries. Although an expected result is to turn China into a new center for accumulation with self-generated dynamics, the restructuring implemented as the state-led corporatization is likely to reinforce many of the existing dynamics because the ensuing spending binges paid insufficient attention to social need—despite qualitative changes the restructuring brought about in the state-dominated realm of communications.

Themes: Chinese Economy, the State, and Digital Capitalism

This book fits into a wider discussion about the information society, network society, and digital economy. What is at stake is the character of change,[8] with systematic reference to China. To borrow from the summary by Randolph Kluver and Chen Yang, the prevalent framing questions in the burgeoning Chinese internet research are: Can the state-guided economy build a free-market internet, and can the authoritarian state control it?[9] Unfortunately, these starting points, either premised on market-based technological modernization or concerned with usage and censorship of new digital technology, have engendered major gaps in research because they force China's communications into a dichotomous state-market and state-information framing. The political-economic dynamics featuring complex, evolving, and contingent interactions among the state, the market, and the society are tantalizingly overlooked, and the role of the state is undeservingly simplified.

In new-media studies on China, research on pluralistic uses of new technology has provided much-needed insight on meanings and practices in highly situated contexts. This "demand-side" or "user-based" approach,[10] however, tends to take the structural power of the production and consumption of new media as a given, abstract, and remote backdrop. Robin Mansell's critique about the state of the field still holds force today: "What the internet means—and for whom it has meaning—is debated in a manner that is detached from the way in which power is embedded in, and experienced through, the new media."[11] In view of complex and even conflicting empirical evidence for abundance and scarcity, pluralism and inequality, and change and continuity, new-media studies on China, in particular, need an updated, structural examination of broader social and economic dynamics.[12]

Like many other developing countries, China, by riding digital networks, is "de-Westernizing" global communications and rejoining the transnational corporate structure at once.[13] Therefore, there is surging demand for repositioning empirical ideas about communications in connection with different yet interrelated domestic and international political-economic dynamics. Rather than reify China exceptionalism in the networked age and posit some intrinsic sociopolitical logic of the ostensibly insulated communications system, this volume situates the contention and difference that China projects within the larger trend of global convergence, attending the tensioned interactions between China's integration with global digital capitalism, on the one hand, and domestic policy and politics of media, technology, and telecommunications, on the other.

Specifically, this volume places the swiftly changing communications landscape of China within the political economy of Chinese-style capitalism, which is intricately intertwined with the world economy. On the one hand, transformation in and around China's communications, or the rise of the digital economy in general, is constitutive of the transformation of global capitalism.

On the other, the global expansion of digital capitalism—led by transnational corporations headquartered in the Organization for Economic Cooperation and Development (OECD) nations—does not generate a singular trend worldwide but intensifies uneven and contradictory development of markets, regulations, and social relations.[14] Therefore, the different, interrelated, and contingent processes of forging the digital economy are the focus of this book, which is intended to illuminate the constitutive role of the state that both contends and overlaps with domestic and transnational corporate dynamics in recasting China's communications ecosystem into a Chinese variant of digital capitalism.

CHINESE ECONOMY

An abundance of literature exists on Chinese-style capitalism, on the one hand, and the Chinese communications industry, on the other.[15] This segmented approach reflects not only disciplinary divisions but also a shared underestimation of communications, across its entire range from telecommunications to broadband and from wireless networks to digital media, as a key economic sector, indispensable infrastructure, and a pivotal site of political-economic transformation. One sensibility that informs this book is highlighting why and how communications is central to Chinese-style capitalism and its ongoing reconfiguration.

A mere recital of figures sheds some light. ICT manufacturing, in 2011, contributed 8.9, 6.1, and 31 percent to China's industrial revenue, industrial profit, and total export and import, respectively. In the world, China is the largest producer of color televisions, mobile phones, and computers, and China's income from software development surpassed 15 percent of the global total.[16] Serving the world's largest number of internet and telephone users, Chinese telecom operators have accounted for a significant share of central state-owned assets since 2003, exceeding 21 percent.[17] In 2014 internet-related business accounted for 7 percent of the country's GDP.[18] Overall, hardware, software, and service production, along with advanced telecom networks, have been central to the Chinese economy.

Communications is also central to China's ongoing economic transformation. As David Harvey reminds us, the vitality of capitalism hinges upon "finding reinvestment opportunities for a portion of the surplus produced yesterday." Opening up new product lines and creating wholly new sectors of industry are major solutions.[19] Critical scholars in North America have problematized such renewal of capitalist growth in the global epicenter, the United States. In *Information and the Crisis Economy* (1986), Herbert Schiller underscores the Western capitalist crises in the 1970s, explicating the beginning of rewiring the whole society as a way of combating acute economic downturns and political crises. Dan Schiller in *Digital Capitalism* (1999) further traces on both the domestic and international fronts the full-blown digital economy expanding to the global scale as well as domestic markets—deepening processes in a range of ICT-penetrated socioeconomic sectors.

Now, a logical extension, in a changed global context, is to examine how China—pressed by its deepened entanglement with the global economy and growing share of capitalist crises—takes up communications to address its own developmental problems. Although China in the past three decades transformed itself into a global production base to absorb transnational capital, it is time for the country to construct its own "strategic" industries. For Chinese ruling elites, communications constitutes a new profitable investment outlet with great consumption and growth potential and with critical geopolitical implications.

Communications industries and policies are integrated into key national strategies for economic restructuring: To build a modern production structure, the state has selected new generations of information technology as one of the seven high-tech industries for prioritized development; to create domestic demand, the state is also orchestrating a society-wide deployment of networked ICT applications in traditional industry and commercial sectors.[20] The large stakes, no doubt, assure communications of prominent places on the policy agenda for the foreseeable future, which also makes assessing and explaining the outcome of China's information-and-communications policy initiatives important.

The crosscutting role designated to communications means that industrial attributes and state-corporate relations specific to the realm of communications have bearing on general economic recovery and development. An ownership overview sheds some light. The commodity chain of communications covers a range of businesses in roughly three symbiotic areas: hardware manufacturing, network operation and management, and digital media.[21] In terms of ownership, they span two distinct sectors in the economic geography: the export-processing economy driven by transnational capital and the state-controlled economy "inside the system." Just as important, media and telecommunications, although by definition inside the system, have been reorganized by policymakers to serve the broader opening-up and market reforms and have varied degrees of transnational entanglement. The state's regulatory capacities in these subsectors, therefore, should not be taken for granted.

In essence, the political economy of communications has never been so important for understanding China's economic transformation. This book documents and analyzes recent policy and political economy changes in communications in connection with the broader context of the crisis and the rebalancing act that must follow.

A STATE-CENTRIC STORY

This book is informed by theoretical work that sees the state as an indispensable agent for capital as well as the machinery for class power. Indeed, so-called Chinese-style capitalism is characterized by a developmental state and its differentiated approaches to various economic sectors. To develop an industrialized market economy, governments at various levels initiate infrastructure construction and urbanization movements. Cheap labor, cheap land, and good infrastructures are used to lure industrial capital from overseas and at home.[22] This capital-friendly economic-growth model reached a pinnacle after China entered the World Trade Organization (WTO) in 2001. By 2002 China had become the third-largest ICT manufacturer in the world, its share in the global trade of electronics rising from 2.7 percent in 1998 to 6.5 percent in 2002.[23] Mainstream economists often blame the Chinese state monopoly over bank credit, land, and administrative power for enriching large state enterprises at the expense of medium- and small-size private enterprises. However, collusion between decentralized state power and transnational corporate interests is also a prerequisite for China's export-processing regime, mainly at the expense of social interests.

In the wake of the 1997 East Asian crisis and after China's accession to the WTO, the state launched a series of commercialization drives in the public service sector of housing, education, and medical care, arguably to stimulate domestic consumption and to expand market activities. Likewise, both the telecommunications and cultural-system reforms set out to corporatize public institutions that the state budget formerly supported—without losing state dominance. Indeed, telecom operators and cultural institutions constitute different geographical and developmental foci from the export-processing side. This book explains how these corporatized branches of the state—with varying degrees of transnational entanglement—develop their own imperatives, ideologies, and practices while maintaining their positions as internal instruments for the state's rebalancing plan.

As critical scholars argue, only the state, despite the limitations and contradictions of public policy, can save capitalism from recurrent crises.[24] Hence, since the 2008 global economic crisis, global media attention has been on how the Chinese state, entangled with outside influences and domestic forces, attempted to regain greater control over China's own development. Indeed, the state retains critical maneuvering levers even in the context of global economic integration. Despite the campaign of corporatization, the Chinese state from 1998 on enforced recentralization and re-regulation in strategic sectors.[25] In strategic sectors from telecommunications to media, the state, through public property rights, administrative interference, and top personnel appointment, retains the ability to enforce its general rebalancing plans.[26] Even in liberalized manufacturing industries, the state's general developmental vision can still guide the increasingly diverse initiatives of both public and private national entities.[27] Just as important, re-regulation and recentralization, new trends in China's market governance, should not obscure that competing bureaucratic imperatives and vested state interests in the economy have created and continue to create nonaligned initiatives and diffused commitments, all under the banner of economic restructuring.

Interrogating the role of the state in a network-based economy also grows out of the agenda of critical political economy in the field of communication research.[28] As Western critical scholars demonstrate, the US government, despite its laissez-faire rhetoric, sponsored the creation and expansion of computer and electronics industries.[29] In the scholarship of Chinese communications, however, the prevalent conceptualization of the state remains limited to either "state failure" as going against the neoclassical ideals of free market or the "propaganda state" judged by the liberal democratic value.[30] These frameworks encourage tunnel vision as they obstruct theoretical and empirical inquires of the state's multifarious involvements in communications development and the underlying political economic dynamics. It is problematic to demarcate the state and the market as separate realms when state-owned enterprises and state entities from local governments to various state authorities all engage in market creation and market development. Highlighting the state's constitutive role in China's evolving networked economy and noting market elements in statist initiatives, this book shows that no simple opposition between state and market suffices to explain contemporary developments.

To move beyond binary framing, we need to see the state as a combination of contending functions and interests rather than a uniform entity. Despite its relative autonomy, the state is partly constituted by contention, collusion, and compromises between regulatory bureaus and corporate actors, public and private sectors, transnational linkages and nationalistic interests, and powerful stakeholders and the rest of the society. Complex and even conflicted relationships rule this commonly shared entity, despite its coherent rhetoric, within its own bureaucracy, with its corporate foundation, and with various nonstate actors. The nonunitary nature of the state, its policies, and its relationships with corporate arms requires a careful political-economic analysis. Thus, this book tells a state-centric story. It underscores the nonunitary nature of the state and documents how the state, entangled with market forces and class interests, tries to reshape Chinese communications for broader yet different economic-developmental purposes.

DIGITAL CAPITALISM

With research on developed nations and the conformist pressures they generate in the interconnected global system, critical studies in the political economy of communications remind us how digital network technology has become part of the capitalist economic system and is even galvanized into "digital capitalism."[31] As a global system, digital capitalism comprises top transnational corporations, the global production networks they have organized, and international corporate governing institutions.[32] From the vantage point of China, this book historicizes precise pressures toward global convergence and argues that the state's actions to leverage communications industries and policies—to relieve structural imbalances and to combat the global crisis—have accelerated China's convergence into global digital capitalism. The tempo of networking the nation is getting intensive, constituting what Dan Schiller calls China's model of "state-led digital capitalism," which contends, collaborates, and overlaps with the US-dominated system of global digital capitalism.[33]

This convergence, however, is subject to contestation. On the global level, after having established itself as a global export-processing center, China during its rise is challenging the barriers that prevent its expansion, as the United States did with its offensives against the United Kingdom–controlled communication networks in the 1910s through 1940s.[34] Communications is central to China's ongoing renegotiation with the global capitalist system. China's demands for a stronger position in global production chains, more power in allocation and control decisions about critical information resources, and more growth space through cultural export all indicate mounting geopolitical tensions centered on communications. Indeed, in view of China's rising position and the underpinning role of communications to the growth of global capitalism since the 1970s,[35] China's full-blown embrace of communications will have a further impact on the global market economy and the global communications order.

China's chance to engage and leverage digital capitalism should not be overstated, because the United States has fortified its economic, military, and cultural hegemony through leading the digital revolution. China's share of the global economy is large, but its position is downstream and peripheral instead of commanding and strong. Because of the three-decade-long, rapid economic expansion, China's growth has built up serious bottlenecks. The long-term trends in the Chinese economy are overproduction in manufacturing and deficiency in domestic demand. Although the state has tried to boost domestic demand by investing in infrastructure projects since the 1990s, it has also been forced to subsidize export-processing companies to maintain the overseas competitiveness of Chinese products and to save export-related jobs.[36] In 1999 electronic products already received the highest rate of export-tax rebates, not to mention cheap land, cheap labor, and lax environmental requirements.[37] Not only is it unwarranted optimism to expect China to bail out global capitalism but the country also may constitute the "single weakest link" in the global capitalist chain.[38]

Positioning China's state-led model of digital capitalism in the global system also requires complicating the developmental-state model pertaining to the digital economy. Well known for its will and resource for making developmental initiatives, the Chinese state is likely to become a key architect of the global digital future as China's digital economy is gaining strength. But the power and unity of the Chinese state should not be overstated. Each nonstate actor, including technocratic communities, business associations, the urban middle class, and peasant and worker communities, presses its case, although with uneven levels of planning, organization, and articulation. As the state is partly open to the influence of nonstate forces, policy solutions in the economic arena are contingent upon conflicting interests, competing edicts, and strategic moves.

With its residual socialist sensibilities and postcolonial historical conditions, the Chinese state is pressured to preserve some space for alternatives to global convergence. But this book underscores the uncertainty and ambivalence of China's ability to blaze a unique developmental path and posits that statist nationalism in the techno-economic arena is contingent upon specific political-economic relations. Intervening factors, such as rivaling regional and bureaucratic imperatives, entrenched transnational dynamics, and the self-aggrandizing impulse of bureaucratic capital, all create conflicted internal dynamics, adulterate national plans, and restrict the state's nationalistic intention and ability.

Chapter Breakdown

The chapters are organized according to the economic geography of communications, spanning two distinct sectors: the export-processing economy driven by transnational capital and the state-controlled economy inside the system. Apart from the economic geography, the 2008 global economic crisis—as a critical juncture—provides a temporal framework for each chapter.[39]

The first two chapters focus on the ICT-dominant export-processing economy and this economy's symbiotic relationship with telecommunications and explore the historical relationships between communications and (under)development characteristic of China's growth pattern since the market reform. Chapter 1 introduces the ICT-dominant export-processing economy and its historical trajectory, spatial features, and new territorial units in western China. Chapter 2 carries forward similar themes into the domain of China's telecom infrastructure and explicates how telecommunications—as state-controlled institutions and resources—responded to the need of this export-processing regime and how this created profound implications for domestic social relations.

After the analysis of the entrenched political economy and its evolution after 2008, chapters 3, 4, and 5 tackle changing policy and structural dynamics. Under the auspices of economic restructuring, China has systemized and intensified its efforts to network the nation. This is not to say that networking only began after 2008—discrete efforts under various authorities had been well underway. However, as the state embraced communications to rejuvenate the economic system, these initiatives coalesced into a new grand strategy of economic restructuring, new in terms of the scale these initiatives operate on and in terms of the qualitative changes the grand strategy is likely to bring out. To capture the broad patterns of what has changed and what hasn't in policy arenas and in business dynamics, chapters 3, 4, and 5 delve into specific topics, such as the broadband internet, third-generation (3G) and fourth-generation (4G) mobile communications, and digital TV, respectively, addressing how communications in its various forms has become a frontier of economic restructuring and analyzing the obstacles the state faces in tackling developmental pitfalls.

To connect domestic efforts with friction-full geopolitical relations, chapter 6 explores likely global implications of the China story in ICT manufacturing, media and entertainment, and internet governance. The book closes by critically conceptualizing the Chinese state as a "developmental" state in the global system of digital capitalism. The conclusion also summarizes the centrality of communications in China's opening-up and in its market reforms, explains the limited effect of China further embracing communications in correcting unbalanced economic dynamics, and assesses what may be learned from China's successes and mistakes.

CHAPTER 1

Driving Capitalism to Western China
IT and the Unwieldy Export-Processing Regime

Over the past three decades, China's economic miracle was built on heavy investment in production-related facilities and infrastructures and was propelled by a China-centric production system capable of assembling large volumes of final products for Western consumer markets. This model of economic growth has not produced equity at home. Western China with its large peasant and worker populations falls far behind the coastal provinces; backwardness is a label separating the hinterland, including Chongqing, Sichuan, Guizhou, Yunnan, Tibet, Shanxi, Gansu, Qinghai, Ningxia, Xinjiang, Inner Mongolia, and Guangxi, from the coastal pursuit of capitalist modernity in the image of Western industrialized countries. In terms of political economy, however, the western China region has always been an integral part of Chinese-style capitalism, as a supply base for cheap labor and natural resources, a virgin territory to absorb large sums of investment, and probably a potential market to consume mass-produced commodities.

The Western China Development Program (WCDP), which started in the late 1990s and was renewed and reenergized in the wake of the 2008 global economic crisis, pushed the region back into the policy stage. After 2008, under structural pressures, export-processing enterprises, many in the business of ICT moved inland with the assistance of hosting governments. While the central state was doing something that had rarely been seen before—critically rethinking development—why did local governments in western China develop an information economy by adopting the coastal model that was denounced for future purposes?

To begin exploring the making of a new, network-based economy in tandem with China's restructuring scheme, this chapter sets up the temporal-spatial positioning of the export-processing regime, underscoring the dominance of ICT manufacturing, and examines the export-processing regime from the perspective of western fringe areas, situating them in the historical and transnational flux. After laying out the historical and structural causes for regional "disadvantages," the chapter examines recent measures of spatial rebalancing, focusing on the dynamics between state policy and transnational capital.

This chapter argues that under the banner of economic restructuring, state authorities endorsed westward relocation of mega ICT manufacturers, but the western relocation does not change the existing political economy of global digital capitalism. Benefits accruing to local communities in western China are dubious and limited. When the regulatory authority on labor conditions remains decentralized, peasants and peasant-based migrant workers continue to take the brunt of the development around ICT export-processing production. Although the westward industrial relocation may temporarily relieve downward pressure on corporate profits, it undercuts the state's capacity for increasing the residential income share of the GDP and, thus, diminishes the prospect of higher domestic consumption—a key ingredient for economic restructuring.

This chapter asks two sets of questions: Why and how do communication-related industries—whether hardware manufacturing or network services—become a vehicle for achieving or not achieving regional development? In light of the post-2008 wave of industrial relocation as a spatial fix, what is the prospect for the export-processing regime? And what does the changing position of western China in the global networks of production tell us about the unchanged character of digital capitalism?

A Brief History

For centuries, China, then known as the middle kingdom, faced trouble from the tribal warriors from inner Asia but little from the sea. In the late nineteenth century, however, invasions over the sea from modern Europe posed devastating threats. Qing rulers were overwhelmed by relentless encroachment from the seaboard and were unable to comprehend the expansionist logic of industrial capitalism. The inertia of the court and the inability of the society to respond to the "pull of Western gravity" eventually led to decades of imperialist coercion, political disorder, and economic devastation.[1] Thus, the great revolution of the twentieth century, in the view of John King Fairbank, a historian of China, was a long series of domestic struggles attempting to adjust China to the new Eurocentric capitalist system.

China was a semi-colonial and semi-feudal country up to 1949. The domestic household economy, including subsistence agriculture and handicraft manufacturing, was dominant. Although they sprouted in foreign-controlled treaty ports, modern factories were exceptional and irrelevant to the rural hinterland. Except during the 1930s when Chongqing became a wartime national center and industrial enterprises moved in from the northeastern fronts, the hinterland was, by and large, a remote, poor, and even alien-looking space. The state power, although modern in urban enclaves, depended on foreign power to rule; its powerful constituents, compradors and the landed gentry, suppressed socioeconomic reforms, and national programs barely favored the rural majority.[2] The turning point did come with the rise of the Chinese Communist Party (CCP) in 1921. As political scientist Lin Chun remarks, the CCP forged a revolutionary alternative against colonial modernity and capitalist integration; succeeded in combating imperialism, feudalism, and bureaucratic capitalism; and established a sovereign socialist nation-state.[3]

This socialist sovereignty gave China a remarkable capacity for self-determination after 1949. An inward-looking strategy prevailed in the face of international isolation Western industrialized countries imposed. In the First (1953–57) and Second (1958–62) Five-Year Plans, the state ramped up heavy industries in the western backwater. During the First Five-Year Plan, out of 156 Soviet-aided projects, 24 were assigned to Shanxi and 16 to neighboring Gansu province. After China's relationship with the Soviet Union went sour in the 1960s, the Maoist state further steered resources to its Third Front project intended to foster heavy and defense industries in the west. As a result, Sichuan, Chongqing, and Shanxi all had good industrial bases, with the bulk in the southwestern region led by Sichuan and Chongqing.[4] This landward strategy, however, rendered these locales dependent on Beijing for material supply, budgetary support, and purchase orders, with little benefit accruing to hosting locales and their residents, especially rural residents.[5]

The 1980s saw China's reentry into the global production and trade system. The changes from the pre-1949 era included the presence of a powerful party state, the absence of indigenous capitalist and landlord classes, and the availability of a self-reliant state industrial sector and millions of peasants free from the feudalistic land bondage. As technocratic leaders survived Mao's political crusades from 1966 to 1976, they moved fast to nullify the Cultural Revolution and to reinstate economic construction as the top priority. In a gradual way, the post-Mao state joggled loose the planning economy to improve productivity at home. To avoid falling further behind Western industrial economies and especially China's outward-looking, export-driven East Asian neighbors, the post-Mao state enabled select areas to experimentally relink with the global system. A coastal strategy was underway to allow local initiatives and global forces to interact in special economic zones and open cities.[6] Empowered by decentralized authority, local governments in these zones harnessed various channels of resources and actively instituted an outward-looking system.

In the 1990s, the selective, "reformist" integration with global capitalism gave way to a "radicalized" version.[7] By 1995 the whole country was virtually open to foreign direct investment (FDI). A biased liberalization policy that gave foreign investors preferred incentives found earnest implementation on the local level. Endowed with incentive and authority to act in an entrepreneurial fashion, local governments at various levels established industrial parks and development zones to ramp up export-processing trade where cheap land, modern infrastructures, friendly administrative procedures, and generous fiscal incentives were available. Transnational corporations and joint ventures, increasingly joined by private enterprises, formed a global logistic network on the Chinese soil.

Also in the 1990s, ICT manufacturing began to spearhead this foreign capital-led, export-processing mode of industrialization. In 1994 the Ministry of Electronics Industry (MEI) encouraged domestic firms to seek foreign, collective, and private capital and to "build a trade structure of importing upscale computers and exporting downscale computers."[8] In 1995 the ministry called upon domestic enterprises to shift from producing household electronics only to making more computer systems and telecom equipment.[9] In 1997 developing ICT production became a general economic objective not only for the MEI: To improve the profile of the national economy and its efficiency level, the State Planning Commission, which was replaced by the State Development and Planning Commission in 1998, decreed to cultivate new growth outlets, especially by developing electronics and housing industries and by furthering opening-up.[10]

Up to 1997, the amount of foreign direct investment in ICT manufacturing was 40 percent of the total industrial investment; between 1990 and 2002, foreign investment in this sector amounted to $70 billion, dwarfing the domestic investment of $22 billion.[11] What came out of this FDI boom was a manufacturing powerhouse—with enormous assembly-and-processing capacities. However, the implications are mixed: If South Korea, Japan, Taiwan, and Hong Kong had achieved industrial upgrading by participating in globalized production in the 1960s and 1970s, the global capitalist system was far less lenient toward newcomers in the 1980s and 1990s—as the global neoliberal reform ushered in an "epoch of unprecedented concentration of global business power"—and the ICT sector was no exception.[12] Becoming a downstream hub in this production system, China saw its domestic spatiality being reshaped and even distorted to an extreme, which is discussed later.

This export-processing regime is predicated on millions of disciplined workers and their significantly suppressed wage. Between 1995 and 2002, electronics and telecom equipment manufacturing was one of only three industrial sectors with positive job growth, whereas traditional industries, including textile, machinery, steel, and transportation equipment production, all experienced common job losses.[13] With foreign-invested enterprises making the majority of sales revenue, ICT manufacturing as a rapidly growing sector for employment fueled the general process of slashing the veteran rank and file in the state-owned sector and expanding the peasant-based workforce in the foreign-dominated sector. Spearheaded by ICT manufacturing, capitalist labor relations were instituted for an externally oriented circuit of accumulation driven jointly by foreign investment and overseas demand.

Although human livelihood was at stake, the attention of top-level leaders was fixated on the "inefficient" economic profile. They noted some undesirable characteristics of the macro-economy, especially the huge waste of natural resources and duplicate construction of low-end manufacturing capacities. In response, the Ninth Five-Year Plan (1996–2000) pledged an economic restructuring.[14] Among others, landmark measures included moving welfare services and public goods into the market arena. On the heels in the late 1990s of monetizing housing, education, and health care in conjunction with privatizing state enterprises, a consumer society was forming among China's urban bureaucratic and professional classes. Yet, the root cause for lagging residential consumption, for example, intense labor exploitation, remained untouched. Between 1995 and 2005, the proportion of residential income in the GDP dropped by 9.8 percent in contrast with the rising shares of corporate and governmental revenue.[15]

China's WTO accession in 2001 conveniently brought in enormous investment from transnational corporations, further expanding China's share in transnational production and global trade. As the export-processing economy continued to heat up, the call for economic restructuring became subdued. As a result, into the 2000s large-volume export-processing trade, fueled by heavy investment in production-related facilities and infrastructures, continued to propel GDP growth. After expanding from 11 percent in 1985 to 55.8 percent in 1996, the share of export processing in total export stayed at 50.7 percent until 2007 and then slid to 39 percent as of 2013.[16] Processing trade was even a bigger fraction for ICT manufacturing at 80.9 percent in 2009 and nearly 61 percent in 2013.[17]

In the outward-looking economy, western provinces collectively have little advantage and are disintegrated with the dominant corridor of economic activities. As early as 1992, the state opened all the capital cities of inland provinces to overseas investment; preferential policies earmarked for certain regions also gave way to an industry-oriented foreign-investment policy.[18] However, industrial agglomeration had already taken effect in the coastal region. The superior ability of coastal provinces to make expansion plans—even when inland provinces suffered from shrinking credits during the austerity years—only exacerbated regional gaps.[19] The comprehensive liberalization did little to help in closing the regional disparity. The following sections discuss infrastructure disconnection and industrial hollowing-out, which are widely seen as the biggest hurdles against the western region's catch-up, to illuminate the structural nature of these hurdles, and examine national countermeasures.

Rewiring the Circuit of Accumulation

In the 1990s, in view of local competition for foreign industrial capital and the ensuing oversupply of low-end export-processing capacities, the central state tried to regulate myriad local investment programs until the outbreak of the 1997 East Asian financial crisis. To mitigate the export slump in the aftermath, the state spent 3.6 trillion yuan (US$434 billion) on basic construction.[20] Amidst active fiscal policies, the WCDP was inaugurated. Zeng Peiyan, then chairperson of the State Development and Planning Commission, called for "developing Western China in the same way as developing the special economic zones in the early reform era."[21] Ever since, the central state has attempted to reshape the domestic spatiality and even to rewire the global circuit of accumulation, hoping to create new spaces for production and consumption.

Drawing upon state bonds and a range of budgetary funds for basic construction, environment protection, poverty alleviation, and enterprise reform and for development in education, health, science, and culture, the WCDP focused on spreading basic infrastructures and modernist institutions to the hinterland. The top task was infrastructure construction, primarily transportation networks and energy-transmission systems. As of 2000, transportation and telecommunications accounted for nearly 32 percent of the fixed-asset spending in western regions.[22] In the WCDP program, the central state earmarked 400 billion yuan (US$48 billion) for construction, culminating in a total investment of 850 billion yuan (US$102 billion) in sixty key projects by 2004.[23]

Supported by new highways and railroads, western provinces attempted to "look West" for international trade. After all, the state wanted to counteract the dominant trade structure with the Global North, comprising developed nations in North America, West Europe, and East Asia; to increase the ratio of interior provinces in international trade; and to tap into newly emerging markets in the Global South, made up of Africa, Latin America, and developing Asia.[24] Geographical vicinity, however, does not guarantee significant interactions. By 2005 Sichuan Province, at the upper reach of the Yangtze River, had less than 4 percent of the trade with neighboring South Asian countries—the lion's share went to Shanghai, Guangdong, Zhejiang, Jiangsu, Shandong, and other coastal provinces.[25] Yunnan and Guangxi, likewise, had less than a 2 percent share each in trade with Southeast Asian nations, but Guangdong alone claimed 37 percent.[26] State-funded transport links could barely tilt the flow of global capital. The Guangxi local government, for example, had to pay $120,000 to induce a foreign ship to upload at its Qinzhou port.[27] The Eurasian continental railway, which started crisscrossing central Asia in 1991, was another stubborn expression of the dominant circuit of capital: It was not fully operational until 2001 because economic powers at both ends of the bridge, that is, Western Europe, Japan, and South Korea, preferred maritime connections.[28]

Accompanying the transportation networks were systems for energy transmission. Although adding budgetary revenue to local governments, mega projects, such as the west-east gas transmission, west-east electricity transmission, and south-north water diversion, channeled natural resources to the coastal area and left damaged ecosystems and displaced peasants behind. Available information sheds light on the limited extent of local benefits. Approximately 120 billion yuan (US$14.5 billion) were earmarked for the west-east gas-transmission pipelines, of which western provinces got 34 billion yuan (US$4.1 billion);[29] of 850 billion yuan (US$102 billion) spent by the WCDP on infrastructures by 2004, 50 percent went to purchasing material and equipment from coastal and central provinces;[30] centrally controlled state enterprises in construction, petroleum, electricity, hydropower, and aircraft manufacturing were the primary handlers of WCDP-related infrastructure projects.

Telecom operators, in support of the WCDP, were instructed to prioritize telecom pipeline construction along the Eurasian continental bridge and Yangtze River waterway and from Guiyang to Kunming and from Hohhot to Nanning.[31] Telecom systems were in place earlier in comparison with transport facilities, for which large-scale investment did not begin until 1997. By 2008 only one double-track railroad connected Xinjiang with the rest of China.[32] In contrast, by 1998 fiber-optic pipelines already connected all provincial capitals and 95 percent of the cities and counties except Lhasa, and every province had had at least two fiber cables running through it.[33] Due to the geopolitical importance of central Asia for China's energy security, the state deliberately built telecom hubs in western China. In 2012 Xinjiang, for example, became the sixth international communication gateway. This gateway significantly reduced the route telecom signals need to travel, say, between Xinjiang and Kazakhstan.[34] Despite the relatively better situation, spatial imbalances still define telecommunications, which chapter 2 discusses.

The state media system, like telecom operators, was not a formal part of the WCDP program but responded to the state mandate by creating satellite channels. Satellite channels make up a media system for spreading party propaganda and, more important, for building a national advertising market. In 2003, thanks to spending by telecom, health, real estate, and financial industries, television and print media earned 154 billion yuan (US$18.6 billion) in advertising revenue. Five coastal provinces, Beijing, Shanghai, Guangdong, Zhejiang, and Jiangsu, claimed the bulk of the market. For western provinces, in view of their small local economies, satellite TV is the window to the national advertising market. Guizhou Satellite TV, for example, earned 87 percent of its advertising revenue from other provinces.[35] To cater to corporate clients based in Beijing, Shanghai, and Zhejiang, in 2002 Guizhou Satellite TV branded itself as the "western TV" channel and gained landing rights in eight western provinces to serve businesses wanting to sell in the region.[36]

As political economist Barry Naughton notes, the WCDP achieved less in closing economic disparity than in integrating west China into the national grids of transportation and energy.[37] Despite the amount of state input, the gap between coastal and western regions expanded: By 2004, the incomes for urban and rural residents in western China fell further behind the coastal and national averages; rural residents in the west earned merely 53 percent of their coastal counterparts. Given China's embedded position in the global capitalist system, the WCDP program—especially its infrastructure-based efforts—presented at best a mixture of contradictory interventions, some potentially challenging the dominant flow of capital and others organizing production resources, including transport and energy, to the benefit of the outward-looking coastal economy.

Fueling Industrial Hollowing-Out

The WCDP program also entailed measures for industrial development that needed local implementation. The measures did not mitigate the regional disadvantages in the outward-looking economy, either. By the late 1990s, the state had decreased its direct investment and involvement in the local economy, and its intervention focused on creating an investment-friendly environment. Relaxed loan conditions, friendly foreign investment and trade conditions, and favorable tax rates on corporate income, industrial land use, and equipment imports were offered by the state. As this section will show, these measures were insufficient to provide an alternative to the outward-looking economy or to resist the hollowing-out of local industrial bases—in the contexts of state asset liquidation and land speculation.[38]

In the 1980s and even early 1990s, western provinces had a strong lead in electronics and machinery production. Sichuan, for example, had 21.8 percent of the enterprises under the purview of the MEI and fulfilled major tasks for the military.[39] As for Shanxi, the electronics and telecom-equipment industry was its third-largest sector built during the Third Front period. Following state policy in the late 1980s and early 1990s, western provinces began breaking the socialist employment system, seeking corporate consolidation, and repurposing military-oriented production capacity for commercial use.

Led by palpable market demand and pressed by declining state input, these provinces sought foreign capital to develop export-processing trade. Since 1978 Shanxi had engaged in compensation trade to restructure its electronics industry; relying upon foreign machinery, mass production of TV sets and refrigerators began. In 1995 when China possessed a large volume of manufacturing capacity for several household appliances, Sichuan was the top production base for TV sets, with its state-owned Changhong Electric Corporation claiming more than 50 percent of the electronics sector in the province of profit and tax. After 1995, however, foreign competition, capacity oversupply, and dropping retail prices plagued the industry.

Under the guise of foreign capital–led industrialization, urbanization unfolded by the late 1990s, making spatial reshuffling a necessary condition for capital accumulation.[40] Urbanization entailed a development-zone rush. Back in the early 1980s, to engage in export processing, small Hong Kong manufacturers had opened up numerous workshops in townships and villages all over South China. Unable to make substantial investment in public facilities in an equally scattered way, local officials soon preferred the formation of industrial zones.[41] Meanwhile, the central government was interested in forming "advanced" manufacturing clusters and, from the late 1980s, began to designate industrial parks and development zones. In this context, inland provinces joined the development-zone rush.[42] The fall of agricultural productivity relative to industrial productivity from 1985 further induced local governments in inland provinces to appropriate large stretches of farmland for large-scale industrial or infrastructure projects.[43] The predatory land practice helped proliferate numerous industrial parks. In 2001, of the forty-three national economic and technological development zones, sixteen were in western cities.

In the late 1990s, during the state-owned enterprises (SOE) reform, a systematic campaign of asset liquidation swept unprofitable state-owned enterprises, the primary ownership sector in western regions. During 2000 and 2001, more than 420 state enterprises in western China went bankrupt or were sold;[44] between 2000 and 2005, the number of state-owned industrial enterprises in Sichuan dropped by more than 56 percent.[45] This campaign exacerbated land speculation—as land was a category of state assets subject to liquidation. Sichuan makes an illustrative case: From the late 1980s, a good number of Third Front enterprises had moved from mountainous areas to central city districts to form new electronics-manufacturing bases;[46] however, in the late 1990s, cities in Sichuan leveraged inflated, state enterprise–owned, centrally located land assets to borrow money from banks for upgrading factory equipment. This is only part of the story. Liberalized units of industrial capital also moved east; of the outward-bound money, the majority sought growth opportunities in commerce, finance, securities, and real estate—but only a small portion went to manufacturing.[47]

Urbanization in western China pushed up land prices, diverting industrial capital to speculative activities. Outside investors also set eyes on the bountiful speculation opportunities when local governments, which were unable to attract industrial investment, sold land leases in suburban and inner-city areas to foreign developers.[48] Capital from Sichuan and Chongqing, for example, found its way to Shanxi; 60 percent went to real estate and 10 percent to construction materials.[49] In 2004, of the inward-bound investment from other provinces to Sichuan, energy, food processing, and construction materials got the largest share—roughly 33 percent, whereas the two state-designated, high-tech industries, electronics and medicine, received 3.3 percent and 3.1 percent, respectively.[50] As for foreign capital, mostly from Hong Kong, 41.6 percent of the total destined for Shanxi went to the hotel and dining business in 1997, while 41.2 percent was spread among textile, petroleum, machinery, and electronics industries.[51] As for Sichuan, less than 50 percent of foreign investment entered its manufacturing industries in 2005, while another 50 percent found its way to retail, dining, entertainment, and real estate.[52]

Overall, under the banner of the WCDP, neither SOE reforms nor land-speculation booms slowed down the decline of the state-owned electronics industry in western China. Instead, they fueled the hollowing-out of local industrial bases.

Export-Processing Regime in Maturity: Pitfalls and Fixes

The 2001 internet bubble and China's official entry into the WTO further induced global brand-name companies and contract manufacturers to downsize production capacities elsewhere and to ramp up a China-centric production system. China, the coastal region, in particular, became a fully fledged global production center for final products, external parts, and electronic components. Between 1998 and 2003, the export value of computers and related peripherals and parts grew nearly tenfold.[53] ICT manufacturing became a mighty industrial sector. In 2002 ICT exceeded all other manufacturing industries in sales revenue, accounting for 12.9 percent of the national industrial total.[54] It also secured the number 1 position in the export-processing business—as the share of machinery and electronic products grew from 65 percent in 2002 to 76.5 percent in 2012, and the share of high-tech products grew from 33.7 percent to 50 percent. In the same period, the share of textile, garments, furniture, shoes, toys, bags, and plastic products dropped from 22.7 percent to 8.7 percent.[55]

The coastal region enjoyed an exclusive boost from the bulking up of export-processing trade in ICT products. In 1999 the Zhangjiang Hi-Tech Park of Shanghai changed its focus from biopharmaceuticals to IT for its "demonstrated global success."[56] Between 2000 and 2007, the share of ICT products in Guangdong's industrial output increased by 7 percent.[57] Gigantic export-processing clusters emerged along the coastline, thanks to the influx of foreign capital. Up to 2005, as much as 91 percent of foreign investment in ICT manufacturing went to eight coastal provinces.[58]

Despites its momentum, this growth model was elusive for western provinces. In 2002 Song Zhaosu, then party secretary of Gansu, confessed that it was hard for western provinces to get central approval for new industrial projects and equally hard for any new projects to attain market share; the only hopeful area would be "advanced" manufacturing of "high-tech" products.[59] However, the hollowing-out of industrial capacity, resulting from the draconian state enterprise reform, sweeping asset liquidation, land-speculation booms, and the technological shift of market demand, left western provinces a no-growth zone. Taking Chongqing and Sichuan as examples, by 2005, they hardly had any foreign-invested production capacities in any of the ICT product categories, except Sichuan being the third-largest production site for discrete semiconductor devices.[60] Sichuan—the top host of foreign investment in the west—actually saw inward-bound American industrial investment decline between 2003 and 2007.[61]

The gigantic export-processing capacity built along the coastline, meanwhile, became a partial liability. Former Flextronics CEO Michael Marks raised alarm back in 2005: "If the China Yuan and Malaysia Ringgit appreciate, manufacturing costs there will increase in dollar terms, potentially deterring companies who are rushing to build factories there. I think China is overdone."[62] As labor cost in China represents a considerable portion of the cost of PC production, Accenture, a multinational management-consulting company, estimated in 2011 that the profit margin of PC production was the most sensitive to wage increases in recent years.[63] Apart from wage increases, labor unrest in the form of frequent and unpredictable job changes, mounting wildcat strikes, and even suicidal displays also posed a threat to the ICT export-processing business, which requires reliable, speedy, and quality delivery. It is no surprise, therefore, that in Guangdong, manufacturing enterprises are hoping to replace inexpensive labor with expensive robots.

In view of all these risks, the Ministry of Information Industry (MII) pledged in 2005 to support western cities, including Xi'an, Chengdu, and Chongqing, to develop ICT manufacturing, welcoming coastal and foreign capital to the hinterland.[64] In 2007 the Ministry of Commerce, along with the National Development Bank, provided a supportive package for interior provinces to attract export-processing enterprises. Its goal was to increase this region's share in national processing trade to 5 percent.[65] Meanwhile, the Asian Development Bank criticized the WCDP in its first phase for falling short in attracting foreign investment.[66] From 2005 and on, as the program entered its second phase, its focus rested less on leveling the playing field for all and more on attracting investment from coastal provinces, building advantageous industries, and prioritizing a few regional areas.[67]

During the 2008 global economic crisis, rising land prices, frequent labor disputes, and slack overseas markets reached a destructive level, hurting powerful stakeholders. The coalition behind the coastal export-processing regime, made up of transnational and local capital, local governments, and trade-related central bureaus, began to split apart. In 2007 the cancellation of the preferable 15 percent corporate income-tax rate and the beginning of a flat 25 percent tax rate for foreign-invested enterprises, including those from Taiwan, made western China a new tax-saving harbor where the 15 percent tax rate is kept for state-encouraged industries.[68] The wave of worker suicides at Foxconn in 2010, the ensuing negative publicity, and wage spikes then led to a drastic turn of attitude among local officials. A top Guangdong leader publically urged Foxconn in Shenzhen to move assembly operations to other regions and even to other countries. The government did act. It facilitated the relocation of labor-intensive enterprises out of the Pearl River delta by differentiating utility prices, financing new industrial parks, and supporting training programs for migrant workers.

Competing for heavyweight companies relocated from the coastal region proved handy for leaders in the interior region, which had missed the windfall and growth opportunity bestowed by the opening-up policy from the outset. Although the central state called for an end to GDP obsession after 2008, GDP growth was still a major evaluation index for local officials, especially those in the investment-driven economy of western China. The profit margin of export processing is certainly slim, resulting in limited corporate income tax to local government coffers, but sales tax levied on large volumes of products is a coveted stream of tax revenue.[69] Investors mostly from Hong Kong and Taiwan relocated enterprises to counties in western China to get closer to the inland market.[70] Industrial parks on the provincial and national levels, on the other hand, have begun to facilitate a systematic spatial restructuring of the export-processing regime inside of China. After 2005 and especially after 2008, outside investors moved in on an unprecedentedly large scale. Between 2000 and 2010, nearly two hundred thousand enterprises from coastal regions invested or set up ventures in the western region, making a combined investment of 2.2 trillion yuan (US$282 billion).[71] Up to 2012, fifty-four American, sixteen French, fourteen German, and twelve British companies, all in the Fortune 500 list, invested in China's west.[72]

New Territorial Units

Mega ICT manufacturers spearheaded the westward industrial relocation. After 2008 the southwestern region rose to be a new base for large-volume PC production. In light of the systematic reshuffling, what is the prospect for the export-processing regime? In what ways, if any, does this mode of economic restructuring—via state-facilitated and capital-led industrial relocation—redistribute power and resources to disadvantaged regions and populations? And what does the changing position of western China in the global networks of production tell us about the unchanged exploitative character of digital capitalism? To address these questions, this section examines Intel Sichuan and Foxconn Chongqing as case studies.

SICHUAN: INTEL'S NEW BASE

In 2003, after China's WTO accession, Intel committed $375 million to build a testing and assembling factory in Chengdu, Sichuan. Welcoming gestures of the provincial government, including several high-level visits to the corporate headquarters, and Intel's intention to show goodwill to Beijing led to the biggest deal by far in China's west. From 2003 Intel invested a total of $600 million in Chengdu. Was Intel's early and ostensibly atypical move a disruption of business as usual? The answer is no: It did not alter the status quo much.

A brief history is necessary here. Thanks to the fragmented character of semiconductor production that enables production processes to be divided among different suppliers in different places, US chipmakers, such as Intel, National Semiconductor, Fairchild, and AMD, became globalized corporations back in the 1960s. Brand-name companies, including Hewlett-Packard, IBM, Motorola, Apple, and Siemens, only followed in their footsteps. Intel located many of its assembly and testing plants in low-cost areas, especially the Asia-Pacific region, including Malaysia (Penang and Kulim), the Philippines (Cavite), and China (Shanghai and Chengdu). Malaysia, among the earliest recipients of Silicon Valley capital, had become the world's third-largest exporter of IC products by the early 1980s, following the United States and Japan.[73] Into the 2000s, however, as China became a global assembly center for ICT final products, the country's explosive demand for IC inputs galvanized leading firms to move the testing and assembling operation of IC production to China. Growing output came out of China.[74] In 2005 Taiwan had eighty-three chip-assembly facilities, Japan eighty-one, and China seventy-nine; however, of the ten new facilities planned worldwide, six would be built in China.[75]

Since its operation, the Intel Chengdu facility boasted the second-lowest cost following the one in the Philippines. The bulk of its products were exported to the parent company.[76] Its importance was on the continual rise, as cost pressure on the IC firm spiked. In 2006, when announcing a plan to open an assembly and testing plant in Vietnam, Intel chairperson Craig Barrett indicated cost pressure in Shanghai as well as in the Philippines and Malaysia.[77] In 2009 the company closed the facilities in Penang and Cavite. In China it closed the factory in Shanghai and expanded the capacity in Chengdu. Up to 2012, the Chengdu facility processed half of the global supply of laptop chips.[78]

Intel had a catalytic effect. After 2003 global IT giants IBM, Microsoft, and Texas Instruments; telecom-equipment vendors Huawei and ZTE; brand-name PC makers Dell and Legend; and Taiwan-based top contract manufacturers Compal, Foxconn, and Wiltron all built factories in Sichuan. In 2007 the local authority decided to leverage the well-placed IC-production chain to build an even-larger production base of consumer electronics. In 2008 investment in ICT saw a boom, growing by 110 percent; in comparison, fixed-asset investment increased 28.5 percent.[79] However, it was not until 2010 that PC makers and contract manufacturers thronged in to ramp up mass production of electronic devices. In 2011 more than 90 percent of products delivered to the Chengdu Shuangliu International Airport for export were ICT products.[80] The same year, ICT enterprises made 93.9 billion yuan (US$14.4 billion) worth of exports, accounting for 63.3 percent of the province's total industrial export; thereof, Intel alone exported 30.1 billion yuan (US$4.6 billion) and Foxconn 52.3 billion yuan (US$8 billion).[81]

Despite the industrial agglomeration in Sichuan, only Intel and Compal supplied key components, such as motherboards, central processing units (CPUs), memory, hard-disk drives, and batteries. Indeed, although China is the largest semiconductor market in the world, rising from 24 percent of the global total in 2005 to 50 percent in 2014,[82] leading firms can still afford to supply the market from abroad, especially because of cheap airfreight costs and the zero-point tariff on IC products as China's WTO commitment.[83] Intel, up to 2007, in Asia, had no fabrication plants, the plants that take up the front-end process of IC production, while two were in Ireland, two in Israel, and the majority, at least six, were in the United States.[84] Intel's new fabrication plant in Dalian received up to $1 billion worth of incentives from the local government, but the plant manufactured technology "at least three generations behind the leading edge."[85]

After 2008 Intel's global production network crisscrossing China changed. Responding to the skyrocketing demand in the southwestern provinces, the IT giant did a major reshuffling of its logistical networks. Instead of shipping products to Shanghai for domestic and international transfer, including those destined for western provinces, the company in 2012 announced a plan to establish a distribution center in Chengdu so that its IC products could reach clients in western regions within two days.[86] However, despite the rising importance of China as a market and a supply base, China's position in the geography of Intel did not change much.

The Chinese state has hoped to convince foreign chipmakers to build more fabrication plants, but the manufacturers hardly responded. Between 2003 and 2008, they accounted for less than 20 percent of the annual fabrication output. The rapid growth of China-based production was mostly attributable to domestic firms;[87] however, this growth did not change China's external position. Notable Chinese companies, such as Semiconductor Manufacturing International Corporation (SMIC), provide IC manufacturing services for global giants, such as Qualcomm and Texas Instruments. However, domestic IC-design firms, capable of designing for smart cards, video decoders, and telecom equipment, rely mostly on Taiwan-based contract manufacturers to turn designs into products.

This convoluted cross-border IC production chain has resulted in a dilemma: Although exports from China increase year by year, trade deficits do not narrow. In 2011, 80 percent of the market demand for IC products and 90 percent for high-end components were met with imports; as the largest item for import, IC products amounted to $170 billion, of which about 50 percent were reexported as part of final products.[88] The rise of Intel Sichuan and the expansion of the already gigantic industrial clusters it supports in China did not give the country missing technological and industrial capacities it has hoped for.

In this Intel-led spatial rebalancing, Sichuan paid a high price for hosting an industrial complex on this scale. Deficit-driven state spending to build modern parks large enough to house industrial clusters proved indispensable—yet burdensome.[89] The Chengdu High-Tech Industrial Development Zone, comprising two parks, expanded from 2.5 square kilometers (nearly 1 square mile) in 1990 to 130 square kilometers (50 square miles) by 2013.[90] It necessitated annual drives to grab land from peasants. By 2009 its west park had repurposed land from nearly forty thousand peasants.[91] About 60 percent of its local labor forces was landless peasants, but less than 20 percent of job openings in the zone were recruiting peasants, who were limited to positions such as janitors, assembly-line operators, and security and property-management staff. The gap between reality and expectation only resulted in resistance and shared disappointment.[92] Collective petitions in the zone, as a result, were frequent and numerous, as land-losing peasants lodged their grievances in groups to the Bureau of Letters and Visits, hoping to get resolution.[93]

CHONGQING: A NEW SPACE FOR VERTICAL REINTEGRATION

In Chongqing a drastic capital influx has been taking place, disrupting the nearly flat growth pattern of foreign investment for the two decades prior to 2008.[94] What led to this sudden expansion, and what are its implications? To break its landlocked destiny, the Chongqing municipal government courted Hewlett-Packard in 2008, encouraging the company to build a capacity for producing four hundred million laptops per year. Chongqing promised HP to localize in three years 80 percent of the upstream capacity required for component production; otherwise, the government would pay for the logistical expenses.[95] Foxconn, Inventec, Pegatron, Wistron, and Quanta Computer, all transnational contract manufacturers headquartered in Taiwan, and brand-name PC makers, including Acer and Asus, then followed in.[96] The state-facilitated formation of an industrial cluster has been a proud boast ever since.

Vertical reintegration in no way is a new thing for ICT industries but characterizes the success of mega contract manufacturers.[97] After brand-name companies achieved a comprehensive outsourcing of production in the 1990s, consolidation of manufacturing resources to a handful of contract manufacturers accelerated in the 2000s. After the 2001 internet bubble, market shakeouts enabled brand-name PC makers to gain more bargaining power over contract manufacturers. The PC makers drove down the net margins for notebooks from more than 10 percent around 2001 to "just 4 percent for leading original design manufacturers (ODM) such as Quanta and a measly 1 percent for a second-tier player."[98]

The pressure precipitated the formation of mega contract manufacturers, who excel in scale production at cost-effective locations. The pressure also accelerated China's rise as the global center for large-volume PC assembly. Flextronics, the world's number 2 contract manufacturer, for example, was among the first to build industrial parks in places like Brazil, China, Hungary, Mexico, and Poland to get all suppliers around to reduce costs. During the 2001 telecom downturn, Flextronics was able to leverage its low-cost facilities to shift from telecom-equipment manufacturing to consumer-electronics manufacturing.[99] Without low-cost locations for vertical reintegration, Flextronics could not manage large-volume production of consumer products—a business with ultrathin profit margins.

The China strategy is even more essential for Foxconn, as the company's traditional focus was PCs and game consoles. As documented by Dennis Normile, freelance writer for *Electronic Business*, Foxconn is "the low-cost leader for building PCs." In 1993 it opened the first manufacturing facility in mainland China; in 2002 it became China's largest exporter; in 2004 it had five industrial parks housing not only its own factories but also those of its suppliers; in 2006 it topped Flextronics to become the world's number 1 contract manufacturer—as it had 70 percent of its manufacturing in China, and its rival stood at 55 percent.[100]

Although Foxconn deliberately kept a low and even secretive profile, its nonstop growth at 30 percent in 2007, 22 in 2008, 10 in 2009, and over 50 in 2010 and 2011 has drawn public attention. During this period, its worldwide employment grew by leaps and bounds from seven hundred thousand in 2007 to nine hundred thousand in 2010 to over one million in 2011. If digital capitalism has degenerated into crises characterized by business concentration, systematic overcapacity, rapidly falling retail prices, and accelerated product cycles, mega contract manufacturers to some extent thrive in these crises. Foxconn is a living example. To beat an annual 30 percent drop in retail prices, it strives to ensure no less than 30 percent annual output growth.[101] To do so, it offers lower prices to win larger orders from brand-name PC makers. Then, savage measures to slash cost and to cut back on time to market and time to volume production ultimately push out smaller competitors and make Foxconn bigger, as these tactics would for any mega contract manufacturer.

In the post-2008 crisis context, western China has become a new platform for Foxconn. As labor sociologist Pun Ngai documents, Foxconn has acquired small companies since the WCDP.¹⁰² Taking production orders in the range of at least one million units, the giant is bound to reshape the landscape of production. In 2005 and 2006, Chongqing only had capacity for telephone and mobile-phone production.¹⁰³ After making a small output of computers in 2009, its PC shipment ramped up in 2011, surpassing Beijing and just behind Shanghai, Jiangsu, and Guangdong.¹⁰⁴ Apart from Chongqing, other central and western cities also host Foxconn's large-scale production facilities, including Chengdu, which produces over forty million iPads yearly, more than half of the global total, with 120,000 workers, and Zhengzhou in Henan, which employs 200,000 workers, making the latter Foxconn's second-largest iPhone production base.¹⁰⁵ By 2012 the southwestern region became the third-largest hub for PC production, 10.6 percent of sales.¹⁰⁶ Because of this regional expansion, China's PC shipments amounted to 96.5 percent of the global total in 2012 and stayed above 80 percent in 2014, climbing continuously from 47 percent in 2008 and 60.9 percent in 2009.¹⁰⁷

The incentive to integrate western China is cost differentials. According to the manager of Chongqing Ericsson, in comparison with the coastal region, electricity in the west was 50 percent cheaper, factory construction 50 percent, natural gas 60 percent, and labor costs 40 percent.¹⁰⁸ As underdeveloped as it has been, western China is a reservoir of cheap labor. In Chongqing, about twenty-three million out of the total thirty-three million people are peasants with a low standard of living.¹⁰⁹ To round up workers for relocated mega ICT manufacturers, local governments campaigned to persuade peasants to stay locally instead of moving to coastal areas. Counties initiated recruitment drives where village heads acted as brokers. Results were remarkable: Employment in the electronics industry soared from 80,000 in 2010 to 850,000 in 2015.¹¹⁰ However, the Chongqing minimum-wage standard, often used by export-processing enterprises as the default standard for base pay, hovered at 1,250 yuan per month (US$198) in 2015, far below the monthly urban residential income of 3,700 yuan (US$587). Without excessive overtime, base pay rarely met a living-wage standard.¹¹¹ In 2014 about a thousand Chongqing Foxconn workers went on strike, demanding better pay and more overtime.¹¹²

In Sichuan, likewise, the demand to ramp up labor supply was delegated to county and village levels of the government.¹¹³ By 2012 more Sichuan peasants had found nonagricultural jobs inside their province than outside.¹¹⁴ Again, low wage rules. At Foxconn, zealous recruiting efforts belied the low base pay of 950 yuan per month (US$151).¹¹⁵ Since 1993 local governments have had the legal right to determine local standards of the minimum wage, leading to the race to the bottom for workers' pay. The post-2008 state campaign of economic restructuring did not change this policymaking setup. As a result, local governments in western China were able to keep the minimum wage from rising too fast despite upward wage pressure. They had a high stake in ICT export processing: In Chengdu, the Foxconn factory that opened in 2010 boosted Sichuan's import and export by "1333.58%" by May 2011;[116] as for Chongqing, ICT exports accounted for 71 percent of the total industrial exports in 2012 and more than 51 percent in 2014.[117]

Cheap labor is important but offers no guarantees. Riots by labor wherever it goes, heavy dependence on Apple for large-volume orders, and high maintenance for paper-thin profit margins all make Foxconn and the larger production system it represents unsustainable. And, the model is too unwieldy to change. Although the company announced a robot strategy in 2010, so far only human nimbleness can handle the delicate process of assembling hundreds of components into smart phones. The technical fix provides little relief. To sustain its business model, Foxconn has had to deepen its immersion in western China and hired an additional hundred thousand workers there for iPhone6 production.

The westward moves of transnational capital have resulted in a more balanced spatial character of China-based global production networks, but benefits accruing to the local society are dubious and limited. By 2007 ICT manufacturing made up 6 percent of Chongqing's GDP, making it a top industry in the area.[118] Whereas two other top industries made most of the sales in the domestic market (table 1.1), ICT manufacturing depended almost exclusively on export. Although

Table 1.1. Chongqing's top three industries, in billion yuan, 2012

	Gross Industrial Output	Sales	Export Delivery	Tax, Extra Charges	Value-Added Tax Payable	Paid-In Capital	
						State	Foreign
Railway, ship, aviation, and other transporting equipment	123	120	19	.878	3.1	1.1	.641
Communication equipment, computers and other electronic equipment	149	146	117	.226	.951	1.5	1.3
Motor vehicle	239	235	7.3	4.6	7.7	4	4.7

Note: Only enterprises with main business revenue at or above 20 million yuan are included.
Source: Chongqing Statistical Yearbook 2013.

state and foreign capital were nearly equivalent in this sector, foreign-invested enterprises, including 6 percent state-owned equity, claimed the lion's share of the industrial output and exports. On the other hand, despite significantly smaller industrial output, domestic enterprises, with 2 percent foreign-owned equity, had a higher pretax profit. As for the taxes as an indicator of how much capital the government can retain—presumably for public spending—ICT manufacturing in comparison with the other two top industries made the lowest level of contribution in Chongqing (see table 1.1).

Conclusion

China's reintegration into global capitalism does not challenge the system but, instead, offers a bailout by diffusing capitalist relations and its crises at the same time.[119] The so-called China model in mainstream discourses, as Lin Chun points out, describes and affirms a developmental state—at the behest of transnational and private capital—making an export-processing economy work.[120] In light of unresolved contradictions, dependency, and exploitation, China's promise for "leading the world by its innovative example" should, indeed, be a subject of critical reflection.[121]

Having been unevenly integrated into global production networks, China suffers an extreme distortion in its domestic spatiality. From the perspective of western fringe areas, this chapter examines the temporal-spatial nature of ICT manufacturing, which is both the frontier and core of China's export-processing regime. In the wake of the 2008 global economic crisis, local and central governments orchestrated a drive to rebalance the economy, first and foremost in the form of westward relocation of mega ICT manufacturers. Although this new trend—in the name of balanced development—provides a temporary relief concerning corporate profits and ramps up industrial clusters in the western region, it is likely to disperse and even deepen the structural crisis emanating from cross-border production that sustains today's labor exploitation and electronic consumerism at once.

The present development of western China around ICT export processing does little to alter the existing political economy of transnational capitalism—or to alter China's domestic institutional setup undergirding the export-processing regime. In the past three decades, decentralization delegated regulatory tasks and law-making power to local governments, equipping them with sufficient autonomy and incentive to act in an entrepreneurial fashion. Without a recentralization of power on critical issues pertaining to labor-capital relations, poor social strata, especially, peasants and peasant-based workers, will continue to bear the price for sustaining the export-processing regime. Although momentarily relieving the upward wage pressure that threatens the export-processing regime, the westward industrial relocation undercuts the prospect of higher residential income and consumption—and thereby entangles the Chinese state in a profound and unresolved contradiction.

Bailing out the export-processing regime is not the only state reaction. Other measures aimed at creating new industries and stimulating domestic demand are meant to reduce the country's reliance on transnational capital, processing operation, and export markets. In all the endeavors, communications plays a unique and almost pivotal role. Chapter 2 begins to explore how telecoms have supported the export-processing regime while becoming an important economic sector in themselves.

CHAPTER 2

Repurposing Telecoms for Capital

Networking and Inequality

Indispensable for creating an outward-looking market economy, Chinese telecom networks were restructured repeatedly in the past three decades to attract transnational capital to China, to give Chinese elites transnational linkages, and, above all, to support impressive GDP increases from China's export-processing regime. For these very reasons, however, telecom development has resulted in unequal distribution of communication resources and reinforced profound rural-urban regional disparities. This chapter explores the repurposing process in telecommunications for capital and considers its implications for the distribution of power and resources. The chapter underscores the constitutive role of telecommunications in China's export-driven market economy while addressing how the forces shaping telecom structures, such as localized transnational market dynamics, the state's opening-up reforms, and new technological developments, interacted with the country's socioregional relations.

This chapter also historicizes telecom development between 1978 and 2005. The first section examines telecommunications' radical reorganization intended to support the coastal export-processing regime at the beginning of the market reforms. The second section examines the local mechanism of rural telephone development in the late 1980s and 1990s. The third examines the fully fledged corporate reforms that began in the late 1990s and continued into the twenty-first century, exploring how market forces, new technology, and the state's attempts at channeling market forces for social purposes have jointly made telecom networks a platform for corporate accumulation—and genesis of the networked economy.

Instituting Coastal Bias in the "Opening-Up" Reform

During Mao's era and before market reforms from 1949 to 1976, China exercised a socialist delinking strategy and maintained a minimum level of interaction with the global capitalist system. Within these decades of domestic upheavals and international isolation, telecommunications received low levels of capital investment, consistently lower than 1 percent of the total capital investments in the economy up to 1983 and at 523 million yuan (US$261.5 million) as of 1983.[1] Supporting nation building and industrialization efforts, telecom investments focused on long-distance and urban telephone lines. With market dynamics missing, China only had four million telephones, and only one-half of 1 percent of the national population had access to telephones in 1984.[2]

In the 1980s at the beginning of global neoliberal reforms, China started its historic reentry into the global market system, primarily by liberalizing foreign direct investment in the manufacturing sector. On the international scene, the United States and other developed market economies, along with multilateral institutions, succeeded in foisting "newly liberalized system development policies" onto the global stage, after having achieved a widespread network extension in their own countries through welfare-state policies.[3] Although China did not liberalize foreign investment in telecom infrastructures or network operation, the state has since the 1980s actively led an outward-looking mode of system buildup.

In the initial "opening-up" reforms, foreign investors swarmed into south China and brought with them not only global commercial linkages but also pressing demand for modernized telecom capacities. For example, the establishment of the Shekou Industrial Zone in 1979, even before the formation of the Shenzhen Special Economic Zone, had attracted hundreds of foreign-invested enterprises. Although the contact with global capitalism was regionally contained, commercial activities in this small enclave created overwhelming demand for telecom services, generating a contagious pressure on the telecommunications system as a whole, which until then had been severely underinvested and subservient to the party state. To change its bottleneck image amidst mounting critiques, local posts and telecommunications (P&T) bureaus in tandem with local governments, especially those in coastal provinces, not only increased construction projects but also adopted cutting-edge technologies in their urban telecom infrastructures.

The first obstacle to meeting corporate demand was the severe shortage of capital investment. In the Sixth Five-Year Plan period (1981–85), the state could only budget 29.8 billion yuan (US$13.5 billion) for transport, posts, and telecommunications, but most of the fund was devoted to railway and harbor construction.[4] To solve the problem, from 1981 through 1990, the Ministry of Posts and Telecommunications (MPT) called for "finding every possible way to make use of all available funds" raised from the state, collectives, and individuals.[5] Coastal regions, especially special economic zones, turned to debt financing. In Guangdong Province, foreign and domestic loans became the biggest source of capital, accounting for 33.8 percent of the budget, followed by funds raised from users, corporate funds self-accumulated by telecom enterprises, and, lastly, national and ministerial budgetary allocation.[6] Nationwide, by the end of 1989, foreign loans had financed 63 percent of basic construction and 55 percent of system improvement.[7]

The budget shortfall did not mean a diminished role for the Chinese state; instead, local governments took an increasingly hands-on approach. A decentralization reform of the MPT system started in the 1980s, responding to the demand of coastal provinces for more authority over local telecom development. In Mao's era, except for a few periods, the MPT had vertically managed telecommunications, treating local governments as clients. Because direct MPT endowments fell short during the reform era, Jiangsu Province, among the first, proposed a policy change. "Although the telecom infrastructure was a national nerve system and should be managed by the ministry, network development at the intra-provincial and sub-provincial levels should be left to the discretional authority of local governments," the then governor of Jiangsu Province argued. Under collective lobbying pressure, the State Council in 1982 allowed urban telephone services and local pipeline construction to be included in municipal developmental plans.

In 1988, the MPT officially stipulated a new model of "coordinated planning, combined central and local [*tiao/kuai*] administration, layered responsibility, and joint construction" to decentralize the vertical hierarchy of the MPT system, to leave each level accountable both to functional administrative superiors in the MPT system and to those within local governments, and to make each level, with a separate account, more responsive to profit incentives in specific localities.[8] At the top of this administrative structure was the MPT, whose responsibility was the construction of interprovincial long-distance trunks. P&T administration in provincial-level municipalities (PTA) was over the municipal and prefectural P&T bureaus (PTB), which were over the county P&T enterprises (PTE). The PTA's responsibility in tandem with local governments was to provide intraprovincial long-distance trunks and urban networks. An example of this coordination is in Fujian Province. Except for telephone lines between the capital city and each prefecture that the provincial PTAs were to fund, with different levels of local governments supporting land use and construction, telephone lines within each prefecture all the way down to the county level were supposed to be joint projects cofunded by the bureaus and local governments.[9]

Meanwhile, the central state compensated investment deficits with favorable policies, authorizing local P&T authorities to turn telecom networks into self-accumulative assets. In 1981 the MPT authorized a separate account for urban telephone lines. From then on, urban lines were no longer involved financially with facilities in other localities. In a Chinese colloquial expression, an urban telecom would "cook its own meal," responsible for its own profits and operational expenses, as well. To relieve possible budget shortfalls, in 1982 the state permitted an installation charge, the rate of which was set by provincial pricing administrations; thereafter, the charge became a major source of revenue for urban telephone expansion. Also in 1982 the central state gave PTAs a 90 percent retention rate of taxable profits and foreign-currency earnings and an exemption from repaying 90 percent of state loans. In 1986 local governments were allowed to levy "supplementary fees." The Shenzhen government, for example, required new construction of factories and office buildings to get authorization from the PTA and even to submit managerial fees.[10] By 1994 coastal provinces had obtained 50 to 60 percent of construction funds from favorable state policies.[11] Up to 1999 telephone-installation fees and other subsidiary charges underwrote about half of the fixed-asset value in the telecom sector.[12]

In this decentralized financial system, coastal provinces harnessed an expanding pool of capital investment drawn from tax credits, installation fees, domestic and foreign loans, and fiscal support from local governments. In 1980 Guangdong was on a par with interior provinces, such as Hunan, in telecom infrastructure.[13] However, because of its strong capital-raising capacity, the coastal province enjoyed a dramatic push in telecom development after 1980, leaving interior provinces far behind. Up to 2006 Guangdong, the frontier of China's opening-up reform and the hub of the export-processing economy, still constituted one-sixth of the nation's telecom revenue.[14]

The rise of south China as a new telecom hub was also attributable to its primary users who could afford frequent telephone use and, thereby, created quicker profitability for local telecom enterprises. Up to 1991 the chief users of P&T facilities were small- or medium-size, collectively owned firms that had proliferated in south China.[15] Migrant workers also constituted a distinct consumer market in Guangdong although no specific percentage of total demand is available. However, from table 2.1, it is safe to infer that the giant jump of telecom revenue from 1992 to 2000 derived from surging business usage but not from the booming number of migrant workers as the "information have-less."[16]

In interior provinces where the biggest telephone users were governmental institutions, however, the permission for supplemental charges was delayed for four to five years until 1992.[17] In these places, the interests of the MPT system and local governments were not well aligned. Local officials complained that local governments only had obligations but no rights: Because of the vertically integrated operation of telecom systems, local governments did not participate in the management of telecom services, not to mention not owning corporate holdings of the expanding assets. As the then mayor of Chongqing argued, while the local government would call upon big enterprises and big users to provide financial support for telecommunications, the existing financial system of the MPT "curbed the enthusiasm" of the local government; decentralized

Table 2.1. The telephone market in Guangdong, 1992, 2000, 2004, and 2008

Market Size	1992	2000	2004	2008
Total provincial population (million)	64.6	77.8*	78.6	110†
Migrant population (million)	3.3	12+	n/a	31+
Total telephone users (million)	n/a	18	58.6	115.8
Fixed-line users (million)	n/a	11.4	21.8	37.4
Mobile-phone users (million)	.274	6.7	36.8	78.4
Telecom revenue (billion yuan)	.940‡	56.3	83.5	121.5

* This figure is for 2001.
† Long-term residents number 95.44 million.
‡ This figure is for 1989.
Note: In 2008 telephone users outnumbered the provincial populations in Guangdong, indicating that even migrant workers were more likely to own and use telephones. Between 2008 and 2010, the increase in telecom expenses for migrant workers in Guangdong was estimated at 10 billion yuan (US$1.4 billion). The heavier telecom usage among migrant workers, either through fixed-line or mobile devices, was not only a result of falling prices but also of the state's campaign of extending telephone access to rural areas in interior provinces, which made calling home possible for migrant workers in Guangdong.
Sources: China Knowledge Resource Integrated Database, http://number.cnki.net/cyfd/IndexNaviALL.aspx#15/; M. A. Yong, "Guangdong shuanxian shixian renjun yi bu dianhua" 广东率先实现人均一部电话 [Guangdong broke the record of one telephone per person], *Southern.com*, December 17, 2008, http://tx.southcn.com/ztch/30years/meiti/content/2008-12/17/content_4775923.htm.

investment should come with, he said, shared profits.[18] Governments in coastal provinces, however, successfully claimed shares of some locally invested urban telephone lines. Specific reasons are unclear, but the PTAs in special economic zones had more autonomy from the MPT. They reported to the municipal governments, first and foremost, which then had direct access to the State Council.[19]

In the decentralized system, local authorities constructed most local lines, but the MPT still took the primary responsibility for long-distance networks. In the national trunk network, the state deliberately created a two-tier system favoring the burgeoning coastal export-processing regime. In 1984 the State Council issued a six-point instruction, stipulating that telecom services should focus on major cities and coastal areas. The MPT vice minister at the time echoed the decision that capital must be spent on cutting-edge areas, referring to regional and urban networks within newly opened coastal cities, economically advanced regions, and major cities.[20] This two-tier telecom infrastructure constituted and reinforced China's grand transition toward an outward-looking economy led by the coastal export-processing regime.

In this economic structure, western China has been disadvantaged by geographical distance. Sichuan, for example, only had 1 percent of the nation's foreign-invested projects up to 1991.[21] The dominant pattern of telecom development did not mitigate this disadvantage. By 1991 the MPT invested only 140 million yuan (US$35 million) in Sichuan's public telephone networks in comparison with 1.6 billion, 1.3 billion, and 1.2 billion (US$400 million, US$325 million, and US$300 million) in Guangdong, Jiangsu, and Liaoning, respectively.[22] As a result, Sichuan, a sizable province in southwestern China, only gained a 5 percent growth in its outward-bound networks, falling behind the increase of long-distance calling.[23] National pipelines along a north-south axis built for political-military communication with Beijing still outstripped those along an east-west axis connecting Sichuan with Guangdong, Fujian, Zhejiang, and other coastal provinces.[24]

Modernization-minded governments and enterprises in the hinterland still participated in the unequal access to transnational activities. Starting in the late 1980s and through early 1990s, inland provinces pursued a strategy of "borrowing ships to go out to sea": By investing heavily in coastal harbors, they wanted to "ensure access to berths, shipping lines, and favorable treatment for their products."[25] Via the "borrowing" strategy, coastal and interior provinces interacted increasingly on a hierarchical basis of "comparative advantages": Coastal provinces played the role of "middlemen" between interior provinces and the global market, whereas interior provinces provided natural resources and cheap workers for the export economy.[26]

In 1993 the market reform entered an accelerating phase. According to the State Planning Committee, during the Eighth Five-Year Plan (1991–95), the geographical division of the eastern, central, and western regions would be abandoned, giving way to building a "national" industrial base.[27] However, the alliance among coastal provinces had already been fortified. At an information-exchange conference among coastal provinces, representatives from local PTAs overtly advocated a dual system to separately manage coastal telecommunications, with the purpose of shedding the regional cross-subsidization obligation based on a differential-rate structure for calculating local incomes from long-distance calling.[28]

As development proceeded rapidly in prioritized regions, the telecom system shed its loss-making image in the 1990s and gained excellent commercial prospects. In this context, the state withdrew its initial support. By 1995 it had cancelled the 90 percent retention rates for taxable profits and foreign-currency earnings. On the local level, unconditional endowments by local governments, along with other low-interest access to capital raised from institutional and residential users, notably declined.[29] This changing environment was unfavorable to interior provinces, where systematic telecom development did not start until the 1990s. So, in the Eighth Five-Year Plan, the coastal bias persisted. The share of eastern and central provinces in fixed-asset investment rose from 87.6 percent in 1988 to 90 percent in 1994, whereas the share of western provinces fell from 12.4 percent to 9.9 percent.[30] Although the absolute amount of capital investment grew in western provinces, the western-eastern gap unmistakably expanded.

Local Development of Rural Networks, 1980–99

The development of advanced telecom infrastructures in coastal and urban enclaves was accompanied by underdevelopment in the vast rural areas, especially in western China. As of 1995, 80 percent of the national population was rural residents, who possessed less than 20 percent of telephones in the country. Up to 2001, when rural populations declined to 62 percent during massive urbanization, their share of local telephones hovered at 38 percent. A dual ownership structure in the 1980s and 1990s, followed by telecom corporatization and liberalization in a period of rapid technological change, explains the structural neglect of rural telephone networks in the general progress of network expansion and modernization.

During Mao's era, the operation of rural lines at and below the county level was delegated to local governments. As political scientist Eric Harwit notes,

Mao's era witnessed a narrowing of the rural-urban penetration gap. In particular, the national movements in the 1950s to establish rural collectives and communes created a steep increase of rural telephone exchanges. However, even the radical "telephone to every township" campaign launched in the mid-1950s was far from eliminating regional disparity. Rural telephone exchanges still lagged behind those in the cities by approximately 50 percent in the 1960s.[31] From 1962 the state turned its attention away from rural telecommunications.[32]

During the post-Mao market reforms, the bias against rural lines became unequivocal among technocrats in the MPT. To prioritize rural telecom development was unrealistic, according to the top leadership. In his conversation with the then governor of Sichuan, the MPT vice minister expected the provincial PTA to spend capital locally in eight economically advanced regions.[33] Urban bias characteristic of market development became such a hegemonic mantra that it dictated telecom development even in those agricultural provinces that had borne the brunt of market-oriented policy overhauls. In Sichuan, an agricultural province with 77.8 percent of the population being rural residents, investment priority went to urban areas. Chengdu and Chongqing together had 75 percent of telecom business in the whole province.[34]

The ownership of rural telephone lines was a policy heritage from Mao's era. In 1979 the state confirmed that rural lines from the county level down to the communes belonged to each province. In this scheme, the finance of rural lines belonging to the local governmental budget was separated from the centrally controlled MPT budget, but the PTAs still managed the daily rural network operation. As the MPT collected surpluses from profitable provinces to subsidize those with losses, the exclusion of rural lines from the MPT budget meant that agricultural provinces were not subsidized as much as they could have been. Indeed, the state excluded rural telephone services from its planning and financing, expecting the narrowly focused development in core economic regions to "trickle down" to the vast rural periphery.[35]

This ownership structure did encourage local governments to provide subsidies to the generally deficit-ridden rural lines.[36] However, local governments in interior provinces had no systematic development plan prior to 1992 and would "build rural networks when there was money and would not when there was no money."[37] In 1991, the 64.1 million yuan (US$12 million) worth of investment in rural telephone lines was only 4 percent of China's total capital investment in telecommunications, up from 21.1 million yuan (US$4.4 million) at 1.2 percent in 1990, though.[38] As a combined result of investment shortfalls in rural areas and investment drives in core economic regions, telecom development demonstrated an extremely lopsided situation along the rural-urban divide:

China's public telephone infrastructure had a 40 to 50 percent rate of annual growth in the early 1990s, and the rural-urban penetration gap was its widest by 1995.[39]

Despite the pervasive urban bias, the state insisted that developing rural networks was its obligation. Local governments, in particular, had a stake in rural telecom development for without the "last mile" connection, they would receive no revenue from incoming and outgoing calls.[40] After 1992 systematic telecom development started in interior provinces. To expand rural networks, provincial governments began to draw construction capital from counties, districts, towns, and villages, on top of permitting free land use, supplementary charges, and lower taxes to the rural telephone bureaus of the PTAs that operated rural lines on behalf of the local government.

To guarantee capital formation, local governments imposed high tariffs. In 1986, rural telephone fees in Sichuan, for example, climbed by an average of 70 percent.[41] In 1992, copying the urban practice, rural telephone bureaus started to charge installation fees and construction fees. To encourage PTAs to build, local governments enforced quotas for telephone installations, which also assured the PTAs a certain amount of that business. After 1995 system expansion sped up in the countryside (table 2.2). However, peasants still had a lower level of initiating phone calls, even if they had access, because of high tariffs relative to residential incomes.[42] With the low frequency of telephone use, expanding rural telephone lines in interior provinces often incurred financial losses and insoluble deficits. In 1999 all rural telecom enterprises, except Fujian Province, were losing money.[43]

Rural lines in coastal provinces, especially those serving the export-processing regime, fared better. They enjoyed relatively abundant investment funds raised from corporate users and reaped more gains by offering services for transnational commercial activities. The then agriculture minister, Liu Zhongyi, observed that in coastal regions, it was township and village enterprises "which pay for development projects so that the farmers do not have to pay any money out of their own pockets. . . . Farmers in prosperous areas could easily afford to pay for the installation of modern telecommunications."[44] Fueled by the booming export-processing economy, rural networks even became a large chunk of local networks in some places where the urban-rural divide actually weakened.

In the Eighth Five-Year Plan period, the MPT began to incorporate rural areas along the coastline into the nationwide long-distance telephone networks equipped with computer-controlled electronic switches. Interior provinces, however, continued to rely on their own lower-level governments. If lower-level

Table 2.2. Urban and rural telephone subscribers and growth rates, 1992–2010

Year	Local Landline Telephones (10,000 subscribers)				Yearly Growth Rate (%)	
	Total	Urban	Rural	Rural (% of total)	Urban	Rural
1992	1,146.9	920.6	226.3	19.7	37.0	30.0
1993	1,733.3	1,407.6	325.7	18.8	52.9	43.9
1994	2,729.5	2,246.8	482.7	17.7	59.6	48.2
1995	4,070.6	3,263.6	807.0	19.8	45.3	67.2
1996	5,494.7	4,277.8	1,216.9	22.1	31.1	50.8
1997	7,031.0	5,244.4	1,786.6	25.4	22.6	46.8
1998	8,742.1	6,259.8	2,482.3	28.4	19.4	38.9
1999	10,871.7	7,463.3	3,408.4	31.4	19.2	37.3
2000	14,482.9	9,311.6	5,171.3	35.7	24.8	51.7
2001	18,036.8	11,193.7	6,843.1	37.9	20.2	32.3
2002	21,422.2	13,579.1	7,843.1	36.6	21.3	14.6
2003	26,275.0	17,109.7	9,165.3	34.9	26.0	16.9
2004	31,175.6	21,025.1	10,150.5	32.6	22.9	10.7
2005	35,044.5	23,975.3	11,069.2	31.6	14.0	9.1
2006	36,231.5	24,585.9	11,645.6	32.1	2.5	5.2
2007	36,563.8	24,859.4	11,685.5	32.0	1.1	0.3
2008	34,080.4	23,199.5	10,881.0	31.9	−6.7	−6.9
2009	31,368.8	21,177.6	10,191.2	32.5	−8.7	−6.3
2010	29,438.0	19,662.0	9,776.0	33.2	−7.2	−4.1

Sources: China Communications Yearbook 2005; MIIT 中华人民共和国信息产业部, "xinxichanyebu fabu 2005 nian zhongguo tongxin fazhan tongji gongbao," 信息产业部发布2005年中国通信业发展统计公报 [MIIT issued the 2005 statistical communiqué of the People's Republic of China on National Telecommunications Industry development] accessed February 16, 2016, http://www.gov.cn/jrzg/2006-02/10/content_185059.htm; MIIT, "wei 'you hao you kuai' fazhan dianding jian shi jichu—2006 nian quanguo tongxinye fazhan tongji gongbao," 为"又好又快"发展奠定坚实基础—2006年全国通信业发展统计公报 [To lay a solid foundation for the "sound and fast" development—2006 national statistical communiqué of telecommunications industry development], accessed February 16, 2016, http://www.cnii.com.cn/20070108/ca398639.htm; MIIT, "xinxichanyebu fabu 2007 nian zhongguo tongxin fazhan tongji gongbao," 信息产业部发布2007年中国通信业发展统计公报 [MIIT issued the 2007 statistical communiqué of the People's Republic of China on national telecommunications industry development], accessed February 16, 2016, http://www.gov.cn/ztzl/2008-02/05/content_883563.htm; MIIT, "2008 nian quanguo dianxinye tongji gongbao," 2008年全国电信业统计公报 [2008 national telecoms statistics], accessed May 19, 2016, http://cn.chinagate.cn/reports/2009-04/27/content_17682020.htm; MIIT, "2009 nian quanguo dianxinye tongji gongbao," 2009年全国电信业统计公报 [2009 national telecoms statistics], accessed May 19, 2016, http://money.163.com/10/0203/14/5UJTRV2000253B0H.html; MIIT, "Gongye he xinxihua bu fabu 2010 nian quanguo dianxin ye tongji gongbao," 工业和信息化部发布2010年全国电信业统计公报 [MII released 2010 national telecoms statistics], January 26, 2011, May 19, 2016, http://finance.sina.com.cn/roll/20110126/16119314512.shtml.

authorities had huge deficits, as was the case in many remote regions, their rural networks had no technical upgrading. With outdated switching and transmission technology, rural users in these places were physically separated from the national automatic trunk networks. Later on, the provincial ownership of rural networks phased out nationwide. More than twenty provinces agreed to transfer ownership to the MPT. Not accidentally, coastal provinces sitting on valuable rural network assets were the most reluctant to follow the order.[45]

In the Ninth Five-Year Plan (1996–2000) and accelerated in the Tenth Five-Year Plan (2001–6), the MPT system underwent a full-blown corporate reform (discussed in the next section). In response to the global ICT-for-development movement, the Chinese state prioritized the installation of fiber optic–cable arteries. However, rural telephone service, especially in the interior regions, was clearly in dire condition: In 1999, rural users accounted for only 10.8 percent of local telephone users in western provinces, lagging significantly behind 30.7 percent in central provinces and 58.5 percent in eastern provinces.[46] The Ninth Five-Year Plan paid some lip service to communicative equality by making "telephone access in all administrative villages" a sideline goal. No actions followed, though, with the result that very few telephones were installed in villages in 2000, the last year of the Ninth Five-Year Plan period.[47]

Matching International "Best" Practices in the 2000s

Into the 1990s the state began liberalizing and corporatizing telecommunications in preparation for China's accession into the WTO. In this phase, telecommunications became a cornerstone of global integration. Measures were taken to match the international "best" practices, such as separating operational and regulatory rights, breaking up monopolies, and introducing competition. In 1998 the corporate reform severed the institutional tie between the regulator, the MPT, and the historical monopoly operator, China Telecom, and introduced new state-owned operators to create competition. In 1994 China Unicom, backed by the Ministry of Electronics Industry (MEI), was established as the first rival to China Telecom. On the regulatory side, the MPT was merged with the MEI to form the Ministry of Information Industry (MII) in 1998. In 2008 the MII was upgraded into the super Ministry of Industry and Information Technology (MIIT).

China Telecom and China Unicom started deploying a global system for mobile communication (GSM) networks in 1995, which mostly business communities, including those affiliated with foreign-invested enterprises, demanded.[48] Both operators gave their mobile communication subsidiaries a greater scope of freedom to operate as profit-oriented enterprises. To compete with China Unicom and to position itself in the mobile communications market, China Telecom set up a digital communications company, a precursor of China Mobile, in Zhejiang Province as a pilot project of reform. Meant for divestiture at the outset, this new company followed a radical market economy principle of "absorbing foreign investment and establishing lean management and specialized operation."[49] Guangdong also established a mobile-communications company and built China's first provincial GSM network, which was then, along with the company in Zhejiang, peeled off and injected into China Telecom Hong Kong in 1997 for overseas public listing. In 1999 China Mobile was separated from China Telecom.

Telecom operators began to prioritize new mobile and data communication technologies for investment. In 1998 mobile communications enjoyed 34.8 percent of total investment, followed by local networks at 28.3 percent, long distance at 8 percent, and data communications at 3.7 percent.[50] Supported by favorable policies, advanced telecom services grew rapidly. In 1999 international and domestic long distance, data communications, and mobile communications together had a 60 percent share of the total revenue for telecom operators, while local calls, calls with the same area code, had a 40 percent share, which continued to decrease.[51] Reflecting China's growing transnational linkages, the number of business-dominated international private-line circuits between the United States and China, excluding Hong Kong, also skyrocketed in the late 1990s.[52]

The telecom corporate reform was a response not only to technological changes but also to the demand from the business community to control the cost of telecommunications. Before the corporate reform, China Telecom kept down the price of local calling by cross-subsidizing, taking profits that long-distance and international calling generated. The rebalancing of tariffs in 1996, 1999, and 2001 authorized by the state regulator dramatically lowered the rates for long-distance calling, international calling, and international leased private circuits and increased the rate for local calling.[53] The tariff changes disproportionately benefited foreign-invested enterprises and foreign-related institutions. In remote counties, residents found it difficult to afford the increases for local calls;[54] in urban areas, middle-class families also had limited use, out of budgetary concerns, of long-distance lines. Underutilization, thus, plagued the public telephone network.[55] However, a concurrent price cut of rural calls did encourage rural telephone installation in the late 1990s, especially in places where rural and township enterprises were prosperous.[56]

Around the year 2000, the establishment of China Netcom and China Railcom and a second splitting of China Telecom into northern and southern companies took place. Following market signals, these new players expanded disproportionately in the most lucrative business categories.[57] Up to 2002, for example, only about 10 percent of China Mobile's users, nearly 11.8 million, were in western China, with the remaining 107 million in eastern China.[58] Although China Telecom continued to expand basic services in nonprofitable areas, competition pressed the historical monopoly operator to undergo internal corporate reforms that enabled its provincial companies to restrict construction in high-cost and low-return rural areas within their jurisdiction.[59] Indeed, the system-expansion mechanism inherited from the MPT monopoly age could no longer hold operators accountable for public-service obligations, finally prompting Wu Jichuan, then MII minister, to require telecom operators to guarantee "no worsening conditions" in rural and western regions before a universal service fund was put in place.[60]

What induced state regulator Wu to endorse the "universal service" concept—primarily in basic telephone service—was exactly a serious regression in the twenty-first century. Although the absolute number of rural telephone subscribers increased, the growth rate dropped considerably after 2001. The global telecommunications crisis following the bursting of the internet bubble and the domestic reshuffling halted rural-access expansion. The urban expansion, however, remained uncompromised (see table 2.2). As a result, the share of rural telephone users declined in a straight line from 35.7 percent to 31.6 percent from 2000 to 2005. Meanwhile, a new round of urban-based adoption of new communication technology exacerbated regional and social inequalities: Nanhai County in Guangdong, for example, started to extend fiber-optic internet service to every village and every elementary school in the mid-1990s; but in 2003, 25.3 percent of administrative villages in western provinces had no basic fixed-line telephone connection, and the mobile-phone penetration rate was also as low as 20.9 percent nationwide.[61]

In this context, the universal-service concept was meant to enact the state's regulatory role in the general process of liberalization and to extract a public-service function from the profit-driven telecom sector.[62] The state's attempt to establish a universal-service fund, however, was thwarted repeatedly. China Unicom resisted on the ground that China Telecom had collected large amounts of installation and supplementary fees before the revocation in 2001, so it was "unfair" for new operators to contribute to the fund; China Mobile also contested the scope of telecom services eligible for the universal-service obligation.[63] The fund proposal, as a result, was suspended.

As discussed in chapter 1, in 2000 the Chinese state started the Western China Development Program (WCDP) intended to reshape regional development. As

Sichuan wanted to become the southwestern hub for transnational capital, telecommunications, as a key capital good, became more responsive to corporate demands. Famously, after the passage of the Telecommunications Decree in 2000, the MII minister received the first complaint about poor service, from Sichuan's largest foreign-invested electronics manufacturer, which produced components at the lowest cost worldwide.[64]

If the WCDP was to "drive capitalist market development to the west,"[65] it did not have enough impetus to intervene with power relations. Enhanced telecom development in the west gave an advantage to external economic interests while redrawing hierarchical boundaries. In Sichuan, 77.8 percent of the population was rural residents, whose telephone subscription rate lingered at 5 percent in 2004, far below the 40 percent urban rate.[66] The gridlock—caused by the miscarriage of the universal-service fund—was not addressed until after the MII divided the telephone-to-every-village task among six telecom operators in 2004. At the end of 2005, staggering changes had taken place, as more than 94 percent of villages were connected.

By 2002 China Mobile, in place of China Telecom, became the market leader and, therefore, had more impact on connectivity. In 2004 the state regulator made China Mobile, because of its growing market power, take the largest share of responsibility in the telephone-to-every-village campaign with mobile connectivity. In the face of the saturated urban voice market, China Mobile also started Blue Ocean Strategy to explore mobile market opportunities in rural areas. Indeed, rural and migrant users became major growth drivers, accounting for half of China Mobile's new mobile subscribers at the end of 2006.[67] However, as Dan Schiller observes in a different context, despite the breathtaking speed of network expansion and widespread adoption of mobile communications, the "institutional character" of telecom operators remained firmly profit-oriented.[68] "How to win new customers without sacrificing profit margins" was an uncompromised corporate guideline. In remote rural areas, China Mobile ran a lean operation, a business practice of reducing input so as to drive down business cost.[69] Network expansion for inclusion of less-profitable areas was not "an end in itself, but a means" of increasing the market value of its networks.[70]

Knowing that new rural subscribers spend less on calls, China Mobile strenuously developed value-added services, such as ringtones, short-message service, and multimedia-messaging service, to boost revenue per user. In 2010 value-added telecom services, of which mobile communications brought in 89.5 percent, generated 217.5 billion yuan (US$32 billion), or nearly 24 percent of the total business revenue.[71] China Mobile was not alone. Fixed-line operators did not wait long either to restructure their capital investment. Competing to accelerate their transition from access providers to service providers, both fixed-line and mobile operators had anxiously lobbied the state for the third-generation mobile-communications (3G) operational licenses from the year 2000 and in 2009 started to build the next-generation networks. To succeed in technology-based competition was an unequivocal priority. Since the launch of the telephone-to-every-village campaign in 2004, China Mobile spent approximately 19.5 billion yuan (US$2.5 billion). By contrast, its investment in 3G networks in 2009 alone amounted to 58.8 billion yuan (US$8.6 billion).[72] All three top telecom operators followed these same investment routes and collectively invested 80 billion yuan (US$11.8 billion) in 3G networks in 2009 up to July but spent 10.3 billion yuan (US$1.5 billion) on rural coverage over the whole year.[73]

Thanks to the state's principled insistence on rural telephone access, falling prices for network construction, and corporate competition for subscriber growth, equality in telephone access experienced great progress, although it was still insufficient, on the heels of the telephone-to-every-village campaign. The Eleventh Five-Year Plan, ending in 2010, achieved telephone access in 94.5 percent of natural villages (which form naturally over time instead of through administrative demarcation). However, the relentless, market-driven, creative deconstruction of networks has made equitable provision of communicative resources a "constantly moving target."[74] From 2005 through 2010, the rural-urban gap of internet adoption widened steadily.[75] It is safe to say that the universal-service project merely passively filled gaps, failing to confront the root causes of market biases.

Conclusion

This historical chapter delineates two stages of telecom reform. In the 1980s and 1990s, telecommunications was radically reconfigured to facilitate the rearticulation with the global production system. As localized transnational capitalist preferences guided—and even dictated—telecom expansion, eastern-western and urban-rural inequalities were built into telecom institutions and policies. Starting in the mid-1990s, telecom development entered the second phase, becoming a central locus of China's convergence with global capitalism. If the earlier phase of the market reform pushed the MPT system to provide capital goods for the export-processing regime, the reform into the twenty-first century further transformed the whole telecom network into disparate, profit-seeking corporate entities competing in upscale market segments.

Predicated upon nationwide, globally connected, and technologically advanced telecom networks, China has achieved an impressive GDP growth atop the export-processing economy. However, this major growth driver, that is, the export-processing economy, created and reinforced some of the most profound social inequalities in telecommunications and beyond. Although the state cannot be underrated as an enabling agent, the mechanisms of producing inequalities in the general process of development also include transnational market dynamics. Instituting an outward-looking telecom system was part and parcel of the social-spatial reconfiguration of China—in accordance with the global capitalist logic.

Academic writings and policy discourses on international telecommunications offer benchmarking schemes, how-to solutions, and effects assessment.[76] In line with the standard international policy recommendations, China, by and large, followed a typical trajectory, beginning with the plan to link coastal cities and focusing on responding to the demands of businesses, then expanding urban residential service, and, only after that, starting to redress a glaring rural-urban disparity. Despite the apparent convergence with the global norm, telecom development by no means has transcended power hierarchies or national differences. Differences in the starting points—albeit within a shared neoliberal political and commercial environment—mean that China, like many other developing countries, had to single-mindedly pursue capital formation and network upgrading before aiming for the most basic universal-service objective.[77]

The market logic of telecom development—to serve the export-processing regime and to become an accumulation platform in itself—has strengthened profound social inequalities, including in telecommunications. This also inaugurated a corporate networked economy, which then became a fix for the global economic crisis. In this corporate, networked economy, what has been progressing forcefully is the commodification of not only the network but also the information it carries. The buildup of wired and wireless broadband networks, as the following chapters discuss, underpins the market of value-added services, content, and applications, which are increasingly sold on the broadband internet. Orchestrated moves to create priced information for consumption, central to the economic restructuring, are likely to reinforce the gap between the information haves and information have-lesses. Thus, although economic restructuring, predicated on telecommunications, constitutes what Marxist geographer David Harvey calls a "fix," it is likely to concurrently aggravate and contribute to some of the structural forces characteristic of the crisis.

CHAPTER 3

Forging Broadband for the Commanding-Heights Economy

State-Business Relations in Networking

China's growth miracle in the past three decades was built upon the export-processing regime organized by foreign direct investment (FDI). Unlike Japan, South Korea, Taiwan, and Singapore, the four East Asian economies that had previously pursued an export-driven model while delaying the entry of transnational capital, China started with the liberalization of FDI in manufacturing, especially but not only in ICT-hardware manufacturing.[1] In the economic geography, however, there exists a parallel economy "inside the system,"[2] where the state keeps its firm grip through ownership control and administrative supervision. Dominated by state-owned enterprises, the realm of communications is such a sector. More important, it is pivotal to the nationalist ambition of creating a new, commanding-heights economy, which entails complex and interactive technologies and dominant business and innovation models capable of exerting crosscutting and catalyzing influence on the rest of the economy.

The 2008 global economic crisis has placed information and communications at the core of economic restructuring. Policy makers around the world turn to broadband internet and its celebrated innovative potential for a growth comeback. The Chinese state is no exception. It regards broadband as a critical infrastructure for the future. However, knowing how to build this infrastructure requires updated understanding of the changed political economy. As we saw, the telecom reforms in the 1990s focused on breaking the planning economy and expanding market relations, resulting in drastically accelerated network expansion while also reinforcing some deep-rooted social inequality. Reflecting this policy agenda, mainstream historical and policy analysis was premised on market liberalism, focusing on benchmarking the scope of market competition as opposed to the level of state control. However, with Chinese telecommunications taking up new characteristics of being a globally integrated and competition-driven field after having undergone a varying degree of liberalization, the perspective from the 1990s is no longer satisfying or relevant today.

To explicate the historical ascent of the internet into a primary site of economic restructuring, this chapter historicizes broadband internet in China, focusing on the evolving political economy of telecommunications and the internet after the neoliberal reform. It asks, Why do the Chinese state and its national champions embrace the internet? How has the internet been deployed? What did the state do with broadband that resulted in exceptional achievements and widespread public discontent? And can the state cope with market failures characteristic of the global digitalized economy—when the critical infrastructure is expected to support economic recovery and restructuring?

Although inside the state-controlled system, broadband development is in no way immune from global structural forces. Techno-economic trends driven by equipment vendors, IT solution suppliers, and global investors have incorporated and penetrated China. On the heels of large-scale network construction motivated by global trends, corporate competition, moneymaking zeal, and nationalistic pride, the state faces the challenge of turning broadband capacity into an engine of information consumption among individual residents and institutional clients, on the one hand, and addressing market failures left behind by its own national champions, on the other. However, the central state and its bureaus of administration are riven by conflicts and rivalries over market and policy objectives and thus have played a compromised role in the broadband-based economy.

Internet Takeoff: Global Movement and Statist Projects

The internet took off during a politically tumultuous and emotionally confounding decade of the 1990s for the Chinese state and its people. In the aftermath of its suppression of the 1989 student movement, the state found itself facing international isolation, while the society was mired in a widespread chilling effect. The partial market reforms since the late 1970s were forced to a complete halt. Elsewhere on the international scene in 1989, the Berlin Wall came down, and Eastern Europe changed its political path. In 1991 the Soviet Union itself was disbanded. The demise of the Soviet Bloc marked the bygone era of the international socialist movement. It also completed the rise of the United

States to the unrivaled global hegemonic status. Capitalism became the only game in the town.[3]

As political scientist Edward S. Steinfeld poignantly explains, all the crises imploding and exploding in the late 1980s and early 1990s persuaded Chinese leaders to reshape the ties between the state and its economic foundation. Unlike the 1980s, when socialist modernity was still the essential objective, the state from the 1990s and on has yielded to a version of modernity defined in the image of Western capitalist economies. Also unlike the 1980s, when export processing was confined to a few special economic zones and when domestic-market dynamics were enlivened through decentralization of control to regions, enterprises, and households, the 1990s witnessed a comprehensive linkup with the global economic order. The 1992 party mandate of establishing a socialist market economy heralded sweeping reform. Landmark changes include the 1993 enterprise law, the 1994 national labor law, a 60 percent drop in tariffs from 1993, and more than $100 billion worth of foreign investment received between 1994 and 1996, doubling the size of the preceding two decades. By restructuring its production system as well as its institutions—at the behest of foreign investors—the Chinese state from 1992 decisively dismantled its planning economy, turning the country into a cog in the global production system.[4]

It is in this context that Western countries, especially the United States, looked more powerful and attractive than ever. Apart from its military and economic prowess, the United States conjured up a global zeal for networks. In 1993 Bill Clinton's administration announced the "information superhighway" concept and put forth a national plan. Soon after, corporate and governmental actors in the United States, Japan, and Europe—despite fierce competition among themselves—drummed up promotional rhetoric and pushed to liberalize domestic telecom markets around the world, hoping to lead network construction within the largest possible scope and to galvanize new rounds of investment and accumulation.

Swept by this trend, debates broke out inside China on whether and how to build information networks when the penetration rate of traditional telephones was still low. A shared desire among ruling elites to incorporate China into the global economy made this debate a short-lived one. It meant that after having taken over a decade to ramp up basic telephone services in the coastal region, the state this time could not wait too long to enter the internet age. Idiosyncrasy, indeed, persisted. Considering the information-superhighway concept unsuitable for China's developmental reality, eminent telecom experts suggested using existing low-speed networks as a quick start while letting institutional clients build their own information systems.[5]

This design created two sites of gravity in the 1990s, the state information network overseen by the Ministry of Electronics Industry (MEI) and the public internet service operated by the Ministry of Posts and Telecommunications (MPT). Their competition manifested tension between national and global modes of system development. In 1993 the State Council set up the National Joint Conference on State Economic Informatization among major economic management departments.[6] The task force led by the MEI initiated its signature Golden Projects, of which the Golden Bridge Information Network was designed to be a "state information road." As a special purpose network, Golden Bridge interconnected proprietary wide-area data networks dedicated for communication within government agencies and state enterprises.[7] The need to harmonize China's trade regime with international standards motivated this project. In the 1990s Australia, Canada, Europe, Japan, Singapore, South Korea, and the United States had all gone "paperless" in international trading, disfavoring trading partners without similar capacity. China's answer to going paperless was Golden Customs, a subset of the Golden Project and an applied information system linking all foreign-trade departments and firms to realize electronic data exchanges. This was only one of many examples.

Although the MEI, the supervisory authority overseeing three-fourths of domestic telecom manufacturing enterprises, led the Golden Projects, its status was declining in a changing political economy of information. The IT revolution in the 1970s and onwards, along with China's system-wide shift toward an outward-looking economy, induced the state to depend on foreign products and foreign-invested production as a so-called intermediary step toward self-reliance and catch-up.[8] The compromise expressed itself fully in telecommunications. As early as 1986, the state had liberalized foreign imports, including electronic telephone switches and fiber-optic cables, first in coastal regions and then for national pipelines. Although lobbying for a "state will" in supporting indigenous industries, the MEI could not stop transnational companies from taking away the majority of the network-equipment market. Its former buyers, mostly military and private network users, shifted their orders to transnational companies.[9] The MEI lost more ground when its Golden Projects clung to the technonationalist principle of Mao's era,[10] intending to give state-sponsored research institutes an opportunity to sell homegrown products.

In contrast to the declining MEI, the MPT thrived in the outward-looking economy, becoming an "internationalist" ministry. Prior to the market reform, the MPT system had played an auxiliary role in the national economy, and its public telephone market was small. From the 1980s, as discussed in chapter 2, the MPT started to commercialize its network assets. By making a drastic departure from its state-oriented institutional tradition, the MPT turned its urban networks into quasi-independent operational entities, free to make monopoly profits while responsible for their own losses and expenses. Driven by galloping demand, favorable policy, and foreign-made equipment, the MPT telecom system shed its loss-making image in the 1990s and gained excellent commercial prospects. Between 1991 and 1995 alone, telecom networks raised investment capital worth 241.4 billion yuan (US$36 billion) to have most networks digitalized and program-controlled switches installed.[11]

It is not surprising that Golden Bridge soon found its competitor. In 1995 China Telecom under the jurisdiction of the MPT built its first commercial network, ChinaNet, an internet service provider, to serve the general public. In order to pool capital and to avoid duplication, the state had affirmed in 1990 the MPT monopoly control over public communication networks, banning burgeoning dedicated networks set up by state-owned enterprises and national ministries from offering public services without the approval of the MPT or interconnection with its system.[12] This authority soon extended to the internet. The 1996 provisional directive on the management of international connections by computer information networks in the People's Republic of China (PRC), which stipulated that all international data traffic must go through the gateway China Telecom provided, fortified the MPT's sole top-level control over commercial internet services.[13]

The rivalry between the MEI and MPT ended in 1998 when both were merged into the Ministry of Information Industry (MII). The merge was part of the 1998 government reshuffling, a major attempt to downgrade industrial administrations inherited from the planning economy, for the purpose of removing organized opposition to the making of the WTO deal.[14] Despite the creation of the MII, the general shift of gravity from the MEI to MPT was clear. It meant that in the following years, nation-centric visions about the information society had to compromise with, if not totally give way to, global structural influences—as telecommunications under the purview of the MPT and then the MII became a bridge to the global capitalist system and, thus, was subjected to global neoliberal politics, as well.

Making the Internet's Socio-institutional Bedrocks

WTO ENTRY AND INSTITUTIONAL OUTSOURCING

Local competition for foreign industrial capital was acute in the 1990s, resulting in oversupply of low-end, export-processing capacities. The breakout of the 1997 Asian financial crisis, exacerbated by dropping disposable income for urban residents as a result of the draconian state enterprise reform, threatened an imminent economic slowdown. The turmoil, however, did not slow down China's merge into the global capitalist economy but, instead, precipitated the process. In view of China's similarity with Southeast Asian countries in terms of low-end export structures, the Chinese state felt the urge to cultivate new industries with sustainable market demand and to keep pace with external technological changes. Bulking up an ICT-dominant export-processing regime along with its supporting industries was seen as an antidote to the redundancy of production capacities. The willingness for China to grow export-processing trade with the Global North also came from the need for managerial expertise and the latest capital equipment.

At this juncture, China's WTO accession in 2001 offered a convenient boost to the export-processing model as the deal brought in enormous investment from transnational corporations, further enhancing China in global production and global trade.

The threat of economic slowdown also called for an economic restructuring plan, which included, as explained by then Premier Zhu Rongji, a speedy development of consumer-friendly tertiary industries, such as housing, tourism, and telecom services.[15] In the telecom sector, the momentum for selective liberalization was building up in the 1990s. As mentioned, the MPT system had been a beneficiary of China's integration into the global economy, both commercially and institutionally. However, its claim to monopoly was contested. After all, reformers at various levels of the government had promulgated decentralization and liberalization since the 1980s. In the voice market especially, the gradual transition to a buyer's market, primarily for urban users, put the MPT under fire for high prices and poor service. To appease critics, the MPT in 1993 opened up the internet-service retail market, along with other value-added services. Domestic investors, such as local governments, proprietary-network operators, financial institutions, and other big clients, were allowed to own up to a 25 percent share in data communications.[16] In the global economic-slowdown context, the pressure to cultivate new consumption hotspots further justified investment liberalization as a way of driving down prices.

The domestic motives for liberalization coincided with the WTO mandates. On the global front, telecommunications was high on the neoliberal reform agenda. By leading the passage of the WTO Basic Telecommunications Service Agreement in 1997, the United States succeeded, in the words of then Federal Communications Commission (FCC) chairman Reed E. Hundt, in "export[ing] the Telecommunications Act of 1996." Backed by telecom industries, the deal was designed to end national monopolies and to create a single, integrated, global telecom market. Covering 95 percent of the world telecom market, the WTO mandate of free market triggered a "snowball" effect—as resisting countries would "see investment dollars flowing to countries with more open economies."[17]

Telecommunications was central to the US-China relationship. Leveraging a $750 billion global telecom market mostly represented by WTO members,[18] the US government pushed broad telecom liberalization as a precondition for China's entry into the WTO. At home, pressed by the Ministry of Foreign Trade and Economic Cooperation as well as the National Development and Reform Commission (NDRC), the MPT eventually gave in to a stronger WTO commitment. During the US visit of Chinese Premier Zhu Rongji in April 1999, the Chinese government vowed a commitment to the WTO basic telecom-services agreement, including the permission for foreign investment in basic telecom services up to 49 percent and in value-added services up to 50 percent.[19] Zhu stated to his American audiences that the Chinese state had recognized telecoms would become a new growth zone in the Chinese economy, thus seeking "international cooperation" in this area.[20]

US negotiators succeeded in subjecting internet operation to the same conditions in the agreement.[21] Earlier in 1999, the second US-China telecommunications summit had expanded its agenda from traditional telephone products to information technology products.[22] The American side urged China to stop developing electrical switches and to adopt internet-protocol switching. In this US-dominated new market, Chinese telecom operators depended on the products of Vocaltso, Cisco Systems, and Clarent.[23] Furthermore, the Chinese side endorsed AT&T's participation in internet-protocol (IP) network and service provision in Pudong District of Shanghai, to indicate China's readiness for market liberalization.

Stemming from external designs, the ensuing institutional reforms changed how state-owned national champions operated, "who populated their senior management teams, what kinds of external stakeholders they were becoming reliant on, and what types of broader networks they became immersed in."[24] Telecom operators, new and old, underwent corporate and shareholding reforms, absorbing foreign capital via stock-market listing and strategic alliances. China Telecom, the colossus from the planning economy, established a stock market–oriented performance-appraisal system. Subjected to market forces, all operators responded favorably to several interest groups, such as transnational corporations, the financial-services sector, trade-intensive businesses, and urban middle-class consumers. China Netcom, a newcomer established in 1999, boasted a technocentric vision of "building the infrastructure for

China's information age," setting its eyes exclusively on high-margin corporate clients and high-end residential subscribers. After implementing neoliberal measures, Chinese operators as market players enjoyed growing profits and emerged much stronger.

BIRTH OF BROADBAND IN A NEOLIBERAL CRISIS

The neoliberal reforms, however, were implicated in the 2001 global telecom crisis. In the 1990s venture capital from Wall Street chased and fueled a dotcom bubble. The bubble, however, was only a fraction of a much-larger problem in global telecom business. As data traffic surpassed voice traffic in volume, American telecom operators, which had been subjected to unbridled competition after the passage in the United States of the Telecommunications Act of 1996, joined an unprecedented frenzy of investment in fiber-optic cable. In particular, newcomers in the local phone market, often financed by the capital market, initiated a long series of spending sprees on advanced technologies, rolling out state-of-the-art data-transport systems.[25] Between 1996 and 2000, equipment spending by US local telecom companies doubled to about $100 billion annually.[26] Global network-equipment vendors, such as Alcatel, Cisco, Lucent, Motorola, and Nortel, were carried away by the buying binge. They sought to accelerate the ostensibly nonstop growth by financing much of the spending.[27] When this model suddenly collapsed under the weight of overcapacity and overcompetition, demand evaporated, and equipment vendors were on the verge of bankruptcy. In 2001 telecom spending fell in the data-networking business by 10 percent, but in 2002 the decline was an "astronomical 43 percent."[28]

In China in the late 1990s, internet companies could "relatively easily" get millions of dollars in venture-capital funding.[29] On the heels of the Sino-US WTO negotiations, listed Chinese web companies saw their stock prices skyrocketing in the New York Stock Exchange; foreign investors, including Goldman Sachs, IDG, and Yahoo, were lining up investments for the Chinese market.[30] Chinese state banks, however, were slow in investing in local internet startups—as state regulators saw the internet more as "a simple extension of telecom services" than a whole new industry.[31] The MII, like Chinese banks, resisted the influence of nonstate web companies. Then MII minister Wu Jichuan repeatedly stressed that nothing other than verifiable use value for "traditional" industries can justify internet development.[32]

Thanks to the nascent status of the internet there, Chinese telecom operators and the Chinese economy were insulated from the internet bubble. The third Sino-US telecom summit in 2004 reflected a changing market situation of the two countries. While China had built one of the largest telecom networks, the United States only began its recovery after its network-equipment market shrank by 75 percent from 2000. The US government continued to promote market liberalization at the forum; the Chinese delegation, however, became assertive about the role of the state, armored with a sense of self-importance in supporting the US technical leadership.[33] Indeed, after the telecom crisis, policymakers in countries where neoliberal reforms had gone extreme and awry started to adopt some "counter-deregulation approaches."[34]

Chinese web companies living on shaky business models, however, were mired in the recession. Although fledglings, web companies had by the late 1990s garnered some elite promoters, who were academics, journalists, and officials.[35] The decision-making stratum, sporting fancy job titles, possessed enviable characteristics of being young, educated, and cosmopolitan and was forming a community unto itself. In the traditional telecom sector, web companies found allies, as well. China Netcom had been a passionate broadband promoter, with internet technology businessperson Edward Tian as its chief executive officer (CEO). Its primary investments, in the first few years, comprised a high-capacity IP network connecting key cities all in the eastern part of China; submarine cables connecting China with North America, Europe, and Asian Pacific countries; and fiber-optic broadband-access networks in metropolitan areas,[36] mirroring the coastal model of export-processing business.

Given the influential supporter base of the internet, it is no surprise that policy makers and corporate leaders in China, like their foreign counterparts, searched for cures for the struggling web business. It was not digital capitalism that was being questioned but, instead, the Western deviation from market principles. In *People's Daily*, one view argued that web companies alone could not sustain a new digital economy; instead, the main driving force should be millions of enterprises in traditional sectors, which use information and communications technology in everyday operation. Broadband, according to this view, would enable such utilitarian functions.[37] Another view called for ending the era of free-of-charge online services; for this purpose, broadband with technical capacity to support interactive and multimedia content was once again singled out as a technological solution.[38]

Both in China and abroad, the global telecom crisis did not chill the elitist passions for a broadband economy. To dig the telecom business from the slump, the Federal Communications Commission (FCC) of the United States proposed in 2002 hastening broadband-service deployment through deregulation measures.[39] Afterwards from 2004, broadband hinged on wired- and wireless-access technology became a top priority on the US president's IT agenda;[40] President George W. Bush set a national goal of promoting broadband technology, which won applause from global vendors. Led by the United States and Japan, fiber-optic wiring, or the so-called FTTx (fiber to the x), scheme became a global trend after 2004. As promulgated by a 2003 International Telecommunications Union (ITU) report with a telling title "Birth of Broadband," broadband represented a route to offset the slowdown in the global telecom business, for both telecom operators and equipment suppliers.[41]

For Chinese leaders, the thriving broadband economy in South Korea emerging out of the Asian financial crisis offered a compelling example. Having no broadband before 1998, South Korea already "far exceeded" all other nations in terms of broadband penetration in the early years of the twenty-first century.[42] After all, the Chinese leadership was searching for approaches to improve the country's economic profile. South Korea's success, along with the relentless efforts by many other Asian countries to resurrect a new digital economy, instigated the Chinese state to move apace with this global trend.

Finding Markets for Broadband

Into the twenty-first century, a broadband gold rush finally began in China. In the late 1990s, industry parks, business districts, office complexes, and gated neighborhoods had mushroomed, catering to corporate tenants and urban elites. Real estate developers used broadband connectivity as a sales booster for high-priced properties. To retain big clients, telecom operators joined the "enclosure movement," ramping up the supply of fiber-optic pipelines and customer-premises networks. The prospect of China becoming a major manufacturing center in the world, the presence of aggressive nonstate competitors in the customer premises–network market (discussed later), the availability of cheap installation workers, and the free rights of way granted by the government all gave extra impetus to the fiber-optic wiring.[43] Equipment providers, both from overseas and at home, also became strong advocates in the Chinese market when other regional markets for staple products, such as optical-network equipment, digital-subscriber-line (DSL) central-office ports, and DSL customer-premises equipment, shrank a great deal after the internet bubble.[44]

CONSUMERIZATION OF BROADBAND

From 2001 to 2003, 5 percent of telecom investment went to data communications, up from 3.7 percent in 1998.[45] Although the estimated sum of 36 billion yuan (US$4.3 billion) was modest,[46] it was a heady start for the Chinese market and portended a steep growth. As figure 3.1 shows, the global telecom crisis and domestic corporate reshuffling did not curb the enthusiasm for long. Into

Figure 3.1. Fixed-asset investment in data communication networks in China in billion yuan, 1999–2008, 2013–15.

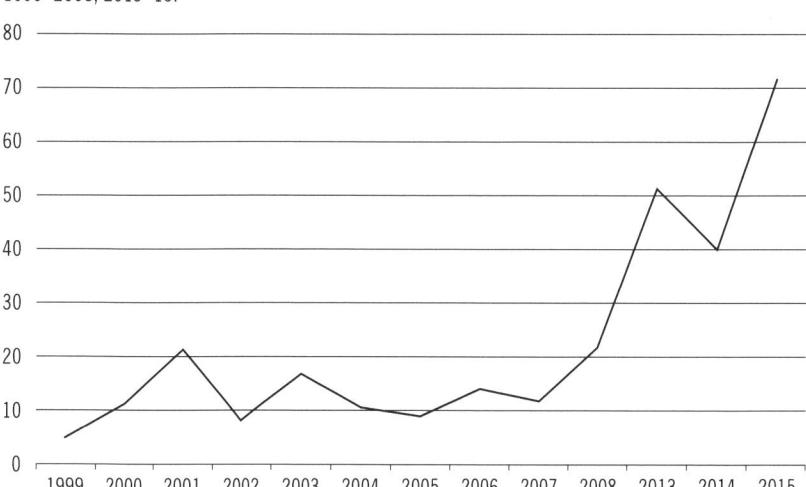

Sources: China Academy of Telecommunication Research 工业和信息化部电信研究院, "Zhongguo dianxingye 60 nian," 中国电信业60年 [Sixty years of China's telecommunication industry] (Beijing: Renmin youdian chubanshe 人民邮电出版社, 2009), 137; MIIT, "2013 nian tongxin yunyingye tongji gongbao," 2013年通信运营业统计公报 [2013 telecoms operation statistics], January 23, 2014, accessed January 12, 2016, http://www.miit.gov.cn/n11293472/n11293832/n11294132/n12858447/15861120.html; MIIT, "2014 nian tongxin yunyingye tongji gongbao," 2014年通信运营业统计公报 [2014 telecoms operation statistics], January 20, 2015, accessed January 16, 2016, http://www.miit.gov.cn/n11293472/n11293832/n11294132/n12858447/16414615.html; MIIT, "2015 nian tongxin yunyingye tongji gongbao," 2015年通信运营业统计公报 [2015 telecoms operation statistics], January 21, 2016, accessed March 2, 2016, http://www.miit.gov.cn/n1146312/n1146904/n1648372/c4620679/content.html.

the Eleventh Five-Year Plan period (2006–10), broadband construction consumed up to 40 percent of telecom capital spending. China Telecom, alone, spent 150 billion yuan (US$20.8 billion), becoming the largest broadband operator worldwide.[47] This steadfast progress in 2007 prompted Zhao Houlin, then ITU deputy secretary-general, to praise China as being "exceptional" in a global context of widening digital gaps between developed and developing countries.[48]

Why could China do this? Loan-financed network expansion had continued into the 1990s to build a national grid of fiber-optic backbones. Bank loans, instead of foreign government loans, underwrote most expenditure. The debt ratio of China Telecom, for example, rose from 35 percent in 1997 to 45 percent in 1999; some provinces, cities, and counties in the interior region went well beyond the 50 percent mark.[49] Into the twenty-first century, a national grid of fiber-optic backbones was already in place, and metropolitan area networks were the biggest site of spending. As the number 1 broadband operator, China Telecom used profit from its mature voice market to subsidize the loss-making data-network business.[50]

The fanfare surrounding broadband contrasted with the slowdown of traditional telecom businesses. Market saturation in urban and coastal markets, coupled with low accessibility and inadequate use in rural markets, had slowed revenue growth in telephone landlines. The decline of long-distance calling, ripped off continually by the popular IP telephone, ushered in a structural crisis for fixed-line operators (table 3.1). Accompanying the crisis of profitability in the traditional voice market, however, was the malaise of underuse in the new broadband market. The utilization rate of China Telecom's fiber-optic resources fell below 50 percent in 2004.[51] Indeed, all the talk about a new digital economy was premised on broadband internet and even fiber connectivity. But the question is, How would state players possibly create organic links between networks and the society at large?

Commodifying data capacity was not an easy task. Inside China, policy makers and researchers often referred to South Korea as the success story in the state-led creation of a broadband-based information economy. What distinguished South Korea, however, was not just sustained state investment in broadband infrastructures but a deliberate program to popularize broadband applications and to amplify consumer demand.[52] While anticipated or even imagined consumer needs justified broadband deployment, the South Korean government carried out a systematic social-engineering campaign to create IT-based governments, businesses, and even citizenship.[53] Likewise, the Chinese state, its telecom operators, and nonstate web companies made some concerted efforts to consumerize the internet.

In the 2000s Chinese operators embarked on sales campaigns, offering discounted monthly rates, free desktops, and even free installation. In 2005 the State-Owned Assets Supervision and Administration Commission (SASAC) began to appraise the performance of China Telecom and China Netcom in terms of broadband subscription, reinforcing the newly found business focus.[54] Sustained marketing efforts triggered market demand. Although limited before 2002,[55] market demand exploded from 2003. That year, broadband subscribers exceeded twelve million.[56] In 2005 broadband subscribers surpassed dial-up internet users.[57] By 2007 broadband users already constituted the majority, marking the coming of a broadband age.

The absolute market size was relatively small, though, unlikely to catch up with the traditional TV and telephone markets in any short term. Economic inequality—and the concentration of computer literacy among urban elites—are

Table 3.1. Distribution of telecom revenue, percentage, for select years 1999–2015

Type of service	1999	2000	2001	2004	2005	2007	2008	2010	2012	2014	2015
Mobile communications*	36.9	41.7	45.7	43.0	45.1	50.9	55.1	69.9	73.7	74.5	73.8
Data communications†	1.5	2.4	3.7	6.2	6.8	8.4	9.8	—	—	13.2	13.6
Fixed-line voice business (domestic and international long-distance, local calling)	49.6	50.3	44.0	50.5	47.9	40.6	34.9	10.3	5.8	4.1	3.6

* Includes income from voice and data business on wireless networks.
† Income from data and internet business on fixed-line networks.
Note: Data communications and fixed-line voice business do not add up to total revenue on fixed-line networks that also includes value-added services.
Sources: "2001 nian dianxin yewu shouru jiegou fenxi, " 2001 年电信业务收入结构发展现状分析 [Revenue structure analysis of the development of telecommunication service in 2001], CCID 赛迪顾问, June 27, 2002, accessed September 1, 2014, http://www.ccidreport.com/market/article/content/402/200206/17859.html; MIIT, "Xinxichanyebu fabu 2005 nian zhongguo tongxinye fazhan tongji gongbao," 信息产业部发布2005年中国通信业发展统计公报 [MII released 2005 telecoms development statistics], February 10, 2002, accessed January 11, 2015, http://www.gov.cn/jrzg/2006-02/10/content_185059.htm; MIIT "Xinxichanyebu fabu 2007 nian quanguo tongxinye fazhan tongji gongbao," 信息产业部发布2007年中国通信业发展统计公报 [MII released 2007 telecoms development statistics], February 5, 2008, accessed January 11, 2015, http://www.gov.cn/ztzl/2008-02/05/content_883563.htm; MIIT, "Gongye he xinxihua bu fabu 2010 nian quanguo dianxinye tongji gongbao," 工业和信息化部发布2010年全国电信业统计公报 [MII released 2010 national telecoms statistics], January 26, 2011, http://finance.sina.com.cn/roll/20110126/16119314512.shtml; MIIT, "2012 nian quanguo tongxinye tongji gongbao," 2012年全国通信业统计公报 [2012 national telecoms statistics], July 23, 2013, accessed May 19, 2016, http://www.scio.gov.cn/ztk/xwfb/2013/25/11/Document/1338200/1338200_2.htm; MIIT, "2014 nian tongxin yunyingye tongji gongbao," 2014年通信运营业统计公报 [2014 telecoms operation statistics], January 20, 2015, accessed May 19, 2016, http://news.xinhuanet.com/info/2015-01/21/c_133934777.htm; MIIT, "2015 nian tongxin yunyingye tongji gongbao," 2015年通信运营业统计公报 [2015 telecoms operation statistics], January 21, 2016, accessed March 2, 2016, http://www.miit.gov.cn/n1146312/n1146904/n1648372/c4620679/content.html.

structurally rooted and have hampered further diffusion. To profit quickly and amply, industry players in the broadband market earnestly searched for killer applications, the kind of popular computer programs that ordinary users are willing to spend time and money on. Interactive and often addictive entertainment services that would generate high data flows, such as online gaming and video-on-demand, received lots of praise from the industry—and from the government—for reducing skill requirements and for increasing individual dependence on broadband. When the market reached 2 billion yuan (US$241 million) in 2003, a drastic jump from 91 million yuan in 2002, the All China Sports Federation enlisted gaming as an official sport and mainstreamed it through state-sponsored events.[58] Also in 2003, gaming-related research projects gained access to the prestigious 863 National High Technology Research and Development Program, a state funding program intended for strategic high technology.[59]

To cultivate a commercial ecosystem for broadband and to build proprietary entrance to this ecosystem, telecom operators also built branded, fee-based gateways to internet applications. These transaction platforms, exemplified by China Mobile's Monternet (*Yidong mengwang*) and China Telecom's Vnet (*Hulian xingkong*), served to aggregate and commodify miscellaneous information services sourced from web companies while authenticating and charging users. After weathering the financial setback in the wake of the internet bubble, surviving Chinese web companies became pragmatic, looking for ways to turn visitors into revenue streams and to institute membership-based pay-per systems.[60] They spared no effort in cultivating new consumption habits—with varying degrees of collaboration and contention with telecom operators. Alibaba, the e-commerce conglomerate, is an outstanding example, leading the roaring online retail market (table 3.2). The company is particularly successful in conjuring a corporate persona, one imbued with market populism and couched in touching grassroots stories told by job-seeking youth, housewives, and disabled migrants who opened online stores. In addition to e-commerce, instant messaging and online gaming became two of the few popular and profitable applications. The symbiotic yet tensioned relationship between telecom operators and web companies proved conducive to market development: By 2004 the internet industry found 73 percent of users spending over 50 yuan (US$6) per month on various services, a notable shift from the free internet era in the 1990s.[61]

As commodity chains built on wired and wireless broadband networks are the bedrock for information consumption, they take up a salient role in the post-2008 economic restructuring scheme, amplifying the importance of network connectivity, speed, and affordability.

Table 3.2. Internet commerce, in trillion yuan, 2004–14

	Volume of e-Commerce	Online Shopping	Cross-Border e-Commerce
2004	.4	—	—
2005	.6	—	—
2006	1.0	—	—
2007	1.7	—	—
2008	3	—	—
2009	3.6	—	—
2010	4.8	.5	
2011	6.4	.8	1.6
2012	8.1	1.3	2
2013	9.9	1.9	3.1
2014	12.3	2.8	3.8

Sources: "Shangwubu: yuji 2016 nian kuajing dianshang jiang zengzhi 6.5 wan yi," 商务部：预计2016年跨境电商将增值6.5万亿元 [Ministry of Commerce: Cross-border e-commerce to reach 6.5 trillion yuan], Ali yanjiuyuan 阿里研究院, accessed January 12, 2016, http://daxue.taobao.com/market/daxue/kuajingdianshang1.php; iResearch 艾瑞咨询, "2013 niandu dianzi shangwu shichang hexin shuju fabu," 2013年度电子商务市场核心数据发布 [2013 e-commerce market statistics], accessed January 16, 2016, http://www.iresearch.com.cn/coredata/2013q4_1.shtml#a2; Zhang Yixuan 张意轩, "Dianzishangwu sheng ji wuxian," 电子商务生机无限 [Unlimited vitality of e-commerce], *Renmin ribao* 人民日报, March 21, 2009, 14; Zhifeng Xu 许志峰, "Zhongguo shekeyuan diaoyan baogao xianshi yu qi cheng wangmin you shangwang gouwu jingli 2005 nian wangmin wangshang xiaofei zonge 135.05 yi yuan," 中国社科院调研报告显示 逾七成网民有上网购物经历 2005年网民网上消费总额135.05亿元 [Chinese Academy of Social Sciences released a report showing that more than 70 percent of netizens having shopped online, 2005 Chinese online sales reached 13.5 billion yuan], 人民日报 *People's Daily*, February 20, 2006, 6; "Zhongguo dianzi shangwu shichang guimo 2007 nian youwang dadao 1.7 billion yuan," 中国电子商务市场规模2007年有望达到1.7万亿元 [E-commerce expected to pass 1.7 trillion yuan in 2007], *Xinhua News*, March 22, 2007, http://www.gov.cn/jrzg/2007-03/22/content_557994.htm; Ma Yun 马芸, "Zheng zhuang dai fa"; iResearch, "2014 niandu zhongguo hulianwang hexin shuju fabu: dianzi shangwu," 2014年度中国互联网核心数据发布:电子商务 [2014 e-commerce statistics], accessed January 12, 2016, http://news.iresearch.cn/zt/246308.shtml; Shu Kang 亢, "2014 nian woguo kuajing dianshang jiaoyi dadao 3.75 wan yi yuan, tongbi zengzhang 39%; qizhong, kuajing dianshang lingshoue dadao 4492 yi yuan, zengsu 44%," 2014年我国跨境电商交易额达到3.75万亿元,同比增长39%。其中,跨境电商零售额达到4492亿元,增速44% [2014 China cross-border e-commerce turnover reached 3.75 trillion yuan, a like-for-like increase of 39%, including 449.2 billion yuan cross-border retail sales with an increase of 44%], *People.com* 人民网—财经, accessed February 16, 2016, http://finance.people.com.cn/n/2015/0517/c1004-27012240.html.

CREATING WEB-ENABLED ENTERPRISES

In the enterprise-networks market, telecom operators along with global IT giants have also promulgated web enablement to encourage the recasting of the economy around information and communications technology.

The business convergence between IT companies and network operators deepened in the past decades. On the supply side, internet-protocol networks, if provided in a competitive market, could offer a combination of voice and data communication at much-lower prices. Coveting this new market, global IT giants transformed themselves into internet-related technology-and-service providers. IBM and Huawei, for example, developed special solutions to support IP infrastructures and made sale pitches whenever they could. On the demand side, transnational corporations, at the height of globalization, wanted cheaper global solutions. As the Global Fortune 500 companies accounted for almost half of the total revenue of the global telecom business as of 2009,[62] it is no surprise they successfully pressed telecom operators into taking up IP transformation. As more transnational corporations came to China after its WTO entry, the country has presented a new telecom market for IT and software solutions.

Telecom operators in China felt the urge to undergo IP transformation. China Telecom in 2005 started to participate in the state informatization campaign intended to promote the adoption of networked information technology in various social and economic arenas. China Netcom earned the bulk of its revenue from corporate product lines, including corporate data, voice-over-IP telephony, and wholesale business, but only 20 percent from residential consumers and small- and medium-size enterprises (SME).[63] Traditionally, data-intensive institutions, such as banks, time-sensitive companies (such as securities markets and stock exchanges), businesses with global reach including import and export, and network-dependent service providers (such as internet cafes and gaming companies), had all been major clients for telecom services. To get involved in more areas, however, telecom operators needed to provide IP network–based IT applications in all walks of life. The telecoms were certainly proud of broadband-enabled synergy. When commenting on the smart-city projects supported by integrated information-and-communications technologies around the country, Lu Yimin, vice chairperson and president of China Unicom, pointed to energy, transport, education, public security, and medicine and health as potential users.[64]

Although web-based applications made inroads into many institutions, manufacturing enterprises were not as receptive as powerful stakeholders had wished. It was particularly an uphill battle to convince China's small manufacturing enterprises to spend money on IT solutions. Since the WTO entry, China has become the global ICT assembly hub, processing components and parts sourced from neighboring countries into final products. This China-centric production system engendered a growing number of SMEs interacting upstream and downstream with transnational giants. China Telecom in Guangdong, for example, set eyes on more than one million such enterprises in the province, hoping to cultivate their demand for services delivered by broadband. Although it was estimated about half of the broadband accounts as of 2002 were set up in Guangdong,[65] SMEs there each spent merely 200 yuan (US$24) each month on communications in 2005.[66] Large-scale enterprises fared better but fell far behind Western counterparts: According to an authoritative survey, IT expenditures increased in a select group of Chinese enterprises, though still at a low level of 0.8 percent of total assets—far below the 8 to 10 percent global benchmark.[67]

Electronic commerce was one hopeful—as it would support and reinforce the export-processing regime (table 3.3; see table 3.2). Back in 1999, Craig Barrett, Intel's chief operating officer, had urged China to rapidly build a strong foundation for e-commerce in order to secure its position in global trade. However, even e-commerce had a slow start when driven only by domestic startups and global IT giants.[68] By 2003 merely 11 percent of 8.3 million SMEs were engaged in e-commerce, making industry observers believe that a self-regulated market provided little incentive for modernization through IT.[69] Recent surveys show

Table 3.3. Major segments of e-commerce by trade volume, 2012, 2013, and 2014

Types of e-Commerce	Trade Volume (%)		
	2012	2013	2014
Business-to-business (B2B) small-and medium-size enterprises	53.3	51.7	50
B2B large enterprises above designated size*	28.3	26.2	23.4
Online shopping	16	18.6	22.9

* In 2011, the benchmark of main business revenue was raised from 5 million yuan to 20 million yuan.
Note: Columns do not add up to 100 percent because the statistics only include major types of e-commerce.
Sources: "2012 niandu dianzi shangwu shichang hexin shuju fabu," 2012年度电子商务市场核心数据发布 [2012 e-commerce market statistics], *iResearch*, accessed January 12, 2016, http://www.iresearch.com.cn/coredata/2012q4_1.shtml; "2013 niandu dianzi shangwu shichang hexin shuju fabu," 2013年度电子商务市场核心数据发布 [2013 e-commerce market statistics], iResearch, accessed January 16, 2016, http://www.iresearch.com.cn/coredata/2013q4_1.shtml#a2; "2014 niandu zhongguo hulianwang hexin shuju fabu: dianzi shangwu," 2014年度中国互联网核心数据发布:电子商务 [2014 e-commerce statistics], *iResearch*, accessed January 12, 2016, http://news.iresearch.cn/zt/246308.shtml.

that by 2013 the ratio of manufacturing enterprises with internet connection was 82 percent, but for those with online stores, it was 25 percent.[70]

Given the lukewarm reaction by manufacturing enterprises, the state acted to push the internet and its applications into the very fabric of the national economy. In 2000 the State Council reenacted the national leadership group to promote the homegrown concept of informatization. It entailed, first and foremost, adapting the government itself to the information age by moving administrative functions online. Xiang Huaicheng, then minister of finance, estimated government IT expenditures in 2002 would amount to 10 billion yuan (US$1.2 billion).[71] At the Sixteenth Party Congress in 2002, the state then announced the so-called neo-industrialization strategy, a plan of using information technology to modernize traditional industries while expanding market demand for ICT products and services through systematic deployment by traditional industries. This marked the beginning of a demand-centric state intervention.

Apart from setting up the new policy framework, the state handpicked large-scale enterprises to be the "dragonhead," as large-scale enterprises, once remodeled with ICT applications, could exert influence via supply chains and customer relations on the rest of Chinese enterprises. Regulatory entities, including the Commission of Foreign Trade and Economic Cooperation and the Ministry of Science and Technology (MOST), put forth favorable fiscal policy to encourage ICT adoption in manufacturing industries that continued to face full-blown global competition. Telecom operators and equipment vendors were also asked to spearhead managerial reform and production reorganization around ICT applications. On the national level, the MII used the level of business-related ICT applications as one criterion in the honorary One Hundred Electronics Enterprises selection. On the provincial level, local bureaus identified one enterprise or two to give guidance to. The overall rationale was to wield corporate ICT use to trigger sector-wide adoption and to propel societal diffusion.[72]

This effort of promoting corporate ICT use was carried forward in 2007 when the SASAC promoted ICT applications in centrally owned state enterprises as a way to create globally competitive national champions. According to the SASAC's 2007 assessment, nearly 7 percent of the enterprises under its supervision reached a so-called advanced level—approaching the level of top transnational corporations, including all telecom operators, while 41 percent were merely "moderate." In the SASAC's Twelfth Five-Year Plan, the goal was to push a majority up to the advanced level.[73]

The Chinese state was instrumental in creating a web-enabled economy. Although the outcomes were insufficient, the state's policies and actions were meant to popularize the idea of using networked applications to retool traditional industry and commerce and to upgrade the standing of Chinese enterprises in the global economic network. As we will see, this agenda took up a central position in the post-2008 economic restructuring, further amplifying the strategic importance of broadband.

Broadband Rises as a National Strategy Post-2008

Networks have never been as important as in the wake of the 2008 global economic crisis. Against the backdrop of stagnation, the capitalist scramble for first-mover advantages has energized a zealous search worldwide for new business opportunities brought by next-generation innovations. Budding business ideas, such as big data, machine-to-machine communication, and cloud computing, all hinge upon a ubiquitous, mobile, and broadband network. In such a milieu, not having ubiquitous broadband deployment, in the words of Michael J. Copps, FCC chairperson, would cause "curbs on innovation, curbs on entrepreneurship, and loss of competitive position" in the global marketplace.[74]

A PIVOT TO A COMMANDING-HEIGHTS ECONOMY

The Chinese state also sees value in broadband for its economic restructuring agenda. While low-end assembly and processing operations make up China's export economy, telecommunications is becoming a pivot in an alternative commanding-heights economy because the internet has enabled information-and-communication technologies to integrate with all sorts of operation from health care to transportation, from manufacturing to agriculture. Similar to the case of the United States, broadband is no longer a matter of telecom operators but is increasingly tied up with national competitiveness and general economic development. To become a leading economic power, China "must become an internet strong country," as a top Chinese telecom executive put it.[75]

Internet-related industries central to the commanding-heights economy are rapidly evolving. In the technical areas of wireless broadband and basic chips, domestic enterprises have shown some signs of reaching a tipping point in innovation and industrialization and, therefore, yearn for top-level design and strategic investment.[76] To achieve a real breakthrough is a tall order, though. With mass production of final products having moved to China, leading IT companies, the majority of which are in countries other than China, are freed up to specialize in innovating platforms, designs, and architectures, ranging from screen technologies to new ways of producing and selling music and video.[77] To harness the internet as a catalyst integrated into general economic development, China needs to address its legacy technological deficits and keep pace with software, terminal, and service innovations.

Equally essential to the commanding-heights economy is its ability to interact and modernize traditional industries. From car electronics to medical electronics and from e-commerce to logistics, information-and-communications technology is seen as the epicenter of a technological revolution and is credited for the outpouring of new industries, new business models, and new consumption hotspots. As industry pundits are eager to tell us, traditional industries have looked to broadband and its applications for a new life. Zhao Houlin, then ITU deputy secretary-general, told his countrymen in 2008 that the reason the term "information society" is elevated to such an unprecedented height is the likelihood for traditional sectors to transform through information-and-communications technology.[78]

Broadband also has a stake in expanding domestic consumption. In 2012, during the Eighteenth Party Congress, *People's Daily* published an authoritative article on economic restructuring, which was tellingly titled "Information Consumption: A New Expansion Engine of Domestic Demand." To encourage information consumption, Miao Wei, MIIT minister, pledged to expand information infrastructures and to cultivate digital-content industries. Network convergence and smart devices have, indeed, boosted electronic consumerism in China. While smart-device sales reached 146.9 billion yuan (US$22.6 billion) in 2011, nonvoice telecom revenue, comprising mostly the incomes from internet access and data communication, passed the critical 50 percent threshold in 2012 when the total telecom revenue for the first time topped 1 trillion yuan (US$159 billion). This category of business then reached 768.5 billion yuan (US$122 billion) at 68.5 percent of the total revenue in 2015.[79] The spending of approximately $193 per capita per year was small in comparison with the American and Japanese standards,[80] but China's huge population still presents an enviable reservoir of information consumerism.

Given all the importance attributed to broadband, how well prepared are telecom operators to undertake this pivotal role? There is no easy answer, given the contradictory positions they occupy. Although Chinese telecom operators are large-scale state enterprises under direct state supervision, they have—over the past two decades—become part of the most globalized business sector in China. Every technological and economic trend on the global scale can be clearly felt at home—via the presence and influence of international equity owners, transnational corporate clients, and IT- and telecom-equipment suppliers who sell solutions around the world. The question becomes, To what extents can the state harness global market dynamics and, in this case, the fiber-optic connectivity fad for economic restructuring purposes?

OBSTACLES ON THE GROUND

The birth and frenzy of broadband took place when telecom operators transformed into globally integrated, competition-driven, and commercially savvy corporate players. Unlike the 1980s, when obstacles against network expansion resided in the planning economy, the post-2008 era has presented a different set of obstacles stemming from a changed political economy of telecommunications.

The quality of broadband services hinges upon access technology. Since 2000 various broadband-access technologies, operated over copper landline networks, including DSL services, have been available. But they do not live up to the idealized high-speed scenario of advanced information societies. Replacing copper lines with fiber-optic cable in broadband-access networks is necessary but is very expensive. In China it is estimated that operators needed to spend 80 percent of investment capital on broadband construction during the Twelfth Five-Year Plan period (2011–15).[81] Indeed, this is a shared challenge for telecom operators worldwide. In response, several countries reversed the market-fundamentalist ethos of the neoliberal telecom reform, bringing back state involvement. After the 2008 global economic crisis, Australia, New Zealand, Singapore, and the United States all announced national broadband programs. Mainstream researchers also urged developing countries to include broadband in stimulus packages.[82]

In China enthusiasm for the fiber-optic broadband access network has ratcheted up since 2008. The MIIT released guiding opinions regarding fiber-optic broadband construction. In 2011 China Telecom launched its broadband campaign in twenty-one southern provinces, aiming to cover all county-level cities and above with fiber-optic networks and to enable direct fiber connectivity with one hundred million households by 2015. To achieve this goal, China Telecom spent 200 billion yuan (US$31.7 billion) from 2011 through 2015 and attracted another 7 billion yuan (US$1.1 billion) worth of nonstate investment.[83] On local levels, many cities aimed to make broadband a trademark. Beijing, Chongqing, Jiangsu, Shandong, and Wuhan all pledged support.[84] The upsurge of investment in data networks in 2008 was a clear indicator (see figure 3.1). By 2014 fixed-line broadband had absorbed an accumulated sum of 220 billion yuan (US$29.7 billion).[85]

However, labor issues complicated this networking program. During the corporate reform in the late 1990s, the state retained ownership control in strategic sectors while freeing its state-owned enterprises from socialist obligations.[86] Telecom operators slashed their formal workforces. To fuel business expansion, they hired nearly one millions informal workers who would sign contracts with labor-dispatching companies.[87] Despite informal status, most of these workers took up jobs essential to everyday operation of the business, including marketing, sales, logistics, customer service, telephone installation, and network maintenance. They received lower pay and were excluded from many benefits reserved for formal employees. This systematic deployment of dispatch workers, however, has caused low morale at grassroots levels, especially when head-to-head competition for subscription growth and when technology-driven network construction on the largest possible scale considerably increased the workload of frontline workers.[88] Small profit margins in the broadband market only made the situation worse, leading to wage stagnation. Poor service, manmade delay, and predatory behaviors as a result have been rampant.

Overcompetition in select urban markets also put the program in jeopardy. In the urban market, telecom operators often let nonstate contractors build the last one-hundred-meter (about 328 feet) connection with end users because in 2001 the state had liberalized customer-premises network construction and operation and delegated the approval authority to provincial regulators.[89] Instead of encouraging competition, however, most Chinese building owners signed exclusive contracts with only one internet service provider (ISP), forming an alliance of control.[90] During the drives to roll out fiber optic–access networks, this lack of control over access networks has left telecom operators vulnerable to rent-seeking property-managing companies, making copper-line replacement difficult and expensive.

The introduction of non–telecom operators further fragmented the market. In 2010 the state permitted mutual market entry by telecom and cable operators, ushering in new competitors in the access market. Although cable networks have not formed a national system, cable operators built access networks while linking up with the public internet system owned by telecom operators.[91] By 2011 cable operators already offered broadband services in more than twenty provinces, accounting for 3.8 percent of all broadband capacities and serving nearly five million users.[92]

Leading web companies have also acquired a stake in the provision of fiber connectivity. Dominant in the Chinese cyberspace, they generate large volumes of data flow, pressing telecom operators to scale up investment in access networks. However, across the expanding broadband network, telecom operators have not been able to trigger commensurate subscriber usage, and their revenue from broadband investment is limited to sales of network access. Unable to share the explosively growing pie of cyberspace business, they see low investment return as a disincentive.[93]

In the rural market, competition did not mitigate shortage and inequality: From 2005 to 2010, the urban-rural digital gap went up steadily, and in 2015 rural users still made up only 28 percent of the whole online community in China.[94] The coexistence of oversupply and shortage is characteristic of the global telecom industry, where operators in saturated markets seek "broadband, mobility, and convergence" to create new revenue streams, while underdeveloped markets still yearn for basic network coverage.[95] However, having been incorporated into all sorts of social and economic activities, broadband services are taking on the importance of public utilities. To ensure that public benefits are widely shared, coverage expansion is essential in any country. This is also true for China. However, the profit-seeking imperative of telecom operators provides little incentive for redistributive network development. Although publishing corporate social-responsibility reports every year, telecom operators are ready to acknowledge market failure with respect to extending bandwidth to rural China. "To make operators build [networks] or force operators to invest is contrary to market rules and unrealistic," one China Telecom source said.[96] Telecom operators still regard rural connectivity as a burdensome duty imposed by their state ownership status and spent more than 90 billion yuan (US$12.3 billion) from 2001 through 2015 on village access to telecommunications,[97] but nonstate providers have no moral or political obligation and only operate in lucrative urban areas.

State authorities do weigh in. The NDRC sets universal service goals for the industry. However, the procedure of formulating the targets requires input from local governments, the MIIT, the SASAC, and even MOST.[98] The involvement of so many stakeholders means that the government-endorsed timeline for network expansion often comes directly from corporate headquarters, leaving telecom operators to support rural connectivity as long as they feel it is proper according to business planning. As the responsible authority, the MIIT has an annual universal service fund of 400 million yuan (US$63.5 million) for allocation to telecom operators, which then each distributes the subsidies to its provincial companies,[99] but the subsidy is too small to influence investment decisions of telecom operators.

DEBATED DEVELOPMENTAL STATE

In 2008 the MIIT released 3G operational licenses earlier than planned to take advantage of the good financial situation of telecom operators. This licensing triggered a spending spree, ramping up fixed-assets investment in support of the broader objective of countering export slowdown.[100] Later, the Chinese state showered infrastructure sectors, except telecommunications, with billions of stimulus money. When the complications of this big spending started to emerge in the macro economy, a debate went on about how to achieve economic restructuring, whether by expanding market logic or allowing governmental investment to return.[101] Neoclassical economic theory limits the role of the state in a market economy to the "letting the market to operate" straitjacket, whereas critics evoke the concept of "market failure" to stress the state's role in providing public service, mitigating negative externalities, and redistributing wealth.[102] In China-area studies, scholars have documented institutional reforms in the "transitional" society toward a market economy.[103] But the question remains, Does the remaking of the state do justice to public service and other developmental goals?

Although broadband is made into a primary site of construction for the commanding-heights economy, the Chinese state has not acted as a unitary whole but is divided by conflicts and rivalries over market and policy objectives. The MIIT was called upon to act as the responsible administration in the rollout of fiber-optic cable. Yet, the MIIT has few levers, as its regulatory authority does not cover business operation. While it can promote technological advance, it cannot enforce unpopular business decisions alone. Provincial communication administrations, which are local branches of the MIIT, play regulatory roles and administer technical matters but are not capable of fulfilling political tasks.[104] In local contexts, therefore, the MIIT has no substantive power to curb predatory behaviors spurred by overcompetition in the urban-access market. In this situation, the MIIT has propagated its technocentric broadband vision, wishing to drum up public pressure on telecom operators.

The State Council's SASAC, established in 2003, is the majority shareholder of telecom operators and has real power over personnel, assets, and business. Aligned with transnational financial capital, which is the minority shareholder, the SASAC upholds the objective of increasing the value of invested capital. Controlling top-personnel assignment and evaluating corporate performance, it is capable of ensuring its agenda through implementation on the corporate level. However, unsatisfied with the efficiency level of telecom operators, the SASAC has not lowered performance expectations, even though knowing that redistributive social policy may affect short-term growth. Indeed, the internal inconsistency of the Chinese bureaucracy is a roadblock to any national broadband plan.

On the demand side, users are another kind of stakeholder. While rural users are neglected and voiceless, urban users have been vocal critics. Residents in major cities, in particular, already regard broadband as a daily necessity, but price-sensitive users are still the majority. Because active data use that 3G and 4G networks encourage still costs more than urban residents want to spend,[105] high expectations for the connectivity and speed of broadband have turned into big disappointment, fueling negative public opinion. Then, mainstream commentators formulated the whole issue in a categorical free-market ideology, affirming the conventional wisdom that insufficient competition causes negative customer experiences. All the assaults resulted in an anticompetition allegation against telecom operators. In 2011, after small ISPs and Tietong under China Mobile logged complaints about high prices for connecting to telecom networks, the NDRC initiated an antimonopoly investigation of China Telecom and China Unicom. State media broke the story of the originally backstage investigation.[106] Suddenly, criticisms about high prices, low speed, and the duopoly flooded from both official and nonofficial sources.

Representing telecom operators, the MIIT was on the defensive. It made a rebuttal, hoping to turn public outrage into possible support for its so-called broadband China program and campaigning for state support from the Ministry of Finance (MOF). The MIIT called for, among other things, policy and financial support from the central government, preferable land and construction policies on the local levels, and a universal-service fund drawn widely from cable operators, ISPs, and web companies. In 2012 the fifth session of the Eleventh National People's Congress reviewed the national strategy—jointly proposed by bureaucratic authorities with unresolved conflicts among them over policy priorities. The same year, to showcase its commitment, the MIIT released guiding opinions concerning a broadband universal-service and upgrading plan. Speaking of social responsibility, the plan assured telecom operators of their principal investor status while throwing its support behind projects targeted for welfare institutions, poverty-stricken areas, the countryside, low-income populations, and the SME sector.

The drafting process had not been smooth because of ideological confusion and rival interests. According to Caixin Media, a Beijing-based media group, the parties involved in drafting the plan disagreed on how to upgrade broadband. Principal issues, such as whether the goal for the national strategy should be universal service or catching up with the countries with high-speed internet and whether corporate investment or state subsidies should underwrite the project, were debated. NDRC sources said the agency "may be inclined toward universal access." Yang Peifang, chairperson of the China Information Economic Society, proposed to treat telecom operators as utilities companies entrusted with social responsibility and permitted to earn low profits only. Tang Xiaoyan, a chief engineer at the China Unicom Research Institute, however, disliked the idea: "Broadband's future direction should be market-oriented so government controls should be consolidated to ensure fair competition and access to resources. And the government should assume responsibility in areas the market cannot profitably reach."[107]

The final plan approved by the State Council in 2013 showed no significant budgetary commitment. The only highlight was the redefined status of broadband as a "strategic public infrastructure," which, presumably, would bring about facilitative treatment from governments at various levels and across different departments. Against the backdrop of accelerated construction cycles, the Chinese state seemed to share the uncertain feeling about "whether fiber optic cable is a fundamental part of the economy and, if it is fundamental, how to intervene without distorting the market."[108] Without substantive commitments on funding and enforceable policy solutions, the network-expansion plan did not solve obstacles and was put in jeopardy. To achieve the stated milestones, it was estimated that the broadband-access network alone would need 570 billion yuan (US$91.9 billion) and to achieve universal service another 500 billion yuan (US$80.6 billion).[109] Telecom operators resisted the job by not doing much. According to the three telecom operators and their equipment vendors, the target for 2013 was likely to fail.[110] As discussed in chapter 6, this gridlock remained unresolved up to 2015. As the state roiled by conflicting imperatives could not act adequately, this amounted to a "policy failure" atop market failure, in this case, of a developmental state.[111]

Conclusions

The Chinese state is lauded for "state-led development in the name of rapid economic growth and the nation's entry to the realms of industrialization and modernization."[112] Like its counterparts in East Asian countries, the Chinese state actively guides economic development and initiates economic global integration at a "gradual, measured" pace.[113] However, its developmental policies have generated serious pitfalls. In export manufacturing, it liberalized the entry of foreign industrial capital while privatizing and letting go the vast majority of state-owned assets. The deep integration with the global economy brought rapid GDP growth but sacrificed maneuvering space for self-determination.

In this globalized economy, as a result, the competitiveness of large industrial companies and small- and medium-size enterprises alike is contingent on advanced information networks. This places communications at the core of the post-2008 economic restructuring.

In strategic industries, including telecoms, the state remains the majority shareholder. By allowing public listing abroad and by instituting competition at home, it inserted incentives and constraints into these state enterprises. As a result, telecom operators, both incumbent and new, have become responsive enough to competitive pressure registered by market rivals, techno-economic trends led by global equipment vendors, and demand for cheaper and better internet connection from residential and business users. However, the technology-driven, fixed-asset investment on an ever-larger scale, which is not so different from the investment-driven economy at large, means that telecom operators need to control operational costs, resulting in antagonistic labor relations and discriminatory network development. It also means in the face of accelerated construction cycles, telecom operators have limited time to turn data capacity into a profitable commodity. Cultivating addictive consumption habits and wiring business procedures, as a result, have become a necessary strategy for China's political economy of communications. Construction-centric policy is now accompanied by systematic efforts at market development and demand management.

Unlike the initial telephone age when the purpose of network development was to support China's transition from the planning economy to an export-driven economy, the take-up of broadband took place when China's outward-looking market economy had become full blown and crisis-ridden. In this new context and especially after 2008, broadband is interwoven into the state's manifold thrusts of constructing for an alternative commanding-height economy. However, the neoliberal reforms have cast telecom operators into globally integrated, competition-driven, and commercially savvy corporate players committed to the market principle of efficiency. New contradictions, such as labor discontent, excessive competition in the urban-access market, and corporate disincentives to expanding networks in the countryside, have hampered broadband from becoming the strategic public infrastructure that state leaders hope to make it.

The old market fundamentalist recipe no longer provides adequate solutions. So there comes the national broadband plan. However, the focus of the so-called national plan is blurred and its intervention circumscribed because of ideological confusion and rival interest fighting. The redrawing of the boundary between the state and the market certainly limits the state's capacity to correct market failures, as many see a supposedly autonomous market as the ultimate arbitrator of developmental policy. In the 2000s the "developmental" state was, indeed, moving toward a "regulatory" state, confining its role more to "formulating, implementing and enforcing rules for markets and their actors rather than directly intervening in pricing and resource allocation."[114] In the realm of telecommunications, however, developmentalism persists despite weakened implementation. What explains the diluted state power is that the state—roiled by competing interests and ideologies—is not a unitary entity regarding "how to do." Even though broadband is made into a primary policy objective for constructing the commanding-heights economy, the state cannot act in a uniform and decisive fashion. Predicated on broadband, the restructuring hatches new contradictions and brings forward new vulnerabilities, as well.

CHAPTER 4

Making a Home-Base Strategy

3G and 4G Mobile Communications and Industrial Policy

During the past three decades, China pursued export-driven economic growth, focusing on building its electronics manufacturing facilities and upgrading communications capacities. The 2008 global economic crisis put a decisive brake on this growth model, which, despite dazzling GDP growth, has created substantial development dilemmas. "Many signs of dependent development," including dependence on exports and limited capacity for innovation, have plagued the Chinese economy.[1] The Chinese state certainly has recognized that information and communications technologies (ICTs) are core to the country's global competitiveness. However, as an industry follower, China creatively adopted existing ICTs but has hardly had any success with independent innovation.[2] The global competition of building a ubiquitous, mobile, broadband network to enable next-generation innovation, business, and consumption further amplifies China's technological deficits in the critical internet-related digital areas.

After 2006 came an outburst of technonationalist discourses, envisioning "Chinese national, as opposed to foreign, control" over the rapidly changing information network when the internet is enabling information and communications technologies to integrate with all sorts of operation, from banking to transport, from commerce to agriculture.[3] Starting in the Eleventh Five-Year Plan period (2006–10), the state took concrete actions to develop proprietary technology standards, striving to achieve leadership in next-generation network technologies.[4] Mobile communications, in particular, has been regarded as "the most likely area within the general information and communication technology field where China can achieve a genuine breakthrough and become a global leader."[5] One MIIT official declared, "We are so close [to the United States] in this area, [i.e., network communications]. . . . [Therefore,] it is worthwhile to mobilize resources of the entire nation to fight for it."[6]

To fortify technonationalist efforts in the wake of the 2008 global economic crisis, the Chinese state stepped up its management of network development. In 2008 amidst the widening global economic crisis, the MIIT under the guidance of the State Council released third-generation (3G) mobile communications operational licenses earlier than planned, to take advantage of the good financial situation of telecom operators. The licensing was built upon the reorganization of the telecommunications market earlier in 2008 when the state had established three operators—China Mobile, China Unicom, and China Telecom—all with the comprehensive capacity to offer both wireless and wired services. China Mobile was given a 3G license to deploy the China-only 3G technical standard, TD-SCDMA, in hopes that its large subscriber base would help establish this new standard and position the standard for sales to overseas operators. China Unicom and China Telecom received licenses to deploy WCDMA, a dominant 3G technical standard widely adopted in Japan, North America, South Korea, and Western Europe, and CDMA2000, a relatively peripheral, Qualcomm-backed 3G standard, respectively. The allocation of 3G licenses then kicked off the largest network construction effort in global telecommunications history.

The 3G policy and deployment, along with the post-2008 restructuring, have drawn well-deserved scholarly attention. Aware of China's unique sociohistorical circumstances, many scholars have written from an institutional perspective, assessing how power relations, competing motivations, and strategic alliances among state regulators, telecom operators, and other stakeholders affected technological development and market conditions.[7] However, without an understanding of China's historical position in global production networks and its sustained efforts to go beyond world factory status, the institutional understanding provides incomplete explanation regarding the state's intentions, methods, and policy outcomes the 3G strategy entailed. The significance of the 3G policy and deployment goes well beyond institutional reshuffling: while promoting the newest network technology, 3G is meant to address legacy problems in telecom-related industries when ICTs are placed front and center in general economic recovery and development. Policy and implementation outcomes not only are likely to shape the future direction of the 4G mobile communications but also serve the analytical purpose of assessing China's re-regulatory capacity after the state already initiated global economic integration to varying degrees.

This chapter traces the evolution of mobile communications as a site of China's "home-base" industrial strategy and as part of geopolitical struggle in the techno-economic realm. It addresses these questions: Why does 3G networks development constitute a unique opportunity for China's industrial development? How does the Chinese state take advantage of the 3G opportunity? And to what extent does the 3G mobile communications development offer opportunities for domestic players? This chapter, first, historicizes telecom development through successive network generations, starting from fixed-line networks to second-generation and then third-generation mobile networks. As the business ecosystem includes network-equipment production, handset production, and content development and distribution, this chapter next explores market-specific trajectories, conditions, and challenges so as to make sense of varying state actions and the obstacles faced under the general 3G developmental framework. Lastly, to underscore the state's diluted capacity to re-regulate, the coda explores how the 3G mobile communications development has affected state strategies and competitive structures in the 4G era.

Altering the Dependent Road

The state initiated global integration at a "gradual, measured" pace, including in telecommunications.[8] Eager to serve the opening-up and market reforms, telecom operators under the auspices of the state adopted foreign network technologies while keeping a ban on foreign ownership and managerial control. This pragmatic, differentiated approach enables the state to have final say in this strategic sector for national-security reasons while allowing localized transnational commercial interests to drive and even dictate the timing and adoption of network technologies. However, when the strategic value of telecommunications increased during the digital transformation of the Chinese economy, which is part and parcel of the economic restructuring, the technological dependence the early policy had created is proving to be hard to overcome, and the state's re-regulatory capacity is proving to be restricted.

THE BEGINNING OF TECHNOLOGICAL DEPENDENCE

The dependent path started with the state's opening-up policy and the economic need to cater to transnational business, first in the coastal provinces. As discussed in chapter 2, in the late 1970s, foreign investors swarmed into south China and brought with them global commercial linkages as well as pressing demand for modernized telecom capacities. During the Seventh Five-Year Plan (1986–90), in the face of central budget shortfalls, the MPT transferred investment responsibility to local P&T bureaus. Under this decentralized investment regime, nonstate financing, including foreign loans and local government–raised societal funds, increased by 30 percent in the late 1980s. Network expansion actually relied on foreign loans. At the end of 1989, for example, loans from foreign governments and foreign banks had financed 63 percent of basic construction and 55 percent of system improvement.[9]

Foreign influence was palpable as loans usually came with strict requirements to buy products from creditor countries, leading to the decline of domestic manufacturers and surging imports of foreign switches.[10] During the Eighth Five-Year Plan (1991–95), domestic products equipped only one-fourth of the newly constructed national fiber-optic trunks. This strategy was particularly problematic because switches are a key locus of telecommunications innovation. The state risked losing national control over network development and trapping China in technological dependence.

However, thanks to its tight grip over network ownership, the state was still relatively capable of implementing the import-substitution policy.[11] Starting in the late 1980s and continuing into the 1990s, the state formed joint ventures with foreign firms to encourage local production and to facilitate technological transfer.[12] Into the 1990s most global vendors established joint ventures in China.[13] By 1998 this import-substitution policy had taken effect and stifled imports: About 50 percent of the switches in the public telephone network were made in China, and locally produced brands—mostly by joint ventures rather than by indigenous suppliers—accounted for 90 percent of all the newly added switches in 1997.[14]

THE RISE: PICKING WINNERS TO PRESERVING MARKETS

A similar pattern marked the deployment of the second-generation (2G) mobile communications. Around 1995 transnational business classes clustered in China's coastal regions clamored for access to the latest digital technology, thus creating market pressure on telecom operators. Foreign equipment vendors also exerted great influence. Ericsson and Nokia lobbied China to adopt the European-backed 2G mobile communications standard, the global system for mobile communication (GSM), while California-headquartered Qualcomm pushed the standard it sponsored, which is code division multiple access (CDMA).[15] Also around 1995 China Telecom and China Unicom started deploying GSM networks.

To exchange market access for technology, the Chinese state encouraged foreign providers to help build advanced mobile networks. In China's 1995 "Government Guidelines for Foreign Investment in Telecommunications," foreign investment was encouraged in digital wireless systems, optical transmission systems, and switching systems. These were then underdeveloped products in China, for which neither domestic suppliers nor foreign joint ventures had acquired sufficient technological capacity.[16] Foreign intention to slow down technological transfer was clear, as global giants wanted to obtain the controlling share in the existing joint ventures before introducing the most advanced technology in mobile and data communications.[17] It is no surprise, therefore, that early orders for mobile base stations and mobile telecom switches went exclusively to foreign vendors.[18] In 1997 when China's GSM subscribers reached 12.8 million, foreign companies, including Ericsson, Motorola, Nokia, and Nortel, owned the market. In 1997 Huawei released China's first domestically built commercial GSM system, but in 1999 the share of Chinese brands for GSM transmission towers and mobile switches remained at 2 percent and 4 percent, respectively.[19]

In 1999 and 2000, the state started its import-substitution policy in mobile communications. It set up special research-and-development (R&D) funds, provided loans to finance industrialization of domestic products, and started to select domestic market winners.[20] This was a critical moment for Chinese firms, as state and nonstate domestic capital followed into the industry of wireless communications after the surge of foreign investment in 1997 (table 4.1). A small handful of domestic companies that had no joint-venture ties with global brands, including Huawei and ZTE, rose above the fray thanks to managerial autonomy and market aggressiveness and were poised to become national champions in mobile and data communications.[21]

Global vendors, however, still managed to limit the growth of domestic players for two more years.[22] It was only in 1999, about four years after the first GSM system was put in service, that four major domestic vendors, including ZTE and Huawei, made their first GSM sale in the Chinese market. Because foreign vendors had dominated the market all the way down to the county level since the large-scale network construction began in 1995, the ensuing network expansion and upgrading had to rely upon locked-in foreign products. By 2005 the share of domestic vendors in the GSM market was still below 10 percent.[23]

Under pressure from the United States, China also adopted the Qualcomm-backed CDMA standard. In 1997 China allowed the CDMA standard to be tried in four cities.[24] In 1999 the MII granted a CDMA license to China Unicom as a

Table 4.1. Registered capital in the telecom manufacturing industry, 1996-99

Subindustry	State Capital (%)				Foreign Capital (%)				The Rest* (%)			
	1996	1997	1998	1999	1996	1997	1998	1999	1996	1997	1998	1999
Wireless equipment	52.7	45.5	43	60.3	13.9	19.6	32	16	33.4	34.9	24.6	23.8
Switches	39.8	41.5	35	32.5	34.9	31.4	25	19.3	25.4	27.1	40	48.3
Wireless terminals	72	61.2	57.6	28.4	24.7	37.2	36.8	42	3.3	1.6	5.6	29.5

* The rest includes legal person's capital and private capital.
Note: Figures may not add up to exactly 100 percent due to rounding.
Source: The Editorial Board of China Yearbook of the Electronics Industry, 1997–2000.

concession to US telecom firms during China's WTO bid. In 2001 China Unicom announced its plan to build a nationwide CDMA network and to become the only operator in the world to run both GSM and CDMA networks.[25] This benefited US-based Qualcomm with royalties from all equipment and handset sales and from a network of equipment manufacturers that had licensed its CDMA technology. In 2001 China Unicom's $1.5 billion worth of contracts for building the national CDMA network was shared by Ericsson, Lucent, Motorola, Nortel, Samsung, and ZTE.[26]

ZTE was the only domestic vendor to get a share of the contracts. Despite China's WTO accession, the state started to support nascent domestic players by reserving part of the home market. To get a domestic vendor in the bidding competition, China Unicom dropped its original plan to adopt CDMA2000 1X and turned to CDMA IS-95, a less-sophisticated standard for which ZTE already had manufacturing capacity.[27] Thanks to this strategic move, ZTE, a traditional fixed-line equipment vendor, succeeded in becoming a wireless, data, and optical communications equipment vendor. These new product lines accounted for 58 percent of its annual revenue in 2001, and CDMA network equipment alone contributed 10.7 percent, 14.8 percent, and 16 percent in 2001, 2002, and 2003, respectively.[28] However, the adoption of an alternative standard to GSM did not change the market structure. In comparison with the GSM market, CDMA had a much-smaller subscriber base in China, about 9 percent of the 2G users as of 2010.[29]

In view of foreign dominance in the home market, both Huawei and ZTE turned to overseas markets, both to avoid head-to-head competition with foreign corporations solely in the Chinese market and to spearhead the state's "go-out" strategy officially promulgated in 2003. To a reasonable extent, Huawei and ZTE were "forced" to focus on overseas markets because "the domestic market was sewn up."[30] Huawei, for example, started foreign operations in 1997 and focused its R&D efforts on making cost-effective products for the developing world. GSM network equipment became the most important early product in overseas markets, despite the difficulty in winning domestic market share.[31] Like ZTE, Huawei's success extended to new product lines, as it became the largest provider of fiber-optic products in Asia-Pacific in 2001.[32] Its full range of products helped Huawei fund R&D investment in wireless communications.

Between 2004 and 2006, the go-out strategy started to pay off for Huawei and ZTE.[33] Their global expansion, supported by products close to Western quality but at competitive prices, challenged leading equipment suppliers. Huawei became an export-driven company, as overseas sales climbed up steadily from 41 percent of its total revenue in 2004 to 75 percent in 2008. Likewise, ZTE's overseas revenue rose in proportion to its total revenue, from 21 percent in 2004 to 60 percent in 2008.[34] Meanwhile, the global telecom-equipment market went through several upheavals, including the 2006 mergers of Alcatel and Lucent and the network-equipment arms of Nokia and Siemens, and the bankruptcy of Nortel in 2009.[35] In 2008 Huawei's annual sales revenue was $18.3 billion, and profit was $1.2 billion, not far behind Ericsson at $24.8 billion and $2.8 billion, respectively.[36] The gap with global market leaders dramatically narrowed.

Although Huawei and ZTE received state support, such as loans from state banks, these companies have embraced global market dynamics and actively participated in international institutions in order to strengthen their positions. As of 2005, Huawei had ten joint research labs with influential partners, all focusing on next-generation mobile communications technology. Huawei has been participating in numerous international standardization organizations.[37]

Along with the overseas expansions of Huawei and ZTE, the state's domestic-protection policy, implemented through its telecom operators, started to take effect. Starting in 2006, both China Mobile and China Unicom adopted a unified approach to equipment buying, in which headquarters negotiated prices with vendors, and provincial operators then followed these prices. One hidden condition of China Mobile's procurement policy was that "if domestic vendors control less than twenty percent of the market in a given province, international vendors must provide prices ten percent lower than those of domestic vendors to win a contract."[38] The effect was conducive to corporate expansion. In 2007 Huawei and ZTE had 13 percent of the Chinese GSM market while Ericsson had 42 percent.[39] In 2008 the combined share of Huawei and ZTE in the 2G market reached about 37 percent, while an about 50 percent market share went to Alcatel-Lucent, Ericsson, and Nokia Siemens (table 4.2).

DELINKING: CHINA-ONLY TD-SCDMA STANDARD

Despite the remarkable success of Huawei and ZTE in gaining traction, foreign vendors still kept a dominant position in the 2G mobile communications

Table 4.2. China's telecommunications-equipment market share, percentage, 2008 and 2009

Year	Generation	Alcatel-Lucent	Ericsson	Huawei	Nokia Siemens	ZTE	Others
2008	2G	12	22	22.5	15	15	13.5
2009	3G	8	12	28	10	25	17

Source: Wedge MKI LLC, cited in Chao, "China's Telecom-Gear Makers."

market. The historical loss taught the state an important lesson,[40] that is, the import-substitution policy within a liberalized, global investment, and trade environment would fail to reverse technological dependence. To support Chinese vendors for technological development in 3G mobile communications, the state leveraged the increasingly important domestic market. Although countries in Europe and Asia started rolling out 3G networks as early as 2000, Xu Yu, deputy director of the China Academy of Telecommunications Research, a think tank under the MII, asserted, "Global 3G development has yet to reach the point at which China would fear it is falling behind."[41] This time the state paused. Unlike its liberal approach during the fixed-line and 2G mobile communications eras, it did not issue 3G operational licenses until after the 2008 global economic crisis.

During the interim years, the state sought to foster advanced production chains among indigenous firms. Since 2004 such companies as Datang, Huawei, Jinpeng Group, and ZTE have all competed in the 3G mobile communications markets. They saw selling to European and Asian markets as an opportunity to gain expertise before the domestic market opening-up. Under the guidance of the China Academy of Telecommunications Research, they negotiated on royalties and other licensing terms with patent-holding global giants.[42] Huawei, for example, signed a cross-licensing agreement with Nokia to cover the production and sales of WCDMA equipment.[43]

More important, China also developed and commercialized the China-only standard, TD-SCDMA. As Ji Zhengkun, director of the Standardization Administration, pointed out, setting technical standards is a key national strategy.[44] As most Western operators were still in recession in 2002, suffering from the burst of the internet bubble, MII deputy minister Lou Qinjian called for taking the opportunity of 3G mobile communications. To establish the China-only standard, the state created an industrial alliance, set up a TD-SCDMA R&D and industrialization fund, assigned favorable frequencies, and took a hardline stance to force China Mobile to adopt it.[45]

However, TD-SCDMA was an awkward and risky standard in many ways. Although the state had spent billions of yuan to support state research centers and to sustain the loss-making Datang Telecom that holds some of TD-SCDMA patents, the TD-SCDMA project suffered from a deep-seated conflict between the state-led program and its underlying nonunitary corporate interests.[46] Leading Chinese equipment vendors, each with global market ambition, provided conditional, at times wavering, support for the China-only standard. Although Huawei set up a joint venture with Siemens to develop TD-SCDMA in 2004 and ZTE put forth the product line in 2005, both were more enthusiastic about

WCDMA and CDMA2000. ZTE clearly gave investment priority to the non-Chinese standards.[47] As discussed later in the coda, the state's apparent success in reining in divergent corporate interests only conceals contingencies and vulnerabilities that then extended to the 4G mobile communications era.

However, given China's "less than impressive record" in carrying out standard strategies in the past,[48] the commercialization of TD-SCDMA was a significant breakthrough in itself as to "showing the way" for other key technologies in indigenous innovation. It began a purposeful buildup of a China-based accumulation regime—despite the stumbling process. Indicating their intention to continue this program in the long run, the state and major corporate stakeholders later facilitated the technical evolution of TD-SCDMA for the 4G mobile communications era.

Indeed, the state's unusual yet unguaranteed ability to tighten management of network development was key at the critical juncture when the state and its technocratic officials saw an opportunity for domestic firms, whether private or state-owned, to collectively alter the dependent path in the network-equipment market. Thanks to the accumulation of corporate competencies overseas in conjunction with the internal preservation of an emerging 3G market, the transition to 3G networks did allow domestic manufacturers to capture market share. In 2009 Huawei and ZTE together controlled more than 50 percent of the domestic 3G network equipment market (see table 4.2). Measured by market share, the outcome is victorious.

Reorganizing the Global Handset-Production Chain

While the telecom policy of exchanging market access for technology entrenched foreign equipment in Chinese telecom networks, the handset market faced a different set of structural conditions. Foreign firms came to China first because of its dramatic domestic market growth. After surpassing the United States to become the largest mobile-phone market in the world, China was critical for any global vendor. However, when China became the global supply base in the 2000s, hosting a world-class supply chain for the global handset industry, dominance of foreign brands in the Chinese market was no longer insurmountable. Chinese companies created their own brands, and some gained traction. Since then, the crux of the problem has been the fact that Chinese companies still relied and continue to rely on imported components.

CHINA'S ENTRY

A new global division of labor reorganized the global handset-production system, leaving space for China to become a low-cost supply base of handset production. Global companies first had outsourced mass production to Taiwan contract manufacturers, who climbed the ladder and became top original-design manufacturers by the early 2000s.[49] In response to the local-content requirement in China, Taiwan contract manufacturers followed the footsteps of global handset vendors and moved production facilities to mainland China.[50] In 2001, thanks to the influx of foreign capital, mobile phones were already the largest item for export in the ICT sector in China. By 2002 China was the home of the largest handset-assembly platform in the world.[51] Its output accounted for 50 percent of worldwide cellphone production in 2004, further up to 81.1 percent in 2013 and above 80 percent up to 2015.[52]

The state proved instrumental in ramping up an export-oriented manufacturing capacity for handsets. In 1998 the MII along with the NDRC issued "Several Instructional Opinions about Accelerating the Development of Mobile Communications Industries," stipulating that the Ministry of Commerce would authorize imports of components and subassemblies according to state production plans and that foreign manufacturers had to meet a 60 percent local-content target.[53] In 2001 the MII began to limit only 50 percent of its planned production output for domestic sales. According to this policy, foreign-invested enterprises should export at least 60 percent of their output.[54] The twin policy of production localization and export push encouraged transnational capital to expand investment in China and to turn China into a global supply base.

The state did use its authority to help Chinese firms but with little effect. In 1999 the MII stopped issuing manufacturing licenses to foreign firms,[55] but by then, foreign-invested enterprises already dominated (see table 4.1), and Chinese handset vendors had merely 3 percent market share.[56] Ericsson, Motorola, Nokia, Philips, Siemens, and Sony all continued to produce and sell in China.[57] By 2004 the MII had issued forty-nine licenses for handsets: GSM, thirteen to domestic enterprises and seventeen to foreign-invested enterprises; and CDMA, eighteen licenses to domestic enterprises and one to a foreign-invested enterprise, Motorola.[58] In contrast to its centralized procurement power over the small handful of network-equipment suppliers, the state's authority was limited over numerous handset manufacturers engaged in free competition.

Although enforcing local production, the state had little leverage to influence what exactly was localized, either.[59] Until recent years, China-based foreign companies, controlling about 83 percent of handset exports, continued to shape the China-based production chain.[60] In 2009, for example, while the majority of China's exports in mobile communications were mobile phones, mobile-phone parts accounted for 78 percent of all mobile communications–related imports; nearly 43 percent of the imports were retouched reimports, indicating that even though China had directly produced more intermediary goods,[61] critical production steps were still missing in China and had to be performed abroad.

LEAPFROGGING TO BRANDED MANUFACTURING

In the 2000s, reflecting the trend of production modularization, global companies, such as Motorola, Philips, and Siemens, sold semiconductor chips, key software, product design, and production testing to any original-equipment manufacturer, thus "flooding" the Chinese market with chipsets and other components. Original design manufacturers in Japan, Korea, and Taiwan followed suit.[62] This transnational supply chain encouraged indigenous companies to "outsource their weakness" in key components, focusing, instead, on assembly and marketing.[63]

Lured by the explosively expanding domestic market, indigenous companies also moved decisively into branded manufacturing in the mature product categories, instead of "moving progressively from manufacturing others' brands to creating their own." Sourcing components and subassemblies from both China-based and overseas suppliers, Chinese companies put forth different models of handsets for the domestic market.[64] This leapfrogging succeeded in terms of market share: In 2003 domestic enterprises managed to attain 30 percent of the Chinese market, up from 10 percent in 2001. Household electronics manufacturers, such as Hai'er, Lenovo, and TCL, also rushed in. They succeeded by selling low- and middle-end handsets in third- and fourth-tier cities as well as in rural areas where first-time users were concentrated.

Imported components made the quick ramp-up possible. Between 2005 and 2010, for example, domestic handset vendors depended on Taiwan-based baseband suppliers to produce low-end GSM phones; Taiwan's MediaTek alone accounted for no less than 70 percent of the GSM-handset IC market.[65] It is no surprise, therefore, that despite the market success of domestic brands in 2003, the government publicly denounced the practice of importing major components and then assembling them into branded final products. This practice, as the MII put it, turned Chinese branded manufacturers into sales agents for foreign companies.[66]

Leapfrogging to branded manufacturing failed to bolster the Chinese handset industry. After 2004 foreign brands equipped with technological prowess curtailed further expansion of domestic brands, which by then had been plagued with excess capacity, overcompetition, and declining profit. In 2009 Nokia took 34.6 percent of the handset market, followed by Samsung at 20.4 percent; the remaining 45 percent was split between Motorola and a variety of Chinese brands.[67] In 2014, after state-facilitated market reshuffles (discussed later),

Huawei, Lenovo, and Xiaomi gained traction, eroding the dominance of Samsung and Apple, but the state authority remained dutifully cautious about the market-share gains.[68]

The lesson from this history remains relevant: Although making China a global supply base, transnational capital localized low-end segments of the supply chain, controlled technological transfer, and created a structural demand for key components in the fledging Chinese handset industry. As one US-based handset manufacturer noted, although global handset vendors can no longer produce all the major components, they are very careful in making "make or buy" decisions; the challenge is to "control key parts of [the] architecture and value network" and to be "able to extract much of the value created in the industry."[69]

DILEMMAS OF THE TD-SCDMA STRATEGY

Busy with surviving cutthroat model changes, Chinese firms had little opportunity to accumulate core R&D and design competencies despite their ostensible success in brand making. Among numerous Chinese handset manufacturers, only a few leading ones, such as Huawei and ZTE, were capable of innovative R&D in handset-baseband processors and radio-frequency modules.[70] This constituted the context of 3G standards deployment in the handset market. The "delinking" strategy embodied by the China-only 3G standard, TD-SCDMA, manifested the state's intention of building missing core competencies but also its restricted capacity to actually achieve this.

As Xiao Hua, director of the MIIT information department, pointed out in 2010, China should use the transition to 3G mobile communications to solve its "weakness" in handset technologies. She noted that in developing chips for TD-SCDMA handsets, corporate efforts were not enough: "They must be accompanied by state organization and implementation."[71] To date, however, state intervention has left mixed results. Although a number of chipset makers emerged, most of them were established in response to the state-sponsored program and, therefore, had weak technological and financial capacities and little market experience.[72]

Commercialization of TD-SCDMA handsets did present an opportunity to form a new supply chain that relies more on domestic vendors. In 2002 the state formed an industrial alliance of Taiwanese and domestic handset makers. However, it was not until 2009 when China Mobile set out to deploy its TD-SCDMA network that the formation of a new supply chain picked up speed under China Mobile's pressure to offer the service as soon as possible.[73] China Mobile's commitment proliferated TD-SCDMA handset models. In 2008 eleven Chinese-made TD-SCDMA handsets were licensed, and by 2009 more than one hundred TD-SCDMA handsets, made by both domestic and global manufacturers, were authorized.[74]

The rapid formation of a new supply chain, however, offered little time for domestic chipset designers to accumulate missing capacities. China Mobile ended up turning to Taiwanese firms, from upstream IC design to downstream handset manufacturing and testing.[75] As a result, MediaTek, also the leading Taiwan-based chipset designer, claimed 46.5 percent of China's TD-SCDMA baseband market.[76] Indeed, there is a disjuncture between the catch-up plan and the hasty execution. The delinking strategy was incomplete because foreign companies continued to play a critical role.

Still, domestic manufacturers performed better in the TD-SCDMA market than in other 3G markets.[77] Chen Haofei, secretary-general of the TD-SCDMA forum, commented, because domestic makers had only about 25 percent market share in China's 2G handset market, it would be "a significant improvement if they can obtain a 50 percent share in China Mobile's first procurement of TD-SCDMA handsets."[78] By 2011 Chinese brands, including Coolpad, Huawei, Lenovo, Tianyu, and ZTE, actually took away nearly 70 percent of the TD-SCDMA handset market.[79] In 2014 six Chinese brands were rated among the top 10 in the worldwide smartphone market. One should not take this progress lightly because the market popularity enables leading Chinese handset vendors to attract users to their proprietary mobile platforms, which has become a new market frontier, as discussed later.

Wireless Applications and Content: Distribution Channels

The state-managed buildup of 3G networks also underpinned efforts to expand the market of value-added services, content, and applications, which all are increasingly sold on wireless networks. In 2007 smartphone applications brought disruption to the global internet market because smart devices upon which applications, services, and software systems operate have become the new gateways to the presumably boundless web; Chinese telecom operators responded to the aggregating power of smart devices by developing proprietary distribution channels, in conjunction with state broadcasters' efforts to transform themselves into multiplatform content providers. These actions within a stronghold of the state and state-owned enterprises were intended to establish a dominant market position for state enterprises in the Chinese mobile internet.

Unlike the network equipment and handset markets, the Chinese internet market is dominated by Chinese service providers and web portals. From the outset, the Chinese leadership has sought to build its own cyberspace, extending import-substitution strategies to create Chinese alternatives to US-dominated internet content.[80] So far, import substitution is remarkably successful. The majority of internet content providers are private or shareholding companies even though they depend on global financial capital to ramp up business. In 2009, for example, the top four web portals, Netease, Sina, Sohu, and Tencent, took away nearly three-quarters of the sector's revenue.[81]

However, the transition from wired to wireless networks created new uncertainties. As of August 2009, China had 710 million cell-phone users,[82] almost twice the country's 384 million internet users.[83] By December 2015, 620 million people used cellphones to surf the internet, accounting for 90.1 percent of all Chinese internet users.[84] Major market players, including telecom operators, traditional broadcasters, global IT giants, and global handset vendors, all vied for dominant positions in the mobile internet market. Dubbing the mobile internet as "the fifth medium," the state wanted to unleash the mobile internet's economic potential while steering market opportunity in favor of domestic enterprises, if not exclusively state enterprises. Thus, the state's intervention had to adjust to the technological change.[85]

When the mobile internet emerged in China, telecom operators were in the driver's seat. In 2000 China Mobile, the market leader in mobile communications, upgraded its GSM network to provide some data applications and launched Monternet, a gateway that aggregates data from major internet portals and content providers.[86] At its creation in 2000, this proprietary, fee-based platform provided internet companies reeling from the internet bubble with the first stream of revenue. To secure the commanding position of this aggregating gateway, China Mobile threatened starting in 2005 to outlaw more than one hundred thousand independent wireless portals that had received in total nearly US$200 million worth of foreign and domestic venture capital.[87]

In 2007 global device manufacturers launched stand-alone smartphone application markets, dramatically undercutting the commanding power of telecom operators. Apple launched its App Store, followed by Nokia's Ovi Store and the Android Market.[88] These vertically integrated application stores changed the power relationship between telecom operators and handset vendors and shifted the general consumption practice from visiting wireless sites through mobile browsers to accessing application stores. Indeed, in the global internet market, "fee-based cultural commodities" organized by "new distribution systems around new software platforms and often proprietary equipment" chipped away the market power of traditional distribution systems and, thus, constituted a major market "destabilizing" force.[89]

Competition among application stores, as a result, drove the global wireless applications market. When Apple opened its App Store to the Chinese market through a three-year exclusive contract with China Unicom, Nokia leveraged its dominant position in the Chinese handset market to gain the largest market share for its Ovi Store (table 4.3). To compete, traditional IT giants also launched mobile operating systems along with application stores. Google created Android as an open operating system paired with the Android Market, which was well received among handset manufacturers. Windows was a latecomer with Windows Phone 7.

Table 4.3. Mobile systems available in China, 2010

Operating System	Market Share* (%)	Handset Maker	Application Market
Symbian	64.1	LG, Nokia, Samsung, Sony-Ericsson	Ovi Store, Mobile Market
Windows Mobile	17.7	HTC (80% globally under different brands)	Windows Marketplace for Mobile
Linux	1.0	Motorola, Samsung	
Google Android	5.4	HTC, Huawei, Lenovo, Motorola, Samsung, Sony Ericsson, ZTE, and others (95%)	Third-party application stores and telecom operators' stores (40%)
			Google Android market (21%)
			Official websites of application developers (12%)
			Discussion forums (11%)
Mac iOS	4.1	Apple	Excluding China's Unicom's Wostore
			Free apps unavailable through the official Apple App Store are downloadable through "jail-broken" Apple devices
Blackberry	3.8	Blackberry (RIM)	

* This column does not add up to 100 percent due to the gray market, where the distribution and sales of mobile phones are not statistically followed.
Sources: Zero2IPO Research Center, "Investment Report of China's Online Application Stores in 2010," August 2010, accessed July 1, 2010, http://tech.qq.com/a/20100908/000445_3.htm; Umeng, "Report on Chinese Mobile Application Stores in 2010," accessed July 1, 2010, http://www.umeng.com/report.

Because China had no competitive edge in either the smartphone market or the operating system market, its telecom operators hoped to leverage control over the wireless network to promote Chinese versions of wireless application stores. China Unicom, for example, launched its app store, Wostore. Although Apple blocked Wostore access in the iPhone, the fact that only 10 percent of China Unicom's more than 15 million 3G users were iPhone users undercut this blockade.[90] By supporting a range of 3G phones other than iPhone, Unicom's Wostore could still reach out to its 3G customers.

Meanwhile, showering customers with subsidy China Mobile led in the 3G market with 27 million subscribers, nearly twice as many as China Unicom's subscribers, as of March 2011. By January 2014, China Mobile's lead weakened, but its 3G subscribers still exceeded 200 million, considerably larger than China Unicom's subscription size of 123 million.[91] China Mobile launched Android and Symbian phones to combat Apple products.[92] Again, offering a wide range of handset models and operating systems worked favorably for Chinese application stores. As table 4.3 indicates, while Google Android was only the third most popular operating system in 2010, Android phones made by different handset manufacturers actually drove more traffic to Chinese application stores, including operators' stores and third-party ones, than to Google's Android Market. China Mobile also launched its own applications store, Mobile Market, and forged agreements with handset vendors, including Nokia and Samsung, to preinstall Mobile Market's minibrowser on their TD-SCDMA devices. Thanks to collaborating with competing handset vendors, Mobile Market became one of the most visible application stores by 2010 (table 4.4).

Table 4.4. Most-visited application stores, 2010

Store	Users (%)
Nokia's Ovi Store	65.2
China Mobile's Mobile Market	57.7
Google's Android Market	13.7
Windows Marketplace	11.0
Apple Store	8.4

Note: Users may visit more than one application store.
Source: iResearch, "2010 nian zhongguo shouji yingyong shangdian yanjiu baogao" 2010年中国手机应用商店研究报告 [Report on Chinese mobile application stores in 2010], January 20, 2011, accessed May 30, 2016, http://news.iresearch.cn/Zt/131993.shtml.

However, this auspicious situation did not last long for the operators' stores. The spread of Android phones has continued to boost the popularity of Chinese application stores but not necessarily Mobile Market. As table 4.5 indicates, the popularity of Google Android phones made by Samsung and leading Chinese vendors was fortified by 2015; however, telecom operators found that their efforts to establish proprietary gateways were outflanked by popular platforms sponsored by Chinese cyber giants and Chinese handset vendors.

While telecom operators tried, with a short-lived success, to establish their proprietary distribution channels for wireless applications, traditional broadcasters, whose interests are represented by the State Administration of Radio, Film, and Television (SARFT), also rushed to create upstream content-aggregating

Table 4.5. Market share of mobile systems available in China, 2015

Operating System Market		Top Handset Maker		Application Market	
System	Share (%)	Maker	Share (%)	Application	Share (%)
Bada	0.01				
Blackberry	0.11				
Google Android	81.4	Samsung	21	Myapp (Tencent)	23
		Xiaomi	20.5	360 Mobile Assistant	20
		Huawei	12.4	Baidu Mobile Assistant	18
		OPPO	8.6	MIUI app store (Xiaomi)	12
		Vivo	8.6	Wandoujia	7
		Lenovo	5	Huawei App Store	6
				Oppo Sotre	6
				Google Play	5
				HiMarket (Android market)	5
				Vivo	5
iOS	11.0				
Symbian	0.06				
Windows	0.43				
YunOS	7.1				

Sources: Data Ape 数据猿, "2015 nian 9 yue zhongguo Android zhineng shouji dashuju baogao," 2015年9月中国Android智能手机大数据报告（上）[Big data report of Android smartphones in China: 2015 September (on)], *Headlines Today* 今日头条, accessed February 20, 2016, http://toutiao.com/i6210566260986102273/; Newzoo, "Top 10 Android App Stores: China," accessed February 20, 2016, https://newzoo.com/insights/rankings/top-10-android-app-stores-china/; Chen Mi 弥尘, "Zuixin zhongguo zhineng shouji shichang caozuo xitong geju: an zhuo zhanbi chao bacheng," 最新中国智能手机市场操作系统格局：安卓占比超八成 [The newest pattern of operating systems of smartphone market in China: Android accounts for over 80 percent], *IT House* IT之家, December 10, 2015, accessed February 20, 2016, http://www.ithome.com/html/android/193777.htm.

platforms to counteract their reliance upon telecom operators for access to cell phone– and computer-based internet users. State-owned TV stations—including China Central Television (CCTV), Shanghai Media Group, South Media Group, and Zhejiang Radio and Television Group—obtained exclusive licenses to build content aggregation platforms for mobile television. As chapter 5 discusses, traditional content providers also tried to establish control over the digital architecture, which stands a chance of becoming a major distributor of digital content. For example, China Satellite Mobile Broadcasting Corporation (Zhongguang weixing yidong guangbo youxian gongsi), the SARFT-appointed national operator, licensed China Mobile to provide mobile TV service, using the homegrown and SARFT-controlled technical system, China Mobile Multimedia Broadcasting (CMMB).[93] Both the licensing requirement and the technical system ensure state control over multimedia distribution systems amidst network and terminal proliferation in the age of convergence.

Conclusions

For Chinese policy makers, the migration to 3G networks presented a critical juncture when a drastic shift from technological and industrial dependence on foreign inputs to a systematic and purposeful buildup of domestic innovation and production capacities became possible. This chapter traces the evolution of mobile communications as a site of China's "home base" industrial strategy and as part of geopolitical struggle in the techno-economic field—with a focus on 3G mobile communications deployment. In this plan, telecom operators are the nodal institutions. The outcomes of such deployment, in turn, are shaping telecom policy in the 4G mobile communications era, which has become the current market frontier.

For many years, the state, in tandem with domestic corporate players, actively negotiated with transnational commercial forces. The interaction between telecom policies and industrial development went through three phases. First, during China's initial move toward the market economy, the state sought to exchange market access for technology. This led to the loss of a rapidly expanding domestic market to foreign companies and stifled fledging Chinese equipment vendors. That failure was followed by the second phase starting in the late 1990s when the state mobilized its licensing authority, required local production, pushed the go-out campaign, and picked national champions. Despite sustained efforts, China barely broke away from technological and industrial dependence. In the network-equipment market, Chinese vendors went abroad to avoid foreign giants at home and barely reclaimed the domestic 2G market.

In the handset market, even though China hosted a world-class supply chain for the global handset industry and some Chinese companies even created their own brands, Chinese companies still relied on imported components.

Entering the 2000s, the Chinese state entered a third developmental phase. In this new phase, the telecommunications sector—a state-controlled key infrastructure and a "pronounced exception" to the global post–World War II historical pattern of privatization and liberalization in telecommunications—has become a most viable sector to implement some unconventional latecomers' strategies, especially when the mobile internet has become a unifying platform for general economic and social activities.[94] Under the state's management, the buildup of massive 3G wireless networks was intended to constitute a China-based accumulation regime for Chinese companies, both public and private. Exerting its ownership control over telecom operators, the state made industrial policies aimed at breakthroughs in related market segments. In the network-equipment market, the state established a China-only technical standard to delink from the global system. In the handset market, the state attempted to reorganize the supply chain by relying more on domestic vendors. Finally, in the new wireless applications market, Chinese telecom carriers went beyond building infrastructures to establishing their own application stores but fortuitously facilitated the ascent to dominance of Chinese proprietary gateways controlled by nonstate companies. All moves were impossible without the state's effective yet unguaranteed control over telecom operators.

The delinking strategy aimed at creating a China-based accumulation regime coexisted with global market forces. After all, two non-Chinese standards, popular in the global market, were also adopted in China. Their adoption met the global aspirations of Chinese companies enmeshed with global market forces. While responding to the state's general developmental planning, so-called national champions, both public and private, are "well-oiled cogs" of the world system, often receiving large investments from foreign sources and doing business overseas.[95] Following their own accumulation imperative and aiming to "beat [foreigners] at their own game,"[96] national champions in no way act as a unitary whole. Nor do they share a uniform relationship with the state.

In sum, struggles over the geopolitics of accumulation have been fought through the deployment of technical standards, especially when the mobile internet becomes a crosscutting strategic platform for socioeconomic development in the twenty-first century. What is new is that in recent years for economic restructuring, China forcefully joined the contention over the transnational circuit of accumulation. So far, China has had some success in the home-base industrial strategy, but this delinking remains incomplete and vulnerable because of the complexity of the wireless industry, in which foreign as well as domestic companies continue to play a critical role. State planning must contend and compromise with transnational technobusiness dynamics. Meanwhile, so-called pillar industries or national champions, as tokens of the state's commanding power, do not have a unitary alignment with the state. Rather than painting China as the poster child of effective state recentralization and re-regulation, it is more accurate to anticipate disjunctions between state intention and actual execution and to underscore the contingent nature of state industrial policies.

Coda

The 3G standards deployment only marked a beginning of China's systematic efforts to build independent innovation and production capacities, the effects of which are unfolding in the 4G era. The centrality of telecommunications to national competitiveness, as well as China's sustained efforts to cope with technological changes in this strategic sector, warrants continuing research attention to the trials of state industrial policy in the convergence age.

The MIIT, China Mobile, Datang, and ZTE actively participated in the evolution of 4G standards. In his reflection of the TD-SCDMA strategy, Wang Jianzhou, former chairperson of China Mobile, regarded the payoff to be the opportunity for China Mobile–headed supply chains to get deeply involved in the technological evolution toward 4G standards.[97] This time, the Chinese authority notably softened the delinking approach from the outset.[98] In 2007 China Mobile proposed to the 3rd Generation Partnership Project (3GPP), an international standard-development organization, to make its sponsored time-division long-term evolution (TD-LTE) the only alternative to the dominant frequency-division long-term evolution (FD-LTE). Following China Mobile's recommendation, the organization also simplified the specification of TD-LTE, resulting in a high commonality between TD-LTE and FD-LTE.[99] This move was meant to make LTE a global standard. For China Mobile, high compatibility between these two variants would enhance global acceptance of TD-LTE networks and create sufficient flexibility in the domestic market, as well.

Still, vulnerabilities extending from the TD-SCDMA program have affected industrial policies intended for 4G mobile communications. To gain early market advantages, the MIIT, China Mobile, and its manufacturers started early to prepare handsets for LTE-based 4G networks. For China Mobile and its handset supply chain, developing a multimode and multiband capacity was a prerequisite for avoiding being pigeonholed. However, the handset-production network powered by Chinese chipset designers did not have adequate capacity yet for serial innovation. In 2012 Qualcomm made such 4G handset chips available, which took Huawei, Leadcore Technology, and Spreadtrum two more years to achieve.[100] As a result, the introduction of 4G mobile communications risked phasing out the limited benefits the TD-SCDMA program brought to domestic chipmakers, which struggled in expanding domestic market share from 0.4 percent in 2014 to over 10 percent in 2015.[101]

As a primary site of industrial strategies, mobile communications is premised on massive fixed-assets investment. Between 2009 and 2015, three telecom operators each spent 200 billion yuan (US$31.3 billion) on 3G networks. After the issuing of 4G licenses in 2013, China Mobile alone spent another 200 billion yuan (US$32.3 billion) on 4G networks.[102] However, despite the hyperbole about information consumption, the single-minded buildup of the most advanced telecom networks faced insufficient residential demand. Even with significantly improved data transmission, 4G networks had a modest pickup in subscription. Although 4G subscribers reached 162 million in 2015, nearly 649 million mobile-phone users still stayed with 2G networks and another 457 million with 3G networks.[103] Smartphone replacement and exorbitant prices for heavy data flow were and still are cooling factors.

This has a bearing on economic restructuring when telecommunications, especially the mobile internet, is part of the solution to retool the economy. Although leftist commentators critical of austerity measures in Western countries tend to regard China's unusual ability to invest in basic infrastructures during the economic crisis as a positive example, one should be aware that the massive construction of cutting-edge networks by profit-sensitive state enterprises did not meet social needs on the ground. The slowly growing subscriber base will prolong the time needed for recouping the vast investment and will even counterproductively undercut corporate willingness to lower the prices for this technological "fix."

CHAPTER 5

Recasting the Media System

Network Convergence and Digital TV

One cannot understand China's network economy in the making without clarifying changes in the media system led by state broadcasters and cable operators. For China's economic restructuring—and its more specific move of making a networked economy—involve corporatizing and digitalizing the media system. In the 2000s and especially after 2008, market enthusiasts in the media sector, who are state policymakers, bureaucratic executives, and mainstream commentators, have seen the predominant enterprise-like model as a restraint. They praise the telecom reform for resulting in full-blown national companies.[1] And they find direct impetus to recast the media system in the global zeal for digital communications technology, which promises to wipe away technological distinctions between telecommunications, internet, and cable networks and to remove regulatory barriers. After the 2008 global economic crisis, the media system, like telecommunications, was integrated into the state program of economic restructuring; unlike telecoms, however, it is subjected to renewed corporate reforms aiming to release growth dynamics and to stimulate domestic demand and consumerism.

This chapter examines why and how the state media system has been reshaped. First, the chapter contextualizes media reforms that are part of the state's cultural-system reform program intended to overhaul the Soviet-style system of cultural institutions. These media reforms use twin approaches: resurrecting public cultural services and forging ahead of the media industry. It then asks, How does this dual agenda articulate the bigger purpose of economic restructuring? After reviewing the national policy trajectory and its underlying political-economic logic, the chapter examines the case of digital TV. To counteract the neutral-sounding, technical expression of network convergence, this chapter explicates the bumpy process of using convergence as a cover to corporatize cable networks and content production. In light of systematic socioeconomic inequality and the resulting deficiency of domestic demand, the chapter also underscores the inherent contradiction of this corporate digital-TV enterprise.

This chapter argues that in this rapidly changing landscape, state-owned digital media companies are increasingly at the forefront of the economic development of China's media and culture industry. Like other state-owned enterprises or national champions, they bear conflicting imperatives—for both maximum profit making and deference to the state's edicts for economic policy and ideological compliance—that engender ambiguity, verging on incoherence, and that, therefore, harbor a fundamental contingency in any policy resolution.

A Brief History of the Cultural-System Reform

China's cultural system as part and parcel of the party-state's ruling structure was established during Mao's era on the foundation of full employment of cultural professionals, including writers and performing artists, and complete dependence of cultural institutions at all administrative levels on state subsidies. This state-centric relationship subjected cultural production to a party-mandated public-interest principle that involved enhancing equitable access to cultural resources for the masses while being fundamentally pedagogic and political.[2] The market reform starting in the 1980s, however, froze state budgetary support, forcing cultural institutions to seek revenue from the market. Despite its peripheral position in market reform, the cultural-system reform still created profound changes in the three-way relationship of the state, the market, and cultural institutions, as culture found a legitimate role in the market economy not solely for the purpose of reinforcing the party-state's value system. Gradually, the state lost its hegemonic claim over cultural authority as the market became an alternative arbiter of cultural production. This not only forced the state to recalibrate censorship standards but also weakened the institutional and budgetary foundations for welfare. Yet, the state never gave up its claim to cultural leadership and continued to have political and policy trump cards over the pace and scope of deregulation.[3]

The pace of the cultural-system reforms, however, was "sluggish and erratic" in the 1980s and even surprisingly in the 1990s, as the government was busy with other areas than the cultural system.[4] Ideological rigidity, institutional conservatism, and intellectual resistance were all restraints to prematurely meddling in cultural-reform affairs.[5] Under the auspices of the Ministry of Culture (MOC), the reform in the 1980s permitted market-oriented reorganization of production, personnel, and distribution—only on a project-by-project basis. Performing-arts groups, for example, were allowed some autonomy in creating performances for sale and to create ad hoc troupes for commercial shows. Only into the 1990s did the reform start to enforce corporate management in employment and distribution at a gradual pace while still allowing state funding for select cultural units.[6]

In the 1990s China's market reform coalesced with the global neoliberal movement. In its peak periods, the neoliberal influence encouraged commercialization of noncompulsory education and nonbasic medical care. However, cautious voices inside the party state resisted a wholesale "industrialization" or "marketization" of culture. "Commercializing the culture sector" never appeared in any policy documents.[7] But a policy of pushing cultural institutions toward the market prevailed. Thanks to greater management autonomy, more operational incentives, and rising market ethos and forced by shrinking state budgets, nonprofit cultural institutions had to develop ways to support themselves. It was common for museums to rent out space to product displays, for libraries to set up photocopy centers, and for cultural centers to introduce pool halls and video games.[8] The limited commercial ventures, however, failed to counterbalance the systematic state underinvestment, which had disabled these public units from guaranteeing basic cultural rights, including access to newspapers and broadcasting programs and rights to participate in public cultural events, especially for nonelitist residents in urban and rural areas.[9]

Meanwhile, media reform, beginning in 1992 and overseen by the State Administration of Radio, Film, and Television (SARFT) and General Administration of Press and Publication (GAPP),[10] partly commercialized media organizations by establishing advertising-dependent media subsidiaries. State media became public institutions managed as business-oriented enterprises.[11] Into the late 1990s, the reform developed a new focus of conglomeration, aiming to create homegrown media groups.[12] By 2005 this effort merged into a wider process of cultural-system reform. Signaling top-level design of a sweeping reform, the state adopted a broad concept of cultural industry, including audiovisual entertainment, news media, and book and magazine publishing; the cultural-system reforms expanded beyond the jurisdiction of the MOC, absorbing a concomitant media reform.

Into the twenty-first century, the first decade was a crucial developmental period during which the culture sector grew important in the country's economic strategy. The Sixteenth Party Congress in 2002 explicitly called for strenuously developing cultural industries (*chanye*) and strengthening public cultural institutions (*shiye*). In 2003 pilot projects of selective corporatization started in selected institutions and regions. In 2005 "Guiding Opinions on Deepening Reform of the Cultural System," a party edict jointly issued by the Chinese Communist Party (CCP) Central Committee and the State Council, marked a more comprehensive implementation nationwide.

After 2008 the culture sector was designated to play a pivotal role in economic recovery and rebalancing. To boost China's service industries, the state sought, among other tasks, to develop innovation capacities in cultural and artistic production.[13] To create effective domestic demand, the state sought to provide more leisure activities for the growing wage-earning classes. As China has had the lowest share of government spending in the GDP among major developed and developing countries,[14] rebalancing also meant that the state should mitigate the hitherto single-minded pursuit of GDP growth and direct more investment from production-related projects to public services.

The earlier phase of the reform had pushed cultural institutions to the market, but the cultural-system reform in the twenty-first century has marked the return of state-financed public institutions. The Sixteenth Party Congress in 2002 officially adopted a conceptual distinction between public cultural institutions and cultural industries, separating "public-interest assets" (*gongyi xing zichan*) from "operational assets" (*jingying xing zichan*).[15] The Eleventh Five-Year Plan (2006–10) increased state budgetary allocations for public institutions, giving priority to the hinterland and the countryside and aiming to establish a "public cultural service" system—the first-time use of this concept.[16] In the broadcasting system, over 1 billion yuan (US$120 million) from the central budget was spent between 1998 and 2005 on the "television to every village" project, accompanied by 2.5 billion yuan (US$301 million) of local budgetary spending.[17] When rural television access showed signs of regression in some places, the central state started in 2006 to underwrite relay stations in prefectural cities and counties. Between 2006 and 2010, central and local governments together spent 8.2 billion yuan (US$1.1 billion).[18] Under the purview of the MOC, a national system of public cultural infrastructures, infrastructures that support basic cultural rights, that reached county (*xian*) and township (*xiang*) levels was built between 2002 and 2011. Governmental spending on the cultural system, excluding construction and administrative expenditures, has grown at an annual rate of 19 percent since 2006. Although the government fund earmarked for the cultural system was worth about 0.4 percent of the 2010 national budgetary expenditure, a historically low point since 1978,[19] the actual expenditures and incremental increases are individually moderate but collectively significant.

As the Sixth Plenary Session of the Seventeenth CCP Central Committee in 2012 stated, the "fundamental task" of the cultural-system reform is to promote socialist core values, lending political support to the state sponsorship of public units. This political narrative does not mention that public units also contribute to market formation. In contrast to the manufacturing industries plagued with overproduction, the culture sector is among the few areas where the output is insufficient to meet people's demand. However, cultural consumerism also faces another structural constraint, as the pool of disposable consumer income is limited and stagnant. Although advertising-financed media constitute the bulk of cultural infrastructures in China, advertising is "neither the sole nor the primary determinant" of effective demand. Ultimately, consumption hinges upon wages and access to public goods.[20] To facilitate China's transition to domestic demand-driven growth with an expanded service industry, the state rediscovered the value of public units in market creation: Libraries and museums, for example, can help promote consumption of cultural products and information services, landmark cultural institutions are part of the building of a tourist industry, and the state-subsidized digital film-exhibition system for underserved rural areas can also help in creating rural markets through fifteen-minute-long commercials before each screening. In the case of digital TV, analyzed later, public-service duties and systems deployed by the state are part of market formation and underwrite technological upgrades of TV-based information services, reduce grassroots opposition to for-profit operations, and contain irrational and controversial corporate behaviors.

Making Cultural Industry

Along with the deliberate policy of supporting public institutions, the parallel cultural-industry drive has taken up a life of its own, reinforced by change dynamics set off by previous phases of the reform. The drive aims to further corporatize partially commercialized branches of the cultural system, deepening the incomplete market transformation. As an archetype of the contradictory results from the 1990s, media groups are, by state definition, public institutions managed as enterprises and involve the participation of commercialized subsidiaries. Subsidiaries, however, continue to be functional components of media groups, enjoying independence in editorial, personnel, and financial matters but without independent legal status.[21] As a way to dilute public ownership, some media groups sought initial public listings (IPOs) of their operational assets but still retain, along with their editorial sections, the upper hand over listed companies. Being "acting" owners on behalf of the state, managers in these quasi-corporate institutions still need to privilege nonmarket obligations for their stakeholders, including the party, the public, and state personnel.[22] Absorbing political pressure and maximizing economic interests, media groups are indeed "unities of contradictions."[23] Such unities neither exist in harmony nor promise stability.

Internal and external market interests have pounded the system for more operational freedom. Overseas investors, among others, have penetrated Chinese media through joint-operating agreements. They seek equity rights as a prerequisite for legal protection of their de facto established position in the market.[24] More important, domestic market actors, seeking capital expansion, also lobby hard for tearing down noncorporate forms of media organization. Beijing Media Corporation Ltd., the first media group to go public in Hong Kong in 2004, for example, complained about being unable to spend the capital raised from its IPO on buying into other provincial markets or into the broadcasting market.[25] Because they cannot shed their public-property status, subsidiaries of media groups are closed to acquisitions and mergers without the party's special permission, which, thereby, constitutes a bulwark against market expansion in this way.

New-digital media have also changed the market structure and, thus, are a change mechanism to the extent that it is no longer possible to live with the planned reform results. In traditional media, thanks to state monopoly over broadcasting outlets, state broadcasters have remained the major providers of content, despite the proliferation of private production companies. However, state broadcasters have faced destabilizing forces registered by proliferating cable, satellite, and online channels. Broadband internet, mobile broadband networks, and other kinds of new distribution channels have not only created a swelling market demand for programs but have also undercut traditional distribution venues. Online video–distribution platforms, for example, were exempted from regulatory restriction on showing foreign TV and films; traditional broadcasting and theater exhibition have far less latitude.[26] Thus, the online-video industry enjoyed rapid expansion, as it did not face fully fledged competition from "an incumbent pay-TV industry already writing fat checks to the content houses."[27] In recent years, leading online-video websites, from Youku-Tudou to iQiyi, all run by private or shareholding companies, have been seeking transition from being major platforms of pirated and user-generated content to legitimate media companies, investing in programming and creating subscription models.[28]

In view of the threats across media segments, the state has treated market share as a political matter. In 2011 the State Council publicized an alarming report, expressing a long-term concern: "For a long time, state-owned cultural institutions were not transformed into corporations, staying outside of the market economy and thus lacking competitiveness and energy. This situation has caused huge waste of state-owned cultural assets, which are facing market marginalization. Meanwhile, all sorts of nonstate enterprises sprang up, dominating distribution channels and consumption platforms."[29] The looming "crisis" justifies the "skin-shedding" evolution of already commercialized public entities into fully fledged corporations. To sustain the state's cultural leadership, state cultural enterprises after going through corporatization are expected to edge out "unruly" nonstate players; when political directives as ideological-control instruments grow unpopular and ineffective, competitive state enterprises will bring the benefits of "economic-financial control."[30] As a note of caution, however, political agreement between the state and state-owned cultural enterprises does not happen without effort. Its maintenance requires continuous input of economic resources, personnel management, and political energy.

In reaction to the changed power dynamics, the cultural-system reforms in the 2000s pivoted on expanding cultural corporations. Policymakers created an accumulation-oriented category of culture, setting free "operational assets" from direct state ownership control and allowing these assets, now with independent corporate legal status, to form subsidiaries.[31] By spinning off corporate subsidiaries from media groups and in some cases from supervisory government departments, the reforms were intended to reduce state support to the vast majority of media enterprises and to let market vagaries shake out the inefficient players while allowing those with market power to achieve further expansion across multiple markets at home and overseas.

The reform stalled momentarily after 2002, not least because state media resisted. At the end of 2002, public assets accounted for 73 percent of the radio, film, and television sector, whereas corporate assets were merely 27 percent.[32] As commercialized public institutions, state media had enjoyed unique privileges, receiving state subsidies, making advertising-based profits, and giving their staff better pension and income benefits. To shun the imposed corporate reform, many state publishing houses and newspapers wanted to keep their public-institution status. However, in the culture sector as a whole, corporate formation accelerated. Between 2004 and 2008, corporations increased by 52 percent, accounting for nearly 83 percent of all registered legal entities in China's culture sector.[33]

After 2008, to make the cultural industry a new economic-growth engine, the state imposed a stringent timeline to complete the wholesale corporate transition in publishing, distribution, film and TV production, performance, broadcasting networks, news websites, and non-news newspapers. In April 2009 the GAPP demanded local publishers become enterprises by the end of the year and those affiliated with central government agencies by the end of 2010. Nonpolitical newspapers, including evening newspapers and metro papers affiliated with major party newspapers, were required to shed their public status and to form corporations by 2012. The MOC, likewise, required arts-and-performance organizations at the top level of their administrative hierarchies to speed up corporate reforms. In the broadcasting sector, the Shanghai Media and Entertainment Group (SMEG)—a public institution—was annulled by the Shanghai municipal government, and SMEG's corporate assets were injected into the Shanghai Media Group Ltd. (SMG) operating under Radio and Television Shanghai. While Radio and Television Shanghai operates broadcasting assets, including stations and channels, SMG, the shareholding company, runs non-news content production, selling to both the domestic and overseas markets. As an important insider confided anonymously, the corporate arm was greatly enlarged while the enshrined public component contracted.[34]

New industrial policies accompanied corporatization. In 2009 the State Council released plans for ten industries, including the Plan for Boosting the Culture Industry. The Twelfth Five-Year Plan (2011–15) set the goal of turning the cultural industry into a "pillar" industry. The Sixth Plenary Session of the Seventeenth CCP Central Committee in 2012 and the publication of the "Decision of the CCP Central Committee on Major Issues Pertaining to Deepening Reform of the Cultural System and Promoting the Great Development and Flourishing of Socialist Culture" fortified this drive in film and television production, publishing and distribution, copying and printing, performance and entertainment, and digital content and animation. Newly emerging industries, such as cultural creative industries, digital publication, mobile multimedia, and animation and gaming, also gained state encouragement.

The following section delves into the processes of forging a corporate digital-TV system, which represents not only traditional media's thrust into the digital economy but also state actors' desire for market freedom.

Digital TV

In the 1990s state media at various levels succeeded in packaging audiences as a commodity for sale. Although enjoying the advertising boom, TV stations did not strictly enforce cost control, sales targets, or efficiency goals in program production. Nor did cable networks generate commercial business.[35] By the end of the decade, claims about convergence enabled by digital technology were widely circulated, promising to wipe away distinctions among "telecommunications, broadcasting, publishing and computing" and to create a network-based cultural industry.[36] As communication scholar Dwayne Winseck notes, in the United States and Canada, the prospect of convergence in the image of a "corporate-run" cyberspace led to a sweeping process of mergers and acquisition.[37] In China, such trends also gave policy makers and media executives the impetus and cover to seek further corporate reforms. After the Sixteenth Party Congress in 2002, they renewed reform in the broadcasting systems. Xu Guangchun, SARFT director, stated that except for advertising revenue, media was still undercommercialized; therefore, the next step was to develop new commercial components, including pay television, pay radio, content production, and program sales.[38] Content sales and network services were designated as the two new poles of market development for TV broadcasting in the digital age.

CLAIMING CABLE'S DIGITAL FUTURE

Corporate reforms began with the cable network.[39] Built in a decentralized manner by municipal, prefectural, and county authorities, cable had provided a socialist welfare service for urban residents,[40] charging only at-cost prices. In the late 1990s, cable was the first in the broadcasting system to feel technology-instigated market opportunity. In 1997 the state began corporatizing cable operators. In 1998 the construction of national and provincial pipelines to connect disparate local cable networks started. In 1999 the Ministry of Science and Technology (MOST), the Ministry of Information Industry (MII), and the SARFT formed a leading group to oversee the development of digital TV. In 2000 the National Development and Reform Commission (NDRC) invested 600 million yuan (US$72.3 million) in pilot projects.[41] Given these big moves, it is no surprise that the telecom system watched cable closely as its biggest potential competitor in the digital age.

Network convergence did not come as anticipated. In 1999, in view of the conflicting interests and duties between telecommunications and broadcasting, the State Council settled on an "anticonvergence" policy—prohibiting telecom and cable operators from entering each other's markets.[42] Although this decree suspended an imminent market crossing, proconvergence sensibilities were kept alive by SARFT officials to justify market reforms in the SARFT system. "Reform pressure and development pressure are high for the SARFT system," said SARFT deputy director Zhang Haitao in 2005. "If not changing the planning economy structure and upgrading the network with digital technology, the SARFT system will scuttle an indigenous industry."[43] In 2005 network digitalization and consolidation became a state-endorsed program. In 2006 International Telecommunications Union (ITU) delegates from 101 nations agreed to switch totally to digital broadcasting by 2015. All these domestic and international developments pressed cable to scramble for its own digital future.

Indeed, between 2001 and 2005, cable operators followed SARFT's call to enforce a complete digital switch. The forced technical makeover aroused widespread complaints among ordinary subscribers. Low-income households and laid-off workers, in particular, were uneasy with price increases following the imposed upgrade. As money talks, they worried that the introduction of commercial services would be a slippery slope, corroding public TV programs.[44] The campaign managed to ease the standoff only after operators across the nation gave away free set-top boxes, although the timing and pace varied considerably depending on local conditions. Either the local government or the cable operator underwrote the expenses: For example, starting in 2003 Qingdao's cable operator used loans from the China Development Bank to finance set-top boxes and then raised subscription fees to pay back the loans; in 2008 the Beijing Municipal Bureau of Radio, Film, and Television earmarked 70 million yuan (US$10 million) to subsidize each household with 100 yuan (US$14.30). In western China, however, numerous small operators could not afford this technical makeover. Even today, as discussed later, digital TV is far from being a national system.

As digitalized cable was slated to become a marketplace trading content commodities, network interconnection on the basis of a shareholding corporate reform was a logical next step. It is requisite for creating a scale competitive advantage over wired and wireless IP networks controlled by telecom operators as well as for reducing costly barriers for content providers.[45] Apart from economic rationality, the motive for "plundering local assets" was present: In 2004, while national- and provincial-level media took the lion's share of advertising revenue, the majority of cable-subscription fees flew to lower-level cable operators.[46] Green-lighted by the SARFT, the corporate model of digitalization entailed network consolidation from above through mergers and acquisitions.

It was not an easy task, though. The drive to form provincial networks fell behind schedule. Although the state had separated cable operators from TV stations in the late 1990s, the former remained subordinate to the local radio and television administration. In places where cable could not make ends meet, the newly consolidated provincial operator had to take over staff and debt from local state budgets. In places where cable revenue had been used to subsidize county-level TV stations and even the radio and TV administration, the task force for consolidation had to raise money to buy out coveted assets and even to challenge the four-tier administrative structure where county-level party organizations perceive local cable networks as an important economic and administrative resource.

Meanwhile, the SARFT wanted to form a national cable company to run provincial branches but failed. In 2004 China Broadcasting Network (CBN) was established, from which all TV stations were to get landing or transmission rights. After failing to secure provincial cable-network assets due to local disputes over asset valuation, CBN was merged into China Cable Television

Network in 2005, which still "possessed little of the estimated 3 million km of cable running the backbone network into homes."[47]

Although the national company was a failure, market development created a few corporate heavyweights on the local level. Wasu, headquartered in Zhejiang, for example, set the goal of becoming a "national" digital-TV provider as early as 2003.[48] Like other heavyweights, Wasu bought equity interests of other cable operators, including those of Xinjiang and Guizhou. Meanwhile, to underwrite digital transformation and ownership consolidation, cable operators in Beijing, Hubei, Hunan, Jilin, Shanxi, Shenzhen, and Zhejiang all went public at the stock markets. In 2014, in the latest try to establish a national cable operator, the state set up China Radio and Television Network Ltd. with 4.5 billion yuan (US$725.8 million) worth of registered capital from the Ministry of Finance. By this time, however, the combined network assets of all local operators were worth 150 billion yuan (US$24.2 billion). This lofty valuation caused by stock-market listing will make corporate takeovers by the nominal national company a thorny process facing lots of pushback.

Despite the bumpy and incoherent process of creating a corporate digital-TV system, the 2008 global economic crisis expedited cable's entry into the market economy. The MOST and SARFT announced a long-range plan to build the next-generation broadcasting network capable of providing digital communication and information services. The State Council decreed to digitalize the broadcasting system, beginning with cable networks. In 2010 the turning point finally came, when the State Council instructed the SARFT and Ministry of Industry and Information Technology (MIIT), authorities in distinct regulatory areas, to tear down market barriers between telecom networks and cable networks in a few selected cities. By 2012 the state had given the green light to all provincial capital cities, enabling triple-play networks that deliver voice, video, and data with a single access subscription, indicating the state's intention to nudge cable operators into a wholesale information economy. In the words of Li Yiqing, Wasu's senior vice president, this decree indicated "the door back to the public service system was completely closed."[49]

COMMODIFICATION OF TV PRODUCTION

The coming of the digital age has given SARFT officials an impetus—and a justification—to forge a "new broadcasting system" on the corporate model. In its four-component design, the national cable company oversees transmission, local operators are the service-providing nodes, SARFT-licensed content-aggregating platforms manage programs, and the SARFT and its local branches supervise the business (figure 5.1). This blueprint, along with the prospect of multiplying networks and proliferating outlets, prodded first-tier TV stations

Figure 5.1. SARFT-licensed corporate digital-TV system, 2007.

Source: Zhou Ting 周婷, "Fufei dianshi pindao xin shangye moshi" 付费电视频道探索新商业模式 (Pay-TV channels explore new business models), *Zhongguo zhengquan bao* 中国证券报, January 31, 2007, accessed May 30, 2016, http://tech.qq.com/a/20070131/000017.htm.

into clamoring for leadership in content provision and platform control. After SMG in 2005 got the first national license to develop internet protocol television (IPTV) with telecom operators, broadcasters' competition with telecom operators commenced.[50] The deregulatory policy in 2010, and the unstoppable rise in popularity of online digital-content platforms, further whipped the broadcasting system, including TV stations, to accelerate digital transformation.

After years of advertising-driven and viewing rates–based competition, the state media system has changed and remained the same at once. Market competition has turned some stations into national and regional flagships while relegating others into obscure status. Despite uneven market power, media organizations still occupy positions along the administrative hierarchy, comply with the territorial administration of the party state, and remain accountable to the Department of Propaganda in the same echelon. In the eyes of aggressive market-oriented stations wanting to override administrative obstacles and to further capitalize media assets, digital technology, along with investment vehicles and global expansion, is a primary wedge.[51]

Combining TV, radio, film, and online media production, top-tier media groups want to make sales to wider markets. They perceive digital technology more as an opportunity than as a threat. As a threat, new-digital media are diverting advertising and audiences away from traditional media. As an opportunity, however, digital technology enabled by the internet allows media organizations to bypass the regulatory constraints on traditional broadcasting and to open a new market window. By collaborating with telecom operators, for example, SMG had eighteen million IPTV subscribers across the nation by 2012. Although many cable operators saw this move as betraying the interests of broadcasters, SMG through its new-media subsidiary BesTV was happy to

Figure 5.2. Revenue streams for Wasu and BesTV.

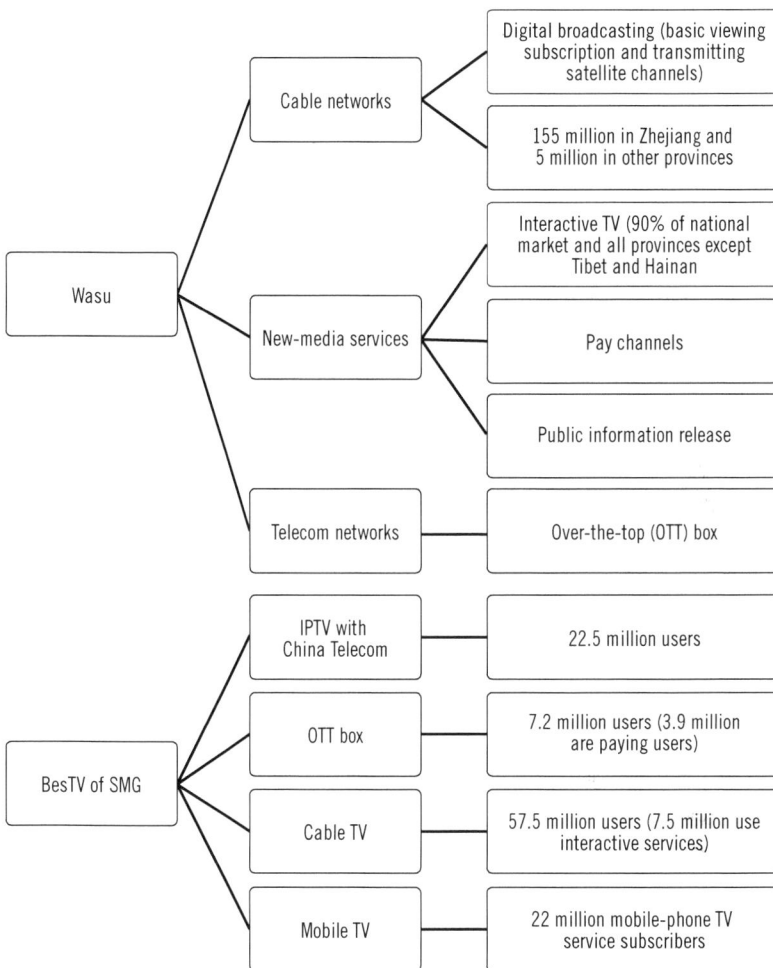

Sources: Shanghai Oriental Pearl Media, "Shanghai dongfang mingzhu xinmeiti gufen youxian gongsi 2015 nian banniandu baogao zhaiyao" 上海东方明珠新媒体股份有限公司2015年半年度报告摘要 (2015 half-yearly report digest of Shanghai Oriental Pearl Media Co. Ltd.), *Securities Times* 证券时报网, August 15, 2015, accessed March 11, 2016, http://epaper.stcn.com/paper/zqsb/html/epaper/index/content_722400.htm; "Hua shu shuzi dianshi chuanmei jituan (hua shu jianjie)" 华数数字电视传媒集团(华数简介) (Introduction to Wasu Digital TV Media Group), *Wasu Group* 华数集团, accessed March 12, 2016, http://www.cncable.com.cn/gsjj/hsjj/hsjj_4840/201405/t20140506_25270.html.

take advantage of the deep pocket of telecom operators to accelerate the digital-TV deployment in which SMG controls content aggregation (figure 5.2).[52]

In the hinterland, market enthusiasts have ample reasons to be unhappy with the administrative system within which they have to operate. At the Hunan Satellite TV, a commercial daredevil in central China, a leader complained: "Our local economy continues to stagnate. So what do we do to maintain the lead that we've built? We are pushing to develop new media, new program content, and the international market. The domestic market is now oversaturated and homogenous."[53]

Marginal media, likewise, seek to blaze a new path out of their territorial limits and to change the "class" composition of their audiences. According to CSM Media Research, a well-respected Chinese audience-measurement company, the main national audience for Guizhou Satellite TV was peasants and other low-income groups.[54] In its home base, however, it had the smallest audience share, actually no more than 10 percent in the countryside, in comparison with China Central Television (CCTV) and other satellite channels.[55] After being licensed to operate the fourth shopping channel in the country in 2007, the Guizhou station set up a company in Beijing, targeting the national market. Its director, Bai Fangqin, spelled out its rationale: "While we can at best make good and fine public programs, in comparison with first-tier stations we are unlikely to be strong and big. However, we can be strong and big in commercial operation [as a shopping channel]."[56]

Inside TV stations, the reorganization of production has been underway, in the spirit of turning state property into media capital imbued with the accumulation imperative. To get ready for the multiplatform digital era, TV stations initiated internal reorganization, aiming to build up an efficient production chain. In a gradual way, the reshuffling delegated program production, acquisition, and operation to channel-based units that then each enforced cost reduction, revenue expansion, personnel downsizing, and channel branding.[57] Non-news channels were then experimentally allowed to be managed as enterprises and even to absorb outside capital.[58] By 2005 stations were permitted by the SARFT to spin off channels for sports, transportation, film, entertainment, music, life, finance, and science and education to subsidiaries on the condition that channels were not publicly listed, rented, or transferred. Although the state retains the public status of TV and radio stations, commercial ethos, rather than the public-service principle, has penetrated the whole broadcasting system with the proliferation of quasi-corporate and corporate-channel units.

In order to unleash industrial development in content production, the state also encouraged separating production from broadcasting, allowing non-news content production departments to form corporate subsidiaries and permitting

TV stations to purchase programs from private sources. Although TV stations did not follow the decree, due to internal resistance, this policy expanded the market space for private and foreign companies, especially in proliferating digital outlets. To provide content that had been unavailable for public viewers, SMG sourced digital content from private entertainment companies, such as Enlight Media Group, and from foreign channels, including Channel V, Discovery Channel, ESPN, HBO, National Geographic, Phoenix TV, and Satellite Television Asian Region (Star TV).[59] In 2009, after years of stalemate, this production-broadcasting separation restarted in subprovincial and provincial cities, spearheaded by SMG. One insider at SMG indicated that in the name of separating production from broadcasting, non-news channels carried out a thorough corporate reform.[60] ToonMax Media, a shareholding company under SMG, for example, signed labor contracts in 2010 with its remaining 170 public employees, completing the most difficult step of corporatization in the realm of employment.[61]

In 2014, to stem internal competition among subsidiaries, SMG broke up channel-based companies and built a centralized corporate model with producers as the heads of basic production units. The producer system had existed from 1995 in state media, responsible by 1998 for nearly 77 percent of programs nationwide. However, because the power of budget allocation rested not with producers but in the higher-administrative echelon of Shanghai's TV channels, which in 2001 merged into SMG, the main economic function of producers was cost control.[62] Cost control is important but is not enough for corporate media. In corporate media, producers are expected to be project managers, responsible not only for budget but also for products and income..Maximizing return on investment is the paramount duty.[63] The narrow cost-control mentality led Sun Yusheng, president of China DTV Media under CCTV, to lament the "oversupply" of TV producers trained for the public media system and his inability to find employees with the right talent and real business acumen.[64] To unleash entrepreneurial spirit, in 2014 Dragon TV, a satellite channel of SMG, gave its producers more control over the budget and personnel and set up an incentive plan to reward producers from profit "without setting upper limits" and even to allow producers to chip in investment for profitable return.[65]

The producer system heralded a systematic expansion of contract-based employment and even temporary employment. Indeed, cost-sensitive and profit-oriented production hinges upon commodification of labor. If media professionals were beneficiaries of the reform in the 1990s that had given state media free rein to run commercials, the rank and file bore the brunt in the 2000s—as corporate reforms made inroads into media organizations, quantifying mental workloads, monetizing welfare services, and making jobs precarious and payment contingent. Between 2001 and 2004, the state launched the personnel-system reform in state media, endorsing corporate labor contracts in China Central Television. As the reform allowed old and new methods to coexist, CCTV, like other state media organizations, has a mix of public, corporate, and temporary employees, making an "almost feudal labor structure" possible.[66] Notably, corporate employees have made up the majority of new-media branches.[67]

Capitalization, financialization, and even privatization of media assets are concomitant with labor and production commodification. Although the press and book publishing spearheaded IPOs in the broader cultural sector, new-media companies were the first in the broadcasting system to get on the stock market. By 2012 eight publicly listed companies under SARFT purview were seven cable operators and BesTV, the new-media company of SMG.[68] Through investment vehicles, state media also incorporated outside investment and branched into new-media arenas in recent years. Wasu, for example, received financial injection not only from the stock market but also from Alibaba as a strategic investor. In this trend of capitalizing and financializing media assets, state media executives have formed a special-interest group advocating partial privatization of state-owned assets—because they are bargaining for an equity incentive plan to extract profits.

After 2008 the so-called mixed-ownership reform coalesced with the state media reform responding to digital threats. Local governments burdened with existing loans have led this new round of state enterprise reform, encouraging the selloff of minority shares of profitable large-scale state enterprises to nonstate investors.[69] In 2014, the "Guiding Opinion for the Converged Development of Traditional and New Media," approved in the wake of the Eighteenth Party Congress, urged state media to embrace the internet in every step of production, distribution, and consumption, encouraging state media to take the helm of converged development. Although information control and cultural security motivated this state decree, media executives and liberal scholars were eager to celebrate it as heralding the end of investment restrictions and ushering in capital-driven, cross-market expansion at full speed.

Media corporations are not under the purview of the State-Owned Assets Supervision and Administration Commission (SASAC), which is leading the mixed-ownership reform. This causes confusion as to which bureau on which administrative level has the final say to give the green light in the cultural system. Jin Bingliang, corporate director of Southern Publishing and Media Corporation, expressed impatience over the lack of breakthrough in approving stock options for top executives—a contentious component of the mixed-ownership reform.

A breakthrough, however, did come in 2014: Although arousing strong critique from the party's department of propaganda, BesTV of SMG announced such an equity incentive plan for a group of 224 people in executive, managerial, and key technical positions, making it the first case in the nation.

Where the Digital Promise Ends

As communication scholar Yuezhi Zhao noted in 2000, the SARFT, a traditional stronghold of public-service principles, evoked the public-interest concept in its turf war with the telecom system and stipulated the "non-commercial nature" of the network.[70] If the public sector undergirds the political economy of socialism, can we infer that the remaining public sector of communications constitutes a space for local alternatives to the global expansion of digital capitalism?[71] The answer is contingent: A careful political-economic analysis will complicate this pristine concept of public service and reveal complex internal dynamics.

In the process of digitalization, the SARFT did expand the public-service system to unprofitable areas by utilizing some new digital technologies.[72] Direct-to-home satellite, for example, charges transmission fees from satellite TV channels but distributes programs to rural and western regions free. As for digital terrestrial TV, the television-to-every-village fund has been used to pay for set-top boxes for rural families. After 2008 the state reiterated the public-service commitment in the sense of warranting people's basic cultural rights and safeguarding national security.

However, public service is an ambiguous concept because it entails multiple objectives beyond altruistically meeting people's needs. These objectives, in some circumstances, are conducive to corporate interests but in other circumstances may serve to discipline state-owned enterprises and to curb their detrimental profit-seeking behaviors. As discussed later, on principle, the SARFT insists on the public duty of transmitting public programs to local subscribers while allowing cable operators to sell new, value-added services to the national market. In actuality, where to draw the line and how to reconcile the two duties are left to the discretion of state-owned companies that manage digital TV. But when the security imperative is compromised by unrestrained market incentives, the state is willing to take action to discipline those state-owned companies in the name of public service.

State intervention in the name of public service has proved indispensable for the corporate model of digital TV. Despite the business hyperbole celebrating a coming windfall of profit, the corporate model faltered. After digital transformation, cable companies have four streams of revenue: basic viewing, pay TV, video on demand, and public information release (see figure 5.2). Up to recently, revenue from basic viewing still makes up the biggest component thanks to price increases and improved ability to monitor and charge subscribers. The Gansu network, for example, earned more than 300 million yuan (US$42.9 million) from basic subscription and 32 million yuan (US$4.6 million) from transmitting satellite channels but less than 10 million yuan (US$1.4 million) from pay TV and 7 million yuan (US$1 million) from other value-added services.[73] For the market leader, Wasu, however, interactive TV was already its second-largest revenue stream after basic subscription, accounting for 19.7 percent of the main business revenue in 2014 (see figure 5.2).[74]

Operators have a particularly hard time in rolling out pay TV channels. In 2002 the first batch of pay-TV channels came along and grew to 136 channels by 2007.[75] In 2003 rolling out pay-TV channels was a state-endorsed strategy to smooth out the pushback against network consolidation, pushback caused by administrative obstacles and economic disputes, as discussed earlier. Up to 2006 SMG invested 100 million yuan (US$12.5 million) on pay TV channels; on the lowest end, CZTV, a video website owned by Zhejiang Radio and Television Group, spent 10 million yuan (US$1.3 million) on one pay channel.[76]

To prevent excessive competition for the limited pool of advertising revenue, the state banned commercials on pay TV. Because pay-TV companies significantly fell behind schedule in audience development, based on high subscription fees, they, in turn, held back content acquisition, worsening their situation—while the advertising-driven public television sector had already provided audiences abundant content. Even today, most such channels have not recouped their investment. "Free TV programs are like a river blocking the acceptance of pay TV," said CCTV's Sun.[77] Socially regressive proposals to downsize the public television sector so as to clear the way for pay TV simmered.[78]

This miscarriage of pay TV forced the SARFT to reinstate the public-service concept. SARFT deputy director Zhang acknowledged in 2004 that it was erroneous to designate pay TV as the only propelling force of digitalization.[79] In making amendments, the SARFT latched digital TV onto the national informationization bandwagon to gain government subsidies and policy support. The Eleventh Five-Year Plan formally stipulated making digital cable a platform for delivering governmental services to the public.[80] Under this technopolitical banner, party secretaries in various cities and provinces, as the commanders in chief, used their political-administrative power to support cable digitalization in the so-called number 1 project. Since then, cable TV has had faster revenue growth than advertising.

Apart from the faltering business of corporate digital TV, the corporate model of digitization has eroded equitable access, turning not-profitable networks into disconnected, inferior information islands. According to the state planning, digital networks should have been available in many prefectural cities in western China by 2008.[81] By 2013 digitalization actually reached 66 percent of all cable subscribers nationwide. Three provinces, Henan, Sichuan, and Tibet, however, fell below the 50 percent mark.[82] Mianyang, the second-largest prefectural-level city in Sichuan, was the first city in western China to make digital cable available. However, to underwrite the upgrade, its cable company became heavily indebted.[83] The high cost prevented smaller operators in western China from carrying out digital transition.[84]

A megacity in southwestern China that had nearly 30 million residents and 4.2 million cable subscribers, Chongqing's situation is instructive. By 2008 the Chongqing Cable Network connected the small yet densely populated city area with nearly 1.1 million household subscribers and two counties each with less than 100,000 subscribers. But the bulk of its territory remained unconnected.[85] Unable to afford the technical transition, most county-level networks became undesirable for the later corporate consolidation, and they faced the techno-economic elimination of public assets.[86] To merge into the Chongqing Cable Network, however, small county networks had to grapple with the disputable issues of asset valuation and converting public employees into corporate ones. Up to 2013 most provincial cable operators had not incorporated county-level networks.

County-level TV stations are the pillars of the rural cultural system, important for covering local current affairs and being the mouthpieces of local government: Rural libraries, with a few hundred old books, tend to be unpopular, and the state-sponsored film exhibition tours only a few times a year.[87] However, many people—especially in western provinces—can no longer view local programs because of digitalization. In 2013 local programs were not incorporated into IPTV programming in most of Yunnan Province.[88] In the countryside, township- and village-level cable networks often have nonstate investments, so they do not transmit county-level programs.[89] As for digital terrestrial TV and direct-to-home satellite-TV broadcasting, both require switching the viewing mode to access local programs.[90] To fill the voids, in 2014 the state pledged more support for county-level TV stations to handle digital convergence.[91] Although it is too early to tell the effects, such a gesture verifies the unexpected yet serious fallout of digitalization.

As in the Canadian case Winseck describes, Chinese liberal scholars have celebrated the internet as a disruptive force challenging state media and propaganda control. This "internet-versus-traditional-media" logic ironically gives the state and its media ample urgency to reclaim "ever large swathes of cyberspace."[92] However, to what extent commercialized state media can safeguard the party state's bottom line in the new-media environment is quite dubious. In a horrifying account of the SARFT becoming a new type of internet service provider under the banner of network convergence, Henry L. Hu underscores the state intention to form a "vertically closed" internet system.[93] To achieve this goal is difficult, though—as state media corporations, along with their shareholding relationship with private-equity holders, make this system porous.

The fiasco involving over-the-top (OTT) technology is illustrative of this porous system. OTT enables users to get internet TV services whether they stay with telecom or cable operators. This fact did not discourage Wasu, a cable operator, from embracing the technology as a gateway to the national market—when the uneven digitalization of cable networks, documented earlier, has slowed down the expansion of its interactive TV business nationwide. BesTV of SMG, another market leader wanting to get ahead in any technology-instigated market enclosure, also applauded this money-burning technology, even though knowing only 30 percent of its OTT viewers were paying subscribers. Like their competitors, both companies preinstalled nonstate, online-video platforms to attract TV viewers. Not until threatening to revoke a license did the SARFT succeed in stopping web companies' inroads onto TV screens, making it a big story for 2014. Although determined to cultivate enterprises under its aegis, the SARFT holds on tightly to the public-service principle, especially the security mandate, to curb overzealous corporate behaviors that would threaten the SARFT's command over the digital-TV system and undercut the system's long-term viability predicated on technobusiness control over subscribers.

Conclusions

At the end of the first decade of the twenty-first century, China was at a crossroads, facing structural pressure to adjust its developmental strategy in a global capitalist crisis economy. Within the state's arsenal, the culture sector, including state media, had become a pivotal arena to facilitate the desired transition to domestic demand-driven growth with an expanded service industry. The push for corporatization in the 2000s was meant, for both political and economic concerns, to unleash state-owned market players from the administratively organized public-service system so as to claim a potentially explosive digital cultural economy. In the post-2008 crisis context, the sweeping corporate reform was an action of expediency to ramp up a new growth outlet in defense against economic slowdown. Through corporatization of non-news content production, first-tier TV stations scaled up market transactions, deepened market principles, created a growing array of state enterprises, and took actions to adapt to the new multimedia era.

Under the guise of "public institutions operating like enterprises," cable networks and TV production were "exceptions to neoliberalism,"[94] shielded by their public and administrative status from excessive market pressure. Market enthusiasts have lobbied to tear down remaining barriers that prevented them from cross-regional and cross-media expansion—and from extracting private profits from the public assets–based accumulation regime. In this struggle, claims and actions of network convergence provided both an ideological cover and a palpable pressure to end this exceptionalism.

While trade journals, echoed by scholarly discussion, are obsessed with the "protracted" process of network convergence, convergence in terms of institutional priority and operational principle has already taken place. Coming out of this bumpy and incoherent process is a corporate digital-TV system made up of a small handful of regional and national corporate heavyweights. Equipped with financial capital, these companies are making loan-financed acquisitions, building state-licensed content-aggregating platforms, partnering with private new-media giants, and plundering the small yet emerging markets of IPTV, interactive TV, internet TV, and pay TV.

The society's unmet cultural need and the party's fear of losing touch with the fragmented society increasingly going online provided the political justification for the capital-intensive enterprise of digitalization. However, cable companies consolidated only networks with commercial promise, while content platforms aggregated mostly nonlocal news and transnational entertainment programs. In light of the dubious economic and social effects, the SARFT realized that the public-service principle and its multifarious objectives are actually indispensable for positioning cable in the digital economy: This reaffirmed public-service duty in basic viewing smoothed out grassroots opposition to the newly acquired for-profit operations while generating subsidies and laying the audience foundation for value-added services; the resurrection of alternative delivery methods, then, helped relieve the undemocratic effects of the corporate model of network digitization led by financial capital in the hands of market leaders; last but not the least, the national-security mandate enabled the SARFT to discipline and even curtail self-aggrandizing yet system-wide detrimental behaviors of leading companies under its aegis.

In view of the ambiguous meaning of public service and its entanglements with the corporate digital-TV enterprise, it is too early and even erroneous to proclaim the state is transforming from an "economic construction oriented government" to a "public service–oriented government."[95] The public-service principle, as abstractly perceived by remote observers, only camouflages fractional relations among state-owned enterprises and obscures the complex relations between the state and its corporate arms.

CHAPTER 6

Building Network Nation

Domestic Thrusts and Global Impacts

In 1995 China's first private internet service provider set up an advertising billboard on White Bridge Street in the Haidian District, Beijing. Its bold characters read: "How far away are the Chinese from the Information Superhighway? 1500 meters up north." The company closed down in a few years. Its upbeat slogan, however, remains a landmark in the Chinese history of building a network nation. In 2014 China boasts 229 million cable viewers, 200 million fixed-line broadband subscribers, 1.27 billion mobile-phone users, and 632 million internet users.[1] *The Internet Age*, a celebrated documentary CCTV aired in 2014, showcases how well poised China is to become a network nation. In its ninth episode, an elegant male voiceover states that if the homegrown network economy draws "one dime of Chinese nutrition" from the population of 1.3 billion people, China will become the only thriving market outside of the United States.

Of course, these statistics and statements are the tip of this iceberg. Focusing on policy and institutional transformation, this book has documented the making and remaking of China's communications system—as the underpinning of a network nation—in the market reform and during the economic restructuring. As the first decade of the 2000s drew to an end, the state formally enlisted communications as a crosscutting platform for economic restructuring in order to deal with the economic crisis overseas and at home. Communications is instrumental for three purposes: fostering information consumption, enhancing innovation and reorganizing production, and spearheading the "go-out" campaign.

This chapter underscores communications as a frontier of economic restructuring. It recaps the profound changes in the political economy of communications and synthesizes organic linkages and interactions among distinct business areas discussed. It argues that the central position assigned to communications in the scheme of economic restructuring has accorded an unprecedented level of importance to network connectivity and networked consumption of products, services, and content. Despite some uplifting effect, investment and profitmaking activities intended to develop network connectivity and network consumption weaken public domination in this critical sector and help little in ameliorating the state's systematic inability in raising residential income. Then, how much advantage would China likely gain from this newly discovered developmental focus? This chapter also explores the global implications of this China story in the fields of ICT manufacturing, media and entertainment, and the internet. It argues that although state intervention characterizes China's global presence, the country has moved steadfastly toward convergence with global digital capitalism.

Recasting the Communications System

A chain reaction was set off when China reintegrated with the global production system. In the 1990s foreign capital from Hong Kong, Macao, and Taiwan, followed by and overtaken by capital from Asian, US, and Western Europe economies, ramped up China's ICT exports. The 1997 East Asian financial crisis further prodded Taiwan business to move the bulk of PC production to mainland China. Since 2000 electronics and telecom-equipment manufacturing has made up a dominant share of China's export-processing economy, making the country a world-class processing-and-assembly hub. As far as electronics is concerned, brand-name transnational corporations and their contract manufacturers, many of which are also transnational in their operation, are in the driver's seat of the hierarchically structured production system. In this system, China acts as a primary final product–assembly hub, importing components and parts from Asian neighboring countries and exporting finished commodities to the Global North.[2]

The ICT-dominant export-processing economy was interlocked with the rewiring and repurposing of telecom networks. In the early reform era, telecom operators in the state-controlled strategic sector were among the first to practice the "exchange market access for technology" approach. Drawing upon foreign network equipment, they ramped up advanced communicative capacity for the outward-looking economy. This left several implications: First, domestic reliance on foreign ICT equipment accelerated the weakening of the homegrown, military-oriented electronics industry. Second, as foreign equipment vendors were encouraged to produce locally in the form of joint ventures, initially for domestic needs and then for export markets, this fed into an export-processing production system. Third, the rewiring and repurposing of telecom networks resulted in communicative inequality along the rural-urban and western-eastern lines.

On the heels of building an export economy, telecoms became an epicenter of capitalist development in the state-dominated service sector. At the Third Plenary Session in 1993, the Fourteenth Party Congress endorsed a state-owned enterprise reform, laying the ground for separating management of affiliated enterprises from administration. During the run-up to the WTO accession, the Ministry of Post and Telecommunications (MPT) announced its long-range plan for 2010, when China was expected to become a global hub for information exchange and a major provider of information services.[3] This ambition lent credence to the corporate and shareholding reforms. Since then the planning and investment in telecoms have been the jobs of telecom operators: By 1998 state budgetary spending only made up less than 0.1 percent of investment in telecommunications; by 2011 telecoms had the lowest share of the state budget at 2.2 percent in comparison with other infrastructure sectors.[4]

In this "lifeline" industry, safeguarding state assets, managing competition, and enforcing redistributive social policy still justify a "state-led system of corporate governance" under the aegis of the State-Owned Assets Supervision and Admission Commission (SASAC) and the National Development and Reform Commission (NDRC).[5] In the 2000s and especially in the wake of the 2008 global economic crisis, the state's intention to harness large-scale state enterprises under the SASAC purview has become explicit. Telecom operation, in particular, became a pivot and lever to support the upgrading of the ICT-dominant export-processing regime—as telecom operators were instructed to assist industrial policy. As remarked by the research director of SASAC, state-owned capital is not in the same boat with ordinary investors but should become the majority shareholder acting out state will.[6] However, the power of those comprehensive regulatory agencies is neither unlimited nor uniform, especially in the face of dramatically growing and globally entangled state enterprises.[7]

If one leg of the economic restructuring scheme is to support indigenous innovation, another leg is to stimulate domestic consumption. In line with the state's call for boosting domestic demand, competing operators—in fear of their slow-growing revenue from the traditional voice market—seek to foster infotech consumerism by tapping into new network possibilities enabled by internet protocol. In the 2000s IPTV was regarded as a golden opportunity to accelerate the transition from network operation to all-around information-service provision. Although IPTV is not yet a self-supporting business, digital set-top boxes channeling instant messaging, e-commerce, online gaming, online courses, and video-on-demand have become a gateway to so-called digital smart homes. After all, this is likely to be a sizable market. As the worldwide IPTV subscribers amounted to sixty-seven million in 2012,[8] China possesses a majority of thirty million.

From the 2000s and especially after 2008, claims and actions about network convergence have accelerated the corporate transition of the broadcasting system—in the image of telecom operators. To join the network economy, cable operators, large or small, self-sufficient or heavily subsidized, made loan-financed upgrading with digital technology. Then, under the banner of creating economies of scale, provincial cable companies were mobilized to acquire network assets at lower administrative levels while being allowed to leave behind those with little commercial potential. To create a national digital-TV system—on a corporate model—is the stated goal of the State Administration of Press, Publications, Radio, Film, and Television (the result of the 2013 merger of the General Administration of Press and Publications and SARFT). However, the political mandate of cultural security, and deficient demand for cultural consumerism rooted in China's socioeconomic inequality, pose twin obstacles to this enterprise. Digital TV by far is not able to dispossess the public TV system of live broadcasting, state channels, advertising revenue, or audience shares but has piggybacked on the established success of the former.

Despite the underdeveloped market for corporate digital TV, a small number of media companies have emerged out of the public broadcasting system, taking away the new digital value-added markets. Wasu and BesTV are two such market leaders. These corporate powers and the production chains they have formed are likely to tilt the public-corporate balance and to move swathes of production resources away from the public system. The most salient sign is scores of star producers from top-tier state media joining or forming private production companies. On the other end of the spectrum, third-tier media organizations also voluntarily jumped onto the digital bandwagon in order to set free their commercial ventures from the public media system weighted in favor of local audiences. New-media companies, regardless of their origins in the public-service sector, are hastening the trend of capitalization, financialization, and privatization. With the aid of investment vehicles, they are more open to absorb industrial capital, societal capital, financial capital, and even private capital from the managerial stratum. Notably, instead of being despised and avoided, private internet giants have become sought-after strategic investors.

The state has made information consumption a national economic policy. However, an MIIT vice minister acknowledged that proper industrial ecosystems and mature business models have yet to come.[9] That is to say, telecom operators and state media, both as anchors of state policies and aspirants to the digital economy, are building platforms for yet-to-explode information consumerism. This gives dominant internet companies, which sit on popular Web 2.0 platforms, a window of opportunity to build their portfolio of proprietary content. Wearing the hat as a member of the Chinese People's Political Consultative Conference in 2014, Robin Li, CEO of Chinese search-engine provider Baidu, called for support to put teaching materials online as a way of relieving regional inequality. He also urged governmental agencies to collaborate with commercial websites as a way of making state-controlled data accessible to the public.[10]

The transition to Web 2.0 has tilted market power further to nonstate corporate platforms, forcing state companies in the telecom and media sectors to reckon these private giants as equal and even formidable players. Leveraging their huge user bases, private internet companies have rushed to build subscription and pay-per-view business while urging state media to quit the online distribution market.[11] In 2014 Alibaba purchased the majority equity of a Hong Kong–based media group, planning to make movies, TV dramas, and web-only dramas every year; iQiyi, a leading online-video site owned by Baidu, planned to make one Hollywood and seven local movies the next year; Youku-Tudou, boasting five hundred million users on both computers and mobile devices, likewise set up a movie production division to feed content to its profitable premium-subscription service.[12] While the box-office revenue of the film industry reached $3.5 billion in 2013, the revenue for the online audiovisual industry surged 41.9 percent to $2.1 billion.[13] The internet giants' chance to beat cable networks and movie theaters should not be dismissed. The resurgence of state-led corporatization, as a response to this digital threat, ironically, is likely to amplify nonstate internet companies and their powerful business models.

Lin Chun's historical framework for understanding China and global capitalism is useful to capture the remaking of China's communications system:[14] As a global manufacturing powerhouse, China "saved" the global capitalist system while spreading exploitation, dependency, and conflict. Inexpensive, made-in-China industrial products, including network equipment and consumer electronics, have helped beat inflation in the Global North. The labor-intensive production regime also drives capital accumulation for transnational corporations and increasingly for domestic enterprises and GDP-obsessed local governments. The circuit does not end there: To make communications compatible with this global convergence, public domination in telecommunications, media, and culture as the political economic underpinning for socialism is fading away. State mandates to occupy the commanding-heights economy, and bureaucratic capitalist impulses to seek market freedom, have coalesced to translate public domination into corporatization and financialization of state assets, making a state-led corporatist system of communications. This is amounting to a "Chinese variant of state-led" digital capitalism.[15] Despite its fading public-service obligation, this corporatist system of communications, still under development, provides some maneuvering space during the global economic crisis.

Communications and Economic Restructuring

Indeed, the global economic crisis propelled the resurgence of state-led corporatization and capital accumulation in the realm of communications. But what kind of macroeconomic conditions have made communications a pivotal lever for economic restructuring? And how effective has this communications-centric approach to economic restructuring been? In general, unable to raise household income in the GDP, the state has extended high investment to the realm of communications, expecting advanced networks to support business innovation and individual entrepreneurship and to stimulate residential consumption in the overall sluggish economy. This move has accorded network connectivity and networked consumption unprecedented importance. But without substantive measures intended for economic justice, limits on residential consumption remain a serious structural obstacle against economic restructuring.

The 2008 global economic crisis exposed China's malaise of structural dependence on transnational capital, foreign technology, export markets, and an externally centered accumulation system. In 2007 before the financial outbreak, China's external dependence rate measured as the ratio of foreign trade in the GDP stood at 63.7 percent.[16] The same year, this index stood at 70 percent for ICT manufacturing.[17] It is no surprise, therefore, that the sudden collapse of the North American and European markets shook the economy. The crisis also led to an explosion of labor disputes, rising 98 percent from the year earlier.[18] After all, the export economy operates on the back of cheap migrant workers. From 2010 through 2013, local governments raised the minimum wage each year—as a gesture to rebalance the economy; however, no region has the minimum wage close to 40 percent of the average urban resident's income.[19] In 2013, for the

260 million migrant workers nationwide, their average monthly pay hovered at 2,609 yuan (US$420.80), which then edged up to 2,864 yuan (US$461.90) in 2014 and 3,072 yuan (US$487.60) in 2015.[20] While the continuous increase was welcomed, it only began redressing long-term residential-income suppression. The low income puts a firm cap on domestic consumption, as household consumption as a share of GDP has remained level around 36 percent from 2011 through 2014.[21]

The government's bailout package worth 4 trillion yuan (US$571 billion) beginning in 2008 had a quick, positive effect but also exacerbated another structural dependence on production-oriented investment. In 2011 investment—nearly 70 percent of which was concentrated in manufacturing industries, basic infrastructure, and real estate—contributed 54.2 percent of GDP growth.[22] This ratio hovered at 54.4 percent in 2013 and fell in 2014 and 2015 in response to serious gluts in real estate and heavy industry and to the state's measures to facilitate overcapacity reduction.[23] Li Deshui, former commissioner of the National Bureau of Statistics, noted China has an "overweight" economy—as the country has built a highway system of more than one hundred thousand kilometers and a power generation capacity of more than four trillion watts, both overtaking the United States, and its steel-production capacity of one billion tons equals the combination of those of Europe, Japan, and the United States.[24] For the purpose of soft landing, investment-driven expansion of infrastructures and manufacturing capacity is a curse.

The mixed needs to ameliorate the volatility of export manufacturing, to stimulate residential consumption, and to channel investment away from fixed assets in traditional industries have encouraged expanding the scope of the market to services. Employment also has some bearing. While manufacturing industries contributed nearly 46 percent of the GDP in 2009, manufacturing's contribution to employment was at a low level of 28 percent.[25] Meanwhile, the number of college graduates shot up from 1.06 million in 2000 to 6.3 million in 2010, and they have flooded the labor market.[26] Available jobs, however, comprise mostly manual and low-paying positions in the manufacturing and traditional service sectors. In this context, modern services are expected to create better jobs while upgrading China's economic profile.

Communications becomes pivotal because both telecommunications and media are strategic service sectors. The global economic crisis has driven the resurgence of state-led corporatization and capital accumulation in the state-controlled realm of communications. The state—jostled by bureaucratic, transnational, and private capital—parlayed the hitherto public assets in production, distribution, and provision into a slew of corporate entities, fortifying the accumulation imperative of the whole communications sector. This was relatively new for the broadcasting system as its grand corporate transformation gained momentum in the 2000s and especially after 2008. As for telecommunications, the sector already had corporations competing in an oligopoly market. In telecoms, the overarching objective is to expand the portfolio of new products and to grow the scope of business to uncharted cyberbusiness territories.

This "birth of industries for profit-making," however, still depends on low-paid workers and, thus, runs the risk of reinforcing the existing economic dynamics.[27] A recent survey reveals that the majority of grassroots telecom workers with ten-year job experience earn less than 5,000 yuan per month (US$806.50) owing to low base pay and unattainable performance expectations.[28] Other surveys reveal that commercialized print media and commercial websites have disproportionately expanded the lower-income rung of journalistic and editorial workforces.[29] The average salary for website editors, whose population reached three million, was 4,000 yuan (US$645) in 2013, with 36.1 percent in the 2,000 to 4,000 yuan range (US$323 to 645) and 32.7 percent in the 4,000 to 6,000 yuan (US$645 to 968) range.[30]

To stimulate information consumption, telecom and cable operators have focused on providing an "effective supply" of networked platforms through heavy investment. Take telecoms, for example: In view of the gaping social inequality at large, heavy investment has driven the spread of broadband. Between 2006 and 2010, fixed-asset investment in telecommunications amounted to 1.5 trillion yuan (US$208 billion). This equals an average annual input of 300 billion yuan (US$41.7 billion), far exceeding the annual input of 200 billion yuan (US$24 billion) in the preceding five years. Between 2011 and 2013, total investment soared again, already reaching the record of 1.5 trillion yuan (US$238.1 billion).[31] No matter how uplifting in some aspects, broadband including mobile broadband is bound to face limits. By 2014 China Mobile, the biggest operator in the world, set up 450,000 TD-SCDMA base stations and close to 500,000 4G base stations, making more than three hundred types of handsets available.[32] By the end of 2015, it set up more than 1 million 4G base stations altogether, making the world's largest 4G network.[33] Although mobile broadband is viewed as a lower-cost-broadband access technology, this operator has not recouped investment from 3G or 4G networks. Nor has the operator's plan panned out to persuade a big portion of mobile-phone users, more than five hundred million, to latch onto the advanced networks following the vast investment.[34]

If telecom operators are still doing the legwork, web companies, especially those focused on e-commerce, are creating new patterns of consumption. Premier Li Keqiang praised the Double 11 (November 11) for illuminating the power of information consumption, as e-commerce giant Alibaba turned the Singles Day, a holiday devoted to single people, into an online shopping festival in 2009. Total online sales on Singles Day exploded from 50 million yuan (US$7.4 million) in 2009 to 36.2 billion yuan (US$5.8 billion) in 2013 and to 91.2 billion yuan (US$14.5 billion) in 2015,[35] more than doubling the combined $3 billion sold in the United States for Black Friday and Cyber Monday.[36] As of 2014, e-commerce claimed 7.5 percent of the retail market, making China the largest online retail market.[37] However, behind the auspicious headlines is an untold story that online shopping has instigated a rapid expansion of express delivery, employing at least seven hundred thousand deliverypeople nationwide and fostering rampant unlawful labor practices.[38] Fierce price competition amidst chronic overcapacity and the shakeout of brick-and-mortar stores have also accompanied the skyrocketing rise of the few monopolistic transaction platforms and lurk as a threat behind the hotheaded spending on "cheaper" commodities sold online.

As far as electronics consumption is concerned, there is a sign of rebalancing thanks to limited state subsidies and improved sales networks. In 2013 domestic sales by ICT manufacturing enterprises reached 4.5 trillion yuan (US$725.8 billion), close to the value of delivery meant for export at 4.8 trillion yuan (US$774.2 billion).[39] Policy initiatives and e-commerce can take some credit. Between 2009 and 2013, the state subsidized domestic purchases of color TVs, mobile phones, and computers in its campaign of sending household appliances to the countryside. In recent years, online shopping fever has flared up on Alibaba and Jingdong Mall, among others—and computers, communications, and consumer electronics are the second-biggest category of products sold online. As a sign of endorsement, the State Council in 2014 pledged to support online shopping and to develop rural logistics in its six-item package for boosting domestic consumption.

As telecom operators, in tandem with global IT giants, drive the whole nation onto digital networks, they are eyeing powerful institutional users—in view of the capped residential income. After promulgating the concept of electronic commerce in 1996, IBM came up with the "smart Earth" concept in 2008 as a rhetorical vehicle to cultivate new commercial opportunity. The hype gave birth to the internet of things, cloud computing, and big data, as IBM envisions a world where everything, alive or not, is connected with networks, and, as a result, inexhaustible data becomes available for storage, digging, and analysis. In China local governments have jumped on the bandwagon: In 2007 about 10 percent of the input for city infrastructures was spent on information applications, 15 percent of telecom investment was on building e-government,[40] and by

2014 China Telecom had built 224 "smart cities" out of its more than 300 local networks.[41] While touting futuristic visions, these moves make no fundamental difference from the heavy-investment model defining China's macro economy.

Apart from building e-governments and smart cities, the central government has the goal of shifting the economy from being dependent on manufacturing to service. The state expects, observed Willy Chiu, vice president of IBM Cloud Labs, to use cloud computing "to bring in outsourcing services business."[42] Telecom operators, troubled by stagnated subscriber growth, have risked jumping in, as the promised shift to networked provision of computing and storage capacity is likely to reposition them favorably in the digital economy. As a result, networked data centers, as the facility for cloud computing, are mushrooming. China Mobile was expected to spend $52 billion in cloud computing between 2012 and 2014, "more than all the US companies have invested in total."[43] Accounting company KPMG estimated that the Chinese government was to invest $154 billion by 2015 to support twenty-five cloud-computing centers.[44] China Telecom alone has built more than 330 data centers.[45] However, the construction fever has so far created an excessive hardware infrastructure, which provides little software-enabled virtualization support.[46] The effect on the economic profile remains dubious, not to mention the effects on employment and the ecosystem.

Manufacturing industries are not excluded from this grand networking project. The "industrial Internet" and the "industrial internet of things," concepts coined by General Electric, that envision a systematic use of networked applications in machinery and industrial operation, have gained currency among top Chinese industrial and technology authorities. The call to ride an unfolding Third Industrial Revolution centered on information and communications technology is becoming a policy discourse.[47] In the first eleven months of 2013, technical upgrading consumed nearly 43 percent of industrial investment.[48] Within China's four major industrial sectors, that is, raw materials, equipment and machinery, consumer products, and electronics, upstream industries, such as steel, construction materials, and shipbuilding, have had serious overcapacity, because large-scale, loan-financed real estate and infrastructure construction are unlikely to continue without evoking financial and environmental backlashes. In the face of a tenacious industrial structure, ICT appears to be one of the few instruments available to the state for achieving gradual transformation. The state authority expects ICT-touched new products, such as green construction materials, new-energy vehicles, industrial robots, and solar batteries, to find future demand.[49]

Building an online nation, or applying ICT products and services to an ever-wide scope of social-economic life, has, indeed, crystalized into a key national strategy. In 2015, echoing a proposal the CEO of social-media giant Tencent made at the National People's Congress, Premier Li Keqiang turned Internet Plus into a new action plan intended for economic restructuring. This plan encompasses a long series of industrial, technology, and spending initiatives along with reform agendas intended to liberalize an information economy. The gist is to boost internet-related businesses and, more important, to use digital networks and computing technologies as basic infrastructures and innovation sources to retool traditional industry and commerce.

This state orchestration, however, covers up lopsided progress. In the remote areas, broadband penetration in rural populations was merely 6.3 percent as of 2013.[50] After much delay, in 2014 the launch of the pilot "broadband countryside" project in Sichuan marked a modest start of budgetary support by the NDRC. After revamping the universal-service mechanism in 2015 to increase central budgetary support and to enlist nonstate and nontelecom enterprises, the state expected 30 percent of rural households to have broadband the same year.[51] In the city, technocentric visions, such as providing online training to blue-collar information workers and making online health care available to the public, have gained currency. Market development in these areas, then, has made the current condition of network connectivity, speed, and affordability less tolerable for slowing down widespread adoption of new applications. When Internet Plus became a new policy mantra, telecom operators came under fire again for dragging their feet on improving broadband services. In May 2015, out of frustration for the lack of progress since the passage of the broadband-China program in 2013, the premier asked telecom operators to make detailed plans to improve the speed of internet services and lower the fees that they charge. The public reprimands of telecom operators, however, only distracted attention from sustainable development goals, such as a living wage and economic justice.

To what extent has economic restructuring been achieved? Economists have divergent views. What is certain is that the enthusiastic embrace of communications has elevated network connectivity, as well as networked consumption of products, services, and content, to a new level. In this sense, China is becoming a new global center where "the pivotal role accorded to information and communications as a solution" for renewing economic growth at home and for rejuvenating global capitalism at large is playing out—a recurrence of what Dan Schiller has documented as a US-led overhaul since the 1970s.[52]

The countries of the Organization for Economic Co-operation and Development, especially the United States, have dominated the global system of digital capitalism. As ICT production and ICT usage are becoming unprecedentedly important in making a sustainable economic recovery in China, how will the state's ambition—backed up by increasingly powerful Chinese corporations and the domestic-market size—make global impact? International relations scholar David L. Shambaugh said, "The rise of China is the big story of our era," but China is still a "partial power."[53] But how much advantage would China likely gain from this newly discovered developmental focus on communications? The following sections explore global implications in ICT manufacturing, media and entertainment, and, finally, the internet.

"Made in China"—"Made for China"

As economist Martin Hart-Landsberg points out, American consumers had spent way beyond their means in the decades before 2008, riding a credit-and-real-estate bubble. The 2008 financial crisis forced them to cut back on their spending in order to fix the broken balance sheet. Despite some adjustments, however, the depression in the Global North—which is a global pole of consumption—did not alter the unbalanced economic dynamics; vested interests have striven to sustain it.[54] To bolster their profit margins under continuously suppressed demand, brand-name companies worked to squeeze out surplus from downstream, China-based partner manufacturers—who constitute a global pole of production.

Indeed, brand-name companies have exploited their commanding positions to adjust the cross-border production system. Samsung, for example, moved half of its production to Vietnam in 2013. Likewise, US PC companies, together with Taiwan-based mega contract manufacturers, also adjusted their China-based industrial clusters. While Southeast Asia presents an option, manufacturers' forays into western China have also helped suppress production costs in response to falling retail prices. After 2008 IT production continued to expand in China. The profit rate, however, was 3.2 percent in 2013 for PC production, down 0.2 percent from the year before,[55] which is the biggest division of ICT manufacturing in China.

To loosen up the unbalanced global economic dynamics pivoting on the "made-in-China" production of electronics, the Chinese state developed a "made for China" strategy to encourage domestic firms to innovate and to sell to the domestic market. The China-only standard as a temporary artificial barrier in the liberalized market dominated by Western transnational capital, and the spending sprees on mobile communications and on internet and data communications, as we saw, helped homegrown vendors regain some market share but not so much in acquiring missing technological competencies.

Import substitution was especially salient for network equipment: By 2014 nearly 70 percent of the domestic telecom-equipment market belonged to homegrown enterprises.[56] This has translated into some global success. In comparison with European and US vendors, Huawei and ZTE together garnered the largest market share in fixed broadband access and optical communications while ranking second and third in mobile communications and in data communications, respectively.[57] The two companies were stymied by the collective weakness in general chips and software innovation and were kept outside of the global enterprise-network market in 2013.[58] However, this systematic deficit in software development, chip design, and chip production did not prevent ZTE and Huawei from enjoying a sales pickup the following year in the Chinese enterprise router market, hurting dominant vendors, such as Hewlett-Packard and Cisco Systems.[59]

The effect was mixed for devices and their production chains. In 2013 the majority of 3G handsets sold in China carried the brands of Huawei, Kupai, Lenovo, and ZTE. However, dependence on chips from Qualcomm, key components from Japan and South Korea, and the Android operating system meant that the profit margins of domestic brands were far below that of global brands.[60] Even the market miracle of the Xiaomi smartphone, reputed for its globally sourced, high-end configuration, did not change its true character of being a high-volume, low-margin business. China Mobile was quick to upgrade to 4G mobile communications systems, but domestic chipmakers that had reaped healthy market share in the 3G era were bogged down by their collective inability to sustain continuous innovation.[61]

If TD-SCDMA and its 4G successor blazed the path, the Edward Snowden exposure of widespread surveillance by the US National Security Agency over global communications has given the Chinese state—along with Chinese enterprises—a strong impetus to restore a proper national industry as far as servers and other storage devices are concerned. The 2013 MIIT annual report declares IT nationalization will be a "long-term trend" encompassing software, hardware, operation, and services.[62] Because semiconductors are used in a wide range of products from smartphones, tablets, and household appliances to automotive, medical, industrial, and military devices, China's dependence on imported chips has been a perennial national security concern. In 2014 the

State Council set up an IC industrial fund, with China Mobile as one of the contributors, signaling a top-level effort to bulk up investment in front-end fabrication plants for the sake of import substitution.

On the software front, since 2007 China has started by far the "largest state-led campaign" of preinstalling Linux-based, homemade operating systems.[63] In 2014 Microsoft's decision to stop technical support for Windows X, the operating system for 60 to 95 percent of the computers used by governmental organizations and state enterprises in China,[64] provided another pretext for the Central Government Procurement Center to ban Windows 8 on government computers. In the nonstate sector, a different type of import substitution is taking place, as homegrown cyber giants, under the auspices of the Internet Plus policy, have acquired applications for retailing, payment service, personal transportation, and e-hospital, aiming to extend their powerful Web 2.0 platforms to organize offline socioeconomic activities.

With the politicization of information and communications, the state's ability to mobilize national champions has improved, despite globalization, financialization, and even privatization of these companies. Auspicious market conditions explain the corporate support for greater state protection—as China's gigantic market size may soon reach critical mass to spur novel ideas, thus placing Chinese enterprises favorably on the frontline of demand-driven innovation.

Still, the sustainability of this techno-economic nationalism is contingent on collaboration among upstream and downstream enterprises, but they often do not work well with each other. In the case of the Loongson central processing unit (CPU), for example, the Chinese Academy of Science, which has been developing the chip in research labs since 2001, started chip industrialization in 2005 and established a company in 2009. Inspur, Lenovo, and Powerleader then developed computers for government use, incorporating the indigenous chip. Again, bad coordination was rife in actual deployment of the homegrown CPU: The CEO of China Electronics Corporation, for example, tellingly indicated that the government should actually "use" homemade products despite their imperfections and high prices, and the Lenovo CEO expressed discontent with homegrown chips.[65]

The made-for-China strategy—limited by internal frictions and incompetence—does not reduce the importance of trade, either. After all, ICT manufacturing based in China is, first and foremost, an integral part of a global production chain, too weighty to break away from the old Global North–oriented trading pattern. According to the Asian Development Bank, the 1996 Information Technology Agreement (ITA), to which China is a signatory, was foundational for the China-centric production system. Because the 1996 ITA eliminated tariffs among member countries on computers, semiconductors, telephones, and other IT goods, it enabled intermediate goods to travel duty-free and, thus, has encouraged the distribution of production processes across different countries. In the hierarchically structured production system, "Japan and the US inject value by providing key components and services directly to the PRC, which is the downstream hub."[66]

The strategy of leveraging the growing domestic market for new generations of technology to forge alternative supply chains among homegrown enterprises has to counter new free-trade agreements for digital products. In 2012, in light of the changing technological composition of world trade, some WTO members sought to expand the scope of the ITA agreement to new ICT products, including multicomponent semiconductors, GPS systems, flat-panel displays, and video-game consoles.[67] In the following rounds of negotiation, China put up a sensitivity list of IT industries that it "wants to either exclude from the talks or phase in over a long time period."[68] This gesture threatening to derail the negotiations faced strong pushback, though. More than eighty global trade associations urged China to back down, and heavy domestic pressure for trade liberalization was also put on China. After the 2014 Asia-Pacific Economic Cooperation meeting, China yielded and reached an ITA expansion agreement. China's share of trade covered by the agreement is the largest among all WTO members, leading those of the United States and European Union. Again, China's "home-base" strategy is incomplete because global giants and foreign products will continue to play critical roles in the foreseeable future.

The politicization of information and communications has spilled over to the international scene, limiting the expansion of Chinese products and capital. The existing high-volume trade with the Global North is one source of geo-economic tension. China has been a focus of antidumping investigations by its major trading partners.[69] Computers and electronic products were and continue to be the dominant fraction of Chinese exports to the United States, at 36.7 percent in 2013 up to November and at 33 percent in 2015 through September;[70] these exports received fifteen intellectual property rights–related complaints in 2014.[71] Apart from Chinese goods, Chinese capital also faces blockades into the highly coveted US market. Huawei and ZTE, for example, are global vendors in terms of revenue—together with 50 percent market share in the Asian Pacific, the Middle East, and Africa and a 25 percent share in Latin America. However, these companies have been precluded from acquiring commercial entities or selling to major telecom operators in the United States. As the global pole of business and technological innovation, the Global North, especially the United

States, still has the will and ability to outflank China's attempts at redistributing power and profits along the global value chain.

To counter the rising protectionism of major trading partners, China is forging alternative geo-economic spaces. By 2015 the country reached fourteen free-trade bilateral agreements mostly with developing countries, including the Association of Southeast Asian Nations, Australia, Chile, Costa Rica, Iceland, New Zealand, Pakistan, Peru, Singapore, South Korea, and Switzerland. In 2014 China established the Silk Road Fund and initiated the Asian Infrastructure Investment Bank, both for funding infrastructure projects in developing countries along the Silk Road over land and at sea. This spatial reorientation is nascent but like the home-base strategy has potential to alter the geopolitics of transnational accumulation. Also like the home-base strategy, this statist initiative may impose unwanted tasks on Chinese enterprises, distracting them by political orders from chasing Western-led innovation trends.

Go Digital and Go Global

The government deploys a network of actors in propaganda, media, and public diplomacy for its "soft power" campaign, a campaign meant to enhance the country's ability to attract and influence others, emphasizing "external propaganda" and "overseas publicity work."[72] This has led the soft-power literature to underscore the statist nature of China's global media presence. Indeed, the campaign has harnessed top-level state media organizations for this purpose, including China Central Television; China Radio International; Xinhua News Agency; *China Daily*, a nationwide newspaper; and *Global Times*, a popular newspaper under the *People's Daily*. However, ideological straitjackets, along with material constraints, such as the lack of local distribution networks, have restrained the statist campaign.[73] As a result, China's global media presence is still nascent and its cultural and ideological influence limited.

This unsatisfying condition has encouraged a decentralized, capital-driven approach to soft power because the policy-making circle began to believe that convergence with the global Hollywood system is a stepping-stone to building a competitive industrial foundation for media and entertainment. The circle's attitudes range from supporting cautious openness to advocating integration to the fullest possible extent. The vice director of the Yunnan Provincial Department of Culture, for example, went so far as to regard "culture as commodity" as a universal value and a prerequisite for global influence.[74] On the ground, the sweeping corporate reform, as documented in chapter 5, is reshaping the political economy of media and entertainment, sending the go-out incentive down to local and nonstate corporations. In this context, instead of the top-level soft-power campaign, market dynamics and capital imperatives need more attention from the state.

To become regional and global media corporate giants, newly minted state enterprises have favored a twin practice of "go digital and go global." With plenty of hot money flowing into the media and entertainment business, Chinese investors are on the lookout for auspicious projects. These investors regard advanced technology as a security blanket for making content digital viewers are willing to pay for. In contrast to the traditional broadcasting system, the new-media business—driven by digital technology—faces fewer regulatory impediments and has lower administrative barriers. First-tier state media, equipped with exclusive operational licenses and an expansionist spirit, have reaped the lion's share of the national interactive TV market. To secure market power on the basis of advanced technology, first-tier state media are forging strategic partnership, setting eyes on enhancing production and distribution capacities across platforms.

As foreign joint ventures are still off-limits for TV, radio, and film production, business ties with Western entertainment technology companies are a detour. As an illustrative example, IMAX's partnership with TCL, a leading Chinese TV company, to build a digital home-theater system for Chinese digital-TV viewers also enlisted Wasu to distribute IMAX-enhanced Hollywood and Chinese content to this system.[75] As for big screens, 3-D and IMAX movies have driven movie theatergoing: In 2014 3-D movies contributed 48 percent of the box office.[76] This market condition explains the decision of China Media Capital, a leading investment fund backed by SMG and the NDRC, to purchase stakes in IMAX's greater China subsidiary in 2014.

Apart from generating an appetite for high-tech content to support digital distribution at home, the domestic political economy of media and entertainment also cultivates corporate desire for an extraterritorial market space to export products and capital to. Take the film industry, for example: Film overproduction relative to the fragmented and uneven domestic market has plagued the industry. In 2013 movie theaters exhibited only 39 percent of all movies.[77] Meanwhile, because domestic box-office successes have depended on big-budget high-tech production, this mode of production instigates a global scope of marketing for recouping high production cost, thus further motivating investment-enabled participation and learning in the global Hollywood system.

In recent years, financing contracted in Western markets, giving China a chance to become a source of investment. The ascent of the Chinese market to the second-largest one, with 44 billion yuan (US$7.0 billion) worth of box-office revenue in 2015, following the United States, further enhanced the attractiveness of Chinese capital. All these trends enabled China Media Capital in 2012 to form Shanghai Oriental DreamWorks Film and Television Technology Corporation with Hollywood's DreamWorks. For Chinese state investors, this unusual partnership is expected to transfer institutional know-how as well as technical and artistic advice to Chinese filmmakers. The goal is to help build a globally aligned industry in China and to make global movies with Chinese elements eligible for theater exhibition in China and popular worldwide.

Aided by the strategy go digital and go global, China has made great strides in content exports. In 2009 China garnered nearly $60 million from overseas sales of over ten thousand hours of film and TV programming. In 2013 overseas sales of Chinese films alone made 1.4 billion yuan (US$228 million).[78] As a reference for comparison, in 2013 South Korea's exports of TV programs and films each garnered $150 million and $59 million, respectively.[79] Despite this expansion, China's overseas market is still limited, unlikely to catch up with the roaring domestic market. In 2015 overseas sales of Chinese films surged again to 2.8 billion yuan (US$444 million), but these takings equaled one-tenth of domestic ticket sales of 27.1 billion yuan (US$4.3 billion).[80]

Indeed, the global appeal of Chinese media and the global footprint of Chinese media capital are both limited. Geopolitical struggle over transnational accumulation is centered in China's explosively growing new-media market. The shift to digital distribution, for example, has created rifts. As of 2006, the worldwide trade in programming rights was valued at $10 billion, and the United States claimed 60 percent.[81] Western programs, however, are hardly present on prime-time television in China—of the thirty imported shows approved in 2011, most came from Hong Kong, South Korea, and Taiwan.[82] In this context, digital-media platforms, such as iQiyi, Sohu, and Youku-Tudou, opened up new market-entry opportunities for Western media content. In 2014, however, the state decided to restrict private online-video platforms and blocked popular internet portals from using OTT to lure living-room audiences away from interactive TV operated by telecom and cable operators. The state also set a quota of foreign programs licensed for online distribution, thereby subsuming video websites under the same regulatory framework with cable and telecom operators while restricting market access for Western programs.

However, market leaders, both domestic and global, are united to combat undesirable user behaviors, such as watching pirated programs. An annual review prepared by the Office of the US Trade Representative claimed 90 percent of China's online music downloads in 2011 were illegal.[83] In installing Netflix-style subscription models, leading Chinese web companies have acted in recent years as good corporate citizens to clamp down on piracy. In 2014 at the International Market of Communication Programs, Charles Zhang, CEO of Sohu, proclaimed that piracy in China was "dead" and that obstacles against the pay-for-view model were removed.[84] For leading online-video websites, capital expenditures on acquiring copyrighted content soared up from 500 million yuan (US$73.5 million) in 2009 to 3.7 billion yuan (US$596.8 million) in 2013.[85] This optimistic trajectory, however, is insufficient: By the end of 2013, merely 11.7 percent of 428 million online-video viewers watched programs for sale, and an even smaller fraction did so regularly.[86] Thus, continuous policy and regulatory inputs from the state and corporate actors are necessary for creating a full-blown new-media market.

Overall, Chinese companies, both state-owned and private ones, have gained strength in China's rapidly growing media-and-entertainment market that is still selectively protected from foreign investment. The state's firm grip on market access, China's astonishing buying power, and leading corporations' spending capacity coalesced into a systematic media power, opening the door to the global Hollywood system and enabling Chinese capital to participate in and learn about transnational projects of production and distribution. This is China's new formula of global participation, aiming to propel top-tier Chinese corporations to regional and even global status in a new digital age.

Contested Convergence

China's internet is becoming an increasingly important portion of the global internet. In view of the internet's strategic importance for the country's national security as well as economic development, the Chinese state is staking out a nationalist position while participating in international standardization organizations and even seeking to influence global internet governance. In keeping up with the popular analogy between Chinese cyberspace and a "giant cage," scholarly attention has disproportionately focused on censorship and the Great Firewall. However, the Chinese internet, driven by a multitude of domestic and international forces, has been converging with the dominant global structure—despite unsettled contention on political and economic fronts.

As Dan Schiller points out, the "free flow of information," along with its assumption of liberal capitalism, has been a defining American foreign policy.[87] This high-minded ideology enables the United States to act as the only legitimate guardian of the "free, neutral, and borderless" platform—while obscuring its disproportionate control over the global network.[88] The Snowden exposure, however, was a slap in the face to this view. In the wake of this 2013 global scandal, *People's Daily* was quick to condemn the absence of international rules, conducive to US hegemonic power.[89]

China has demonstrated an evolving strategy toward US unilateralism in internet governance. Starting from an "extremely peripheral" position in the late 1990s but becoming notably "outspoken" after 2001,[90] the state has stepped up efforts in this crucial field. First, standing with the United Nations and a majority of developing countries, China has challenged the US-centric Internet Corporation for Assigned Names and Numbers (ICANN) that gives US private business interests—and the US government—de facto, top-level control over the naming and addressing system. Although oversight over ICANN continues to stay exclusively with the United States, the UN-sponsored World Summit on the Information Society (WSIS) built a case for other sovereign authorities to work themselves into global internet governance.[91]

The development-oriented nature of the WSIS process has also resulted in a holistic approach to internet governance that goes beyond ICANN-related issues; as Milton L. Mueller points out, the topic now encompasses all policies associated with the internet, including technical-standard setting, interconnection of internet service providers, telecom infrastructures, freedom of expression, and multilingual issues.[92] To shield its unilateral power over ICANN, the US government conceded that "there is no one venue to appropriately address the subject in its entirety."[93]

China shares this holistic view—and, thus, promotes alternative platforms of governance, even as it also works with ICANN. Although China rejoined the ICANN Government Advisory Committee in 2009 and has eased its resistance to the renewed Internet Governance Forum—a nonbinding, multistakeholder forum mandated by the WSIS process—the country's diplomatic focus seems to concentrate on the International Telecommunications Union (ITU).[94] In 2014, backed by the MIIT and the Ministry of Foreign Affairs, Zhao Houlin, veteran ITU official, became ITU secretary general. As Zhao revealed, this success showcased China's capacity and determination to acquire greater responsibility regarding global communications and technology development.[95] Zhao argued that given the globally distributed nature of the internet as well as its integration with the existing public telecom infrastructure, the ITU, with its strength in fully involving developing countries, has potential to become a new coordinating platform for the span of internet governance issues.[96]

The country has spent a fortune to ameliorate the structural imbalance of internet resources, but, as *People's Daily* stresses, without a long-term plan for massive investment, resistance to the unbalanced status quo is futile.[97] After the party state made "indigenous innovation" a guiding policy in 2006, setting national technical standards has been a primary strategy to reverse one-way market liberalization, with emphasis on encouraging ICT-based innovation. With the launch of the China Next-Generation Internet equipped with Chinese IPv6 routers and other homemade technical standards in 2003, the call for housing IPv6 root servers in China was a high-profile gesture because the IPv4 servers are housed mostly in the United States and in Britain, Japan, and Sweden. In 2007 the China Internet Network Information Center (CNNIC) deliberately lowered the registration fee for .cn domain names from 100 yuan (US$13) to 1 yuan (US$0.10) to speed up adoption.[98] By December 2015, .cn domain names had exceeded sixteen million, accounting for 52.8 percent of all domain names inside China.[99] According to the State Council Information Office, China spent 4.3 trillion yuan (US$537.5 billion) on internet infrastructures by 2009.[100]

Apart from scaling up domestic capacity and volume, China has succeeded in becoming a, if not the, network hub in the Asia Pacific region. According to British Telecom's global survey in 2014, Chinese enterprises ranked the highest in terms of going-out ambition, but the majority of them, along with other Asian Pacific clients, regarded the shortage of IT infrastructures as the top obstacle.[101] China Telecom Global Ltd., a wholly owned subsidiary of China Telecom, has worked to spearhead and facilitate corporate global-expansion initiatives. Spending 10 billion yuan (US$1.6 billion) per year on submarine cables while collaborating with more than two hundred foreign operators, this company oversees a China-centered global optical network that interconnects Asia from inside, with Europe, and across the Pacific. Its goal is to catch up with top global network operators in 2016 and 2017.[102]

Accompanying IT industrial policy, IT trade policy has also became a pressure point. With the development of cloud computing, data centers are becoming the heart of trade disputes. As the Chinese government prohibits local companies, especially banks operating in China, from storing data in another country, data centers built in China may claim a potentially huge market.[103] However, on the international scene, transnational corporations, including Google, IBM, Intel, and Microsoft, advocate framing internet access and data flows as trade issues in order to prevent privacy and security policies from becoming onerous trade barriers. The US-led Trans-Pacific Partnership (TPP) negotiations unmistakably incorporated digital products and information flows into a trade framework. The stated commitments include barring custom duties on cross-border data flows and prohibiting data-localization requirements that constitute restriction on trade.[104]

Although trying to maintain "Chinese" cyberspace, the state has willingly accommodated cross-border corporate applications—as an "open" internet is key to garnering commercial benefits. This means China-based data centers welcome externally originated, cross-border data flows. According to president of China Unicom, his company runs "lots" of data centers not only for Chinese clients but also for global corporations, such as "Amazon, Google, and Microsoft." Japanese companies also began to use China-based facilities.[105] This pragmatic attitude toward cyber trade, however, is likely to cultivate domestic interests for trade liberalization, encourage foreign demand for reciprocal treatment, and undercut the state's future claim over cyberspace sovereignty.

Despite its critique of ICANN, China has acquiesced to the multistakeholder model—in a version of a state-corporate partnership.[106] Despite widespread concern regarding the US unilateral power over ICANN, the multistakeholder model of ICANN has gained backing not only from Western countries but also, as acknowledged by *People's Daily*, from corporations, civil society, and nongovernmental organizations.[107] In recent years the state has eased its head-on challenge but participated in debating the substance. This debate has two positions: One is a private sector–based, transnational model of governance, which in practice has operated contradictorily under the US corporatist hegemony and a "free spirit" libertarian tradition;[108] the other one is a development-oriented model driven by nation-states and intergovernmental organizations that seeks inputs from corporate giants but is less open toward small business and civil society. China has come to support the latter. At home, the state evokes "cybersovereignty" and "rule of law" to impose a hierarchical structure, emphasizing the government, corporations, civic organizations, and individual users all as "obligated" entities.[109]

A state-corporate partnership is forming, as the increasingly competitive Chinese internet industry has played a visible role, especially in business and technical operation. In 2014 the Central Leading Group for Cyber Security and Informatization chaired by CCP secretary general Xi Jinping was established. Its office held a study meeting for over sixty internet-related companies. For invited private web companies, this was "unprecedented political treatment."[110] Remember that back in 2010, private cyber entrepreneurs sang a chorus of dismay at exclusion from both the People's Congress and the Political Consultative Conference despite high-profile presence of representatives from telecoms, media, and even IT-equipment manufacturing. The internet industry's ascent in the policy-making arena has parlayed into the state's adoption of the Internet Plus action plan in 2015 and a state-assisted global expansion. In July 2013 Jack Ma, Alibaba Group chairperson, and Robin Li, Baidu CEO, joined President Xi Jinping's official delegation to South Korea and Brazil. In Brazil, Li unveiled the Portuguese version of the Baidu search engine. It is no accident that in 2014, Baidu bought control of the largest Brazilian e-commerce company. According to *China Daily*, it was the first time a Chinese leader helped promote an internet service—because internet services are now on the top leaders' overseas-marketing list, which also includes basic goods, mechanical and electrical products, high-speed railway systems, and nuclear power plants.[111]

China's explosively growing internet market along with the new state-corporate partnership has pressed the existing US-dominated global governance regime to give Chinese cyberspace more legitimacy. In 2015 Ma was elected cochair of the Global Internet Governance Alliance, which ICANN cosponsors. This signified "trust in China's Internet, and how China governs the Internet," said Ma.[112] Despite this success, the honeymoon between the state and private web giants may not last long. New rifts can arise anytime. This likelihood puts forth uncertainties in China's global internet agenda.

Conclusions

As the fastest-growing economic sector, communications broadly conceived has become a fulcrum in the geopolitics of transnational accumulation. International rivalry, which is on the rise after the economic downturn, increasingly centers on communications industries, infrastructures, and policies. Placing communications at the center of its economic restructuring, China—the fastest-growing economy—is, thus, becoming a new epicenter of geopolitical contention over communications.

As a downstream manufacturing hub in the Asia-centered global production network, China derives its economic-growth miracle from an externally centered accumulation system. Although China is far from threatening the United States' position of being "the consumer of last resort,"[113] global integration has fostered outward-looking institutions committed to efficiency and given rise to a growing middle class. Despite its fragmented and uneven character, the country presents an important market for internet-related business. In 2014 Qualcomm earned 50 percent of its revenue from China, while Apple attracted 50 percent of its new consumers from China.[114] This interlocking relationship means that in the time of global economic depression, the world—and the US-led global digital capitalism—anxiously looks at China and its economic prospects. It also means that although it is possible for China to increase household income in the GDP and, thereby, to shift the center of gravity in global accumulation, a pragmatic compromise is possible, which is to cater to the tastes of China's middle class and its outward-looking institutions. The latter approach of prioritizing the needs of outward-looking strata and institutions makes global convergence a preference.

During its continuous rise as an economic power, China was demanding and continues to demand a stronger position in global production chains, more growth space through cultural and capital exports, and more power in allocation and control decisions about critical information resources. Forging alliances with corporate aspirants at home and like-minded counterparts in emerging economies, the Chinese state has transnationalized its stance on many policy fronts. Leveraging the domestic market, it has sought to control more strategic factors of transnational production. Indeed, actions of economic nationalism are becoming deliberate and firm at the time of China becoming a bigger part of the world economy.

This is not to say, however, the economic restructuring centered on communications will reverse China's opening-up. Although in many categories unrestrained liberalization and privatization are unlikely and foreign investment and operation are off limits, the state's determination to cultivate new growth engines in the realm of communications actually stipulates that convergence with the global dominant structure make headway. Foreign capital, market access, technical know-how, and managerial practices have been indispensable for bolstering the global standing of Chinese corporate power. More important, China's state and corporate communities both need to participate globally to hone their ability to deploy these key production factors and to gain more command over the transnational accumulation system. Thus, strategic involvement of Chinese capital in transnational production, distribution, and governance is encouraged atop selective market protection at home. This is China's new strategy for reshaping the geopolitics of transnational accumulation and for redistributing power and resources along the global value chain.

Conclusion

Communications and China's Political Economy

At the intersection of China's rise as a global power and its internal quest for transformation, digital economic development in China is one of the most significant stories of the twenty-first century. Ultimately, this book is about China's state-led model of digital capitalism, which contends, collaborates, and overlaps with the US-dominated system of global digital capitalism.

Since the 1970s, communications has taken up a growing role in the global political economy, accelerating cross-border capital flow, dispersing production activities, and facilitating transnational corporate management. Driven jointly by global structural forces and domestic market reforms, China is deeply integrated into the global political economy. What is new is that the country's expanding global entanglements have resulted in mounting contradictions, acutely manifest during the 2008 global economic crisis, which forced the Chinese state to act. The deliberate efforts for economic restructuring have centered on communications industries and policies, pivoting on building a new, networked economy. How much chance China has to shape this networked economy in relation to the global system of digital capitalism led by transnational corporations is a profound problem. The state's unprecedented enthusiasm—and China's arguably symbolic triumph with Alibaba's record-breaking initial public offering (IPO) at the New York Stock Exchange in 2014—seem to portend an auspicious era.

This book historicizes, disaggregates, and analyzes the relationship between the state, its communications systems, and the global digital economy for forging a network-based economy and, in view of many moving parts, provides a holistic and sobering understanding of communications development in China and its recent past and present and outlines the parameter of contradictions that are likely to affect its future. Rather than treat communications as a distinct realm some intrinsic law rules, this volume characterizes communications industries and policies as interwoven with Chinese-style capitalism—and with its continual adjustment in response to structural tension and conflicts characteristic of global capitalism.

First of all, one cannot emphasize enough the importance of communications in China's market reform—as the former has supported and *reinforced* the latter. The market reform started in the margin, where transnational capital and private capital were ushered in to jumpstart an export-processing industrial economy. Meanwhile, state ownership—either in the form of public property or majority shareholding—has retained its dominance in strategic industries.

Comprising ICT manufacturing, telecommunications, and media, communications is no exception to this reform trajectory. It spans two distinct sectors in the country's economic geography: the export-processing economy driven by transnational capital and a parallel economy "inside the system."[1] The former has rendered the country and its people vulnerable to all the ruinous effects of an unruly global capitalism, from labor abuse to environmental pollution. The latter—the state-controlled realm of communications—has mirrored and supported the former. Into the 2000s and especially after 2008, the state-controlled realm of communications has further formed a new epicenter of profound political and economic changes. In the post-2008 context of crisis and in the following restructuring act, communications is becoming a crosscutting, general-purpose instrument for fixing structural imbalances and for rejuvenating economic growth.

A lesson can be drawn here: communications, as an "exception to neoliberalism" that is shielded from unrestrained liberalization and privatization, gives a developmental state a political-economic foundation for restructuring policy while affording the country some maneuvering space in the context of crisis.

The ownership distinction, however, is unstable. It has created a mounting pressure on the political economy "inside the system" to the extent that it is no longer possible to live with the planned reform results. The internal demands to recast the communications system on a corporate model—to be "compatible" with the liberalized industrial economy, on the one hand, and to become "competitive" against thriving, private, new-media companies, on the other— have grown irresistible. In acceleration after 2000, a corporate reform swept network operation and content provision, driven by nationalistic aspirations for a stronger position in the global techno-economic network as well as by elite demands to profit from the dangerous opportunities presented by digital technology. Except in a few selected, unprofitable areas, the state has spared no effort to expand the scope of the market.

Under the veneer of developmental rationality and technological inevitability, the campaign, however, has created social deficits. The policy-making process, framing communications as technocratic issues, largely excluded ordinary people, especially the worker-peasant communities.[2] Labor in a variety of occupations hitherto regarded as holding "golden rice bowls" and reaping monopoly benefits has come to grief. As employment is expanding in the service sector, the corporate wage-earning class now includes telecom workers, website editors, rank-and-file journalists, express-delivery men, software testers, call-center representatives, short-message authors, and online store salespeople. Under the banner of mixed-ownership reforms, state executives as "entrepreneurial bureaucrats" are advocating partial privatization of state-owned assets.[3] As for the new digital communicative ecosystem shaped by a few national multimedia, aggregating platforms, it is increasingly disembedded with local communities. How rank-and-file communications workers react to the new working conditions, how local worker-peasant communities experience this emerging ecosystem, and how they organize grassroots alternatives are worth future research attention.

Secondly, communications has played a pivotal role in the restructuring, as a national strategic infrastructure, a new investment outlet with great consumption and growth potential, and as a general-purpose catalyst for innovation, industrial modernization, and export upgrades. Unable to challenge head-on the low-wage mode of accumulation, the state gave an unprecedented priority to network connectivity and networked consumption for the purpose of making a sustainable economic recovery. But how successful has this been? Although signs of restructuring are taking place, they fall short of making a qualitative break from the entrenched economic dynamics. The ICT-dominant export-processing regime has undergone some spatial reconfiguration. Cost differentials between the coastal and western regions help relieve the downward pressure and even sustain the profit margins of transnational corporations in the economic downturn. However, the accumulation system based on cheap labor has proven too deep-rooted to change—in the absence of progressive state policy and unified labor resistance. The participation of western fringe areas in globalized production is likely to worsen chronic overcapacity and disperse labor disputes while adding little to the disposable income of the worker-peasant community.

In the sector of modern services intended for encouraging domestic consumption and diverting capital from production-related fixed-asset investment, the state's double-pronged approach has achieved mixed results as well. To expand so-called effective supply, the state has unleashed profit-making industries from the hierarchically organized public-service system through corporate reforms. In a changed technological environment, activated market players inside the system divert investment to less-regulated markets, such as new media and cultural real estate. Building proprietary-content collections, setting up online premium-service platforms, and creating upscale or large-scale cultural-consumption spaces are all capital intensive. These have accrued to a higher level of contribution by cultural industries to the GDP. However, investment-driven industrial development, diverging little from the structural dependence on investment, does not meet social needs on the ground.[4] It adds to the binge in investment.

To manage demand, the state has used budgetary support to buttress social-redistribution projects, hoping to ameliorate market failures characteristic of global digital capitalism. However, the rise of cross-platform corporate giants, rapid market-instigated technological replacements, and the dismantlement of local infrastructures can easily drown out welfare-oriented, corrective efforts. In 2014 the China Academy of Social Science published two authoritative reports indicating that between 2004 and 2012 the ratio of cultural consumption to the GDP declined.[5] Given long-suppressed wages, an incomplete social safety net, and the rising cost of living for the majority of the population, the growing expenditure on marketed information, cultural commodities, and communications consumption is likely to be widely perceived as an unpleasant economic burden—despite more choice, sociability, and participation.

This communications-centric approach to economic restructuring as currently implemented is likely to reinforce, rather than correct, the existing economic dynamics. To create sustainable economic recovery, state intervention should go beyond the supply-demand neoclassical economics equilibrium in order to rebalance capital-labor relations.

Lastly, transnational corporate dynamics both contend and overlap with the state in shaping China's communications ecosystem, as communications is central in China's renegotiation with global capitalism operating increasingly in a networked fashion. The US-dominated global digital capitalism comprises top transnational corporations, the global production networks they have organized, and the international corporate governing structure.[6] This global system of digital capitalism is not something external to China but has unevenly and selectively integrated the country on hierarchical terms. In the global systems of digital capitalism, China is first and foremost a downstream manufacturing powerhouse. During China's opening-up and market reforms, a whole range of governmental and economic institutions has come to depend—in a systematic way—on Western-controlled, advanced information-and-communications technology. Of course, localized global production chains and a booming market also attracted domestic capital, fostering homegrown enterprises and even cultivating a handful of competitive transnational corporations.

The Chinese state wants to play the global game on its own terms, but it also yearns for governing influence inside the existing systems of digital capitalism. Its domestic corporate allies, for disparate business reasons, seek to obtain commanding positions in the global production network and to get well positioned in new commanding height industries. This state-business agenda encourages a techno-economic convergence of Chinese communications into the global capitalist structure, a general trend acquiesced to, facilitated, and even enthusiastically pursued by Chinese political and business leaders. Thus, the domestic corporate reform in the state-controlled realm of communications has a global purpose. Although the state still keeps direct foreign investment or management off limits in many categories of communications, convergence for the purpose of becoming globally competitive takes place on multiple levels, in terms of institutional priority, targeted audiences, the organization of production, and the terms of access. If the high-speed train is China's sale to the world, communications, reconfigured in a transnational business fashion, are expected to be the next offer.

As external dependence and internal imbalances characterize China's relationship with global capitalism, the state has played a new role in resetting the terms of participation by encouraging strategic positioning in transnational accumulation and governance, on the one hand, and leveraging domestic market protection, on the other. It is an uphill battle to overhaul the domestic economy and to reshape the global economic dynamics. However, determination and prowess to forge a state-business alliance, on the one hand, and to engineer new information consumption hotspots, on the other, are on the side of the Chinese state. Not only has the state repurposed communications resources under its ownership control to unleash corporate development, it has also facilitated market development around digital technology in numerous socioeconomic realms.

Then, does the state's demonstrated ability to influence business dynamics in the realm of communications constitute a successful China model? Rather than positing a success recipe for other countries to duplicate, this book underscores uncertainty and ambivalence. For one reason, the state has to work with powerful corporate giants that embody outward-looking interests and imperatives. Even when the purpose is to reassert nation-centric control over the unbalanced global structure of accumulation, statist initiatives contain global elements, including globally financed state enterprises, homegrown transnational corporations, and a true transnational technobusiness network.[7] Thus, the state, not a unitary entity itself, has to put up with constraints, contention, and loopholes. National plans, pillar industries, and national champions, all tokens of state power and nationalistic intention, only conceal complex and even conflicted internal dynamics. Therefore, cyber nationalism or networked nationalism, concepts developed by Milton L. Mueller, among others,[8] is useful to encapsulate state initiatives orchestrated around networked communication—but only with the crucial qualification that statist nationalism is neither monolithic nor guaranteed but, instead, is contingent upon specific political-economic relations. Neither should this concept obscure the larger trend by which China is converging into the global capitalist structure.

The diluted sovereignty is an important dimension of the Chinese state, pertaining to the digital economy. Indeed, the state is a strong developmental state—in the sense that it blazed an economic growth pathway by hosting an export-processing regime and in recent years by trying to mitigate contradictions born of such global entanglements. As China's digital economy is gaining strength, the Chinese state is likely to become a key architect of the global digital future. If the so-called China model refers to a developmental state as such, it is important to avoid overstating the power, unity, and rationality of the state and its actions in setting the scope of global integration, on the one hand, and in redressing pitfalls born of it, on the other. The current volume demonstrates that although the state has attempted to manage varied basic problems, from economic disparities to deficient consumption, from persistent dependence on foreign technology to the outsized role played by foreign investment in China's development, the state is itself partly constituted by these multifarious structural imbalances. Among others, the incentive of local governments to ramp up local GDP and employment, the strategy of centrally owned state enterprises to use global resources for rapid development, and the fortuitous trajectory of local companies driving cable digitization have all imbued the so-called national policy of economic restructuring with a range of local, bureaucratic, and corporate special interests.

A political commitment to carving out a genuinely unique Chinese path, however, remains important. The stakes are high. Given the Chinese state principally insists on equality and justice as core socialist values, communications is pivotal to building a socialist democracy. What kind of China story is likely to prevail out of corporate media with mixed-ownership structure? Will communications-related corporate investment help create sustainable economic recovery widely shared by the worker-peasant community? Capitalist crises in the global system emanate from chronic industrial overcapacity, exploited global labor, unprecedentedly high efficiency, and an unmatched scope of the market, all of which are fortified by the communications industry.[9] If the rise of China is the story of the twenty-first century, the country's embrace of communications with unprecedented enthusiasm is likely to accelerate this process. It is not going to be a simple rise to power but a continual effort to tamp down crises and manage contradictions. The country needs a progressive policy to avoid dragging the world further into incessant stagnation. Looking forward, China and communications will be two leading engines generating decisive dynamics in the global system.

Appendix

Yearly average exchange rate for USD$1 to Chinese yuan (CNY), 1981–2016

Year	CNY Average Rate
1981	1.8
1982	1.9
1983	2.0
1984	2.2
1985	2.9
1986	3.5
1987	3.7
1988	3.7
1989	3.8
1990	4.8
1991	5.3
1992	5.5
1993	5.8
1994	8.6
1995	8.4
1996	8.3

Year	CNY Average Rate
1997	8.3
1998	8.3
1999	8.3
2000	8.3
2001	8.3
2002	8.3
2003	8.3
2004	8.3
2005	8.2
2006	8.0
2007	7.6
2008	7.0
2009	6.8
2010	6.8
2011	6.5
2012	6.3
2013	6.2
2014	6.2
2015	6.3
2016	6.6

Sources: US Forex Foreign Exchange Services, "Yearly Average Rate," accessed May 19, 2016, http://www.usforex.com/forex-tools/historical-rate-tools/yearly-average-rates; "Shuju jianbao: 1950 nian yilai renminbi dui meiyuan huilv bianhua ji dashi yilan" 数据简报：1950年以来人民币兑美元汇率变化及大事一览 [Statistical report: Historical exchanges rates for USD$1 to the Chinese yuan and review of major events], *Zhongguo jingji wang* 中国经济网, February 21, 2014, accessed May 21, 2016, http://intl.ce.cn/specials/zxxx/201402/21/t20140221_2350673.shtml.

Notes

Introduction

1. Martin Hart-Landsberg, *Capitalist Globalization: Consequences, Resistance, and Alternatives* (New York: Monthly Review, 2013), 39–40.

2. Emily Kaiser, "G20 Support Builds for Rebalancing World Economy," *Reuters*, September 22, 2009, http://uk.reuters.com/article/uk-g20-sb-idUKTRE58K4E720090922; Jan Nederveen Pieterse, *Development Theory: Deconstructions/Reconstructions* (Thousand Oaks, CA: Sage, 2004).

3. Carl E. Walter and Fraser J. T. Howie, *Red Capitalism: The Fragile Financial Foundation of China's Extraordinary Rise* (Singapore: Wiley and Sons, 2012).

4. Dan Schiller, *Digital Capitalism: Information Technology and Economic Crisis* (Urbana: University of Illinois Press, 1999), 5, 13–26, 43–56.

5. Wanning Sun and Jenny Chio, *Mapping Media in China: Region, Province, Locality* (New York: Routledge, 2012).

6. Philip C. C. Huang, "Profit-making Firms and China's Development Experience: 'State Capitalism' or 'Socialist Market Economy'?" *Modern China* 38, 6 (2012): 591–629.

7. John Bellamy Foster and Robert W. McChesney, *The Endless Crisis: How Monopoly-Finance Capital Produces Stagnation and Upheaval from the USA to China* (New York: Monthly Review Press, 2012); Jeb Sprague and Grazia Ietto-Gillies, "Transnational Corporations in Twenty-First Century Capitalism: An Interview with Grazia Ietto-Gillies," *Critical Perspectives on International Business* 10, 1–2 (2014): 35–50.

8. Terry Flew, *New Media* (South Melbourne: Oxford University Press, 2014).

9. Randolph Kluver and Chen Yang, "The Internet in China: A Meta-Review of Research," *Information Society* 21, 4 (2005): 301–8.

10. Francis L. F. Lee, Louis Leung, Jack L. Qiu, and Donna S. C. Chu, *Frontiers in New Media Research* (New York: Routledge, 2012).

11. Robin Mansell, "Political Economy, Power and New Media," *New Media & Society* 6, 1 (2004): 96–105.

12. For earlier, exemplary works, see Yuezhi Zhao, *Communication in China: Political Economy, Power, and Conflict* (Lanham: Rowman and Littlefield, 2008); Eric Harwit, *China's Telecommunications Revolution* (Oxford: Oxford University Press, 2008).

13. Jack Linchuan Qiu and Wei Bu, "China ICT Studies: A Review of the Field, 1989–2012," *China Review* 13, 2 (2013): 123–52, 123.

14. Luis Felipe Alvarez León, "The Digital Economy and Variegated Capitalism," *Canadian Journal of Communication* 40, 4 (2015): 637–54.

15. See Huang, *Capitalism with Chinese Characteristics*; Michael Pettis, *Avoiding the Fall: China's Economic Restructuring* (Washington, DC: Carnegie Endowment for International Peace, 2013); Guobin Yang, *The Power of the Internet in China: Citizen Activism Online* (New York: Columbia University Press, 2009).

16. Ministry of Industry and Information Technology (hereinafter referred to as MIIT), *2011 nian dianzi xinxi chanye tongji gongbao* 2011年电子信息产业统计公报 [Public statistics report on telecommunication industry: 2011], February 27, 2012, accessed May 21, 2016, http://www.cnii.com.cn/tjfx/content/2012-02/22/content_1012827.htm.

17. Yukyung Yeo, "Between Owner and Regulator: Governing the Business of China's Telecommunications Service Industry," *China Quarterly* 200 (2009): 1013–32, 1026.

18. Zhu Changrui 朱昌瑞, "Yilan tongxin shi: Hulianwang jingji GDP zhanbi chuang xingao" 一览通信事：互联网经济GDP占比创新高 [Review of telecom news: Internet economy's GDP contribution reached a historical high], *CWWEEKLY* 通信世界, January 23, 2015.

19. David Harvey, *The Enigma of Capital: and the Crisis of Capitalism* (London: Profile, 2010), 111, 94.

20. Yu Hong, "Reading the Twelfth Five-Year Plan: China's Communication-Driven Mode of Economic Restructuring," *International Journal of Communication* 5 (2011): 1045–57.

21. Dan Schiller and Vincent Mosco, "Introduction: Integrating a Continent for a Transnational World," in *Continental Order? Integrating North America for Cybercapitalism*, ed. Vincent Mosco and Dan Schiller (Lanham: Rowman and Littlefield, 2001), 1–34.

22. Zhang Yuling 张玉玲, *Gei Zhongguo Jingji Bamai* 给中国经济把脉 [Discussion of China's economic issues] (Beijing: Contemporary China, 2007); Andong Zhu and David M. Kotz, "The Dependence of China's Economic Growth on Exports and Investment," *Review of Radical Political Economics* 43, 1 (2001): 9–32; Kai Yuen Tsui, "China's Infrastructure Investment Boom and Local Debt Crisis," *Eurasian Geography and Economics* 52, 5 (2011): 686–711.

23. Yu Hong, *Labor, Class Formation, and China's Informationized Policy of Economic Development* (Lanham: Lexington, 2011), 5.

24. Adam Przeworski, *The State and the Economy under Capitalism* (London: Routledge, 2014).

25. Andrew C. Mertha, "China's 'Soft' Centralization: Shifting Tiao/Kuai Authority Relations," *China Quarterly* 184 (2005): 791–810; Roselyn Hsueh, *China's Regulatory State: A New Strategy for Globalization* (Ithaca: Cornell University Press, 2011).

26. Sebastian Heilmann and Elizabeth J. Perry, "Embracing Uncertainty: Guerrilla Policy Style and Adaptive Governance in China," in *Mao's Invisible Hand: The Political Foundations of Adaptive Governance in China*, ed. Sebastian Heilmann and Elizabeth J. Perry (Cambridge: Harvard University Press, 2011), 1–29.

27. Ruben Gonzalez-Vicente, "The Internationalization of the Chinese State," *Political Geography* 30, 7 (2011): 402–11.

28. Nicholas Garnham, "Contribution to a Political Economy of Mass-Communication," *Media, Culture, and Society* 1, 2 (1979): 123–46.

29. Herbert Schiller, *Information and the Crisis Economy* (Norwood: Ablex, 1984).

30. Kluver and Yang, "Internet in China"; Qiu and Bu, "China ICT Studies."

31. Vincent Mosco, *The Pay-Per-View Society: Computers and Communication in the Information Age* (Westport: Greenwood, 1989); D. Schiller, *Digital Capitalism*; Graham Murdock and Peter Golding, *Digital Dynamics: Engagements and Disconnections* (Cresskill: Hampton, 2010); Robert McChesney, *Digital Disconnect: How Capitalism Is Turning the Internet against Democracy* (New York: New Press, 2013); D. Schiller, *Digital Depression: Information Technology and Economic Crisis* (Urbana: University of Illinois Press, 2014).

32. D. Schiller, *Digital Capitalism*.

33. Dan Schiller, "Digital Capitalism: Stagnation and Contention," *Open Democracy*, October 13, 2016, https://www.opendemocracy.net/digitaliberties/dan-schiller/digital-capitalism-stagnation-and-contention.

34. Anthony Smith, *The Geopolitics of Information: How Western Culture Dominates the World* (New York: Oxford University Press, 1980).

35. Dan Schiller, *How to Think about Information* (Urbana: University of Illinois Press, 2007).

36. Huang, *Capitalism with Chinese Characteristics*, 620; Chi Lo, *Understanding China's Growth: Forces That Drive China's Economic Future* (Basingstoke: Palgrave Macmillan, 2007).

37. Cui Zhiyuan, "China's Export Tax Rebate Policy," *China: An International Journal* 1, 2 (2005): 339–49, 343.

38. Foster and McChesney, *Endless Crisis*, 158.

39. McChesney, *Digital Disconnect*, 67.

Chapter 1. Driving Capitalism to Western China

1. John King Fairbank, *The Great Chinese Revolution, 1800–1985* (New York: Harper and Row, 1986), 36–41.

2. Yu Hong, "Colonial Legacies and Peripheral Strategies: Socio-spatial Logic of China's Communications Development since 1840," *Global Media and Communication* 11: 89–102.

3. Lin Chun, *China and Global Capitalism: Reflections on Marxism, History, and Contemporary Politics* (New York: Palgrave Pivot, 2013).

4. Yue-man Yeung, introduction to *Developing China's West: A Critical Path to Balanced National Development*, ed. Yeung Yue-man and Jianfa Shen (Hong Kong: Chinese University Press, 2004), 12.

5. Lijian Hong, "Sichuan: Disadvantage and Mismanagement in the Heavenly Kingdom," in *China's Provinces in Reform: Class, Community and Political Culture*, ed. David S. G. Goodman (London: Routledge, 1997), 199–236.

6. George C. S. Lin, *Red Capitalism in South China: Growth and Development of the Pearl River Delta* (Vancouver: UBC Press, 1997).

7. Lin Chun, *The Transformation of Chinese Socialism* (Durham: Duke University Press, 2006).

8. Hong, *Labor*, 41–42.

9. Yu Yikuan 余义宽, "Xiaofei lei dianzi chanpin chukou zhuan shuai dianzigongye jiang tiaozheng chukou jiegou" 消费类电子产品出口转衰电子工业将调整出口结构 [Export of electronic consumer products declines, electronic industry adjusts export structure], *Xibu dianzi xinxi bao* 西部电子信息报, March 9, 1995, 1.

10. "Quanguo jihua huiyi zai jing zhaokai qiangdiao jiji tuijin jingji jiegou zhanlve xing tiaozheng" 全国计划会议在京召开强调积极推进经济结构战略性调整 [National planning meeting held in Beijing promoting strategic adjustment of economic structure], in *Zhongguo zhong xibu diqu kaifa nian jian 1979–92* 中国中西部地区开发年鉴 [Yearbook of China's central and western region development], ed. Liu Jiang 刘江 (Beijing: 中国财政经济出版社), 12–13.

11. Hong, *Labor*, 41–42.

12. Peter Nolan, *China and the Global Economy: National Champions, Industrial Policy, and the Big Business Revolution* (New York: Palgrave, 2001), 134.

13. Robert H. McGuckin, Matthew Spiegelman, Jianyi Xu, Yaodong Liu, and Yan Jiang, *China's Experience with Productivity and Jobs: Benefits and Costs of Change*, Research Report R-1352-04-RR (Conference Board, 2003), 5.

14. Wei Jie 魏杰, *Zhongguo jingji zhuanxing* 中国经济转型 [China's economic transition], (Beijing: 中国发展出版社, 2011), 97.

15. Su Hainan 苏海南 and Liu Bingquan 刘秉泉, "Gongzi Fenpei pian" 工资分配篇 [On wage distribution], Zhongguo laodong 中国劳动 11 (2008): 16.

16. China International Electronic Commerce Center, "1981 nian–2007 nian jiagong maoyi jinchukou tongjishuju" 1981年–2007年加工贸易进出口统计数据 [Statistics of the processing trade import and export: 1981–2007], http://jm.ec.com.cn/article/jmtjsj/jmzhtj/200810/662713_1.html; Ministry of Commerce, People's Republic of China Comprehensive Department, "2013 nian zhongguo duiwai maoyi fazhan qingkuang" 2013年中国对外贸易发展情况 [2013 development of China's foreign trade], http://zhs.mofcom.gov.cn/article/Nocategory/201405/20140500570675.shtml.

17. Ministry of Science and Technology, People's Republic of China, "2013 nian woguo gaojishu chanpin maoyi zhuangkuang fenxi" 2013年我国高技术产品贸易状况分

析 [2013 analysis of China's high-tech products trade], *Science and Technology Statistical Report* 558 (2015), http://www.most.gov.cn/kjtj/201508/P020150817335226567384.pdf.

18. Sze-yueh Wang and Lee-in Chiu, "The Impact of Mainland China's Open-Door Policy on Regional Industrial Development," in *China's Regions, Polity, and Economy: A Study of Spatial Transformation in the Post-Reform Era*, ed. Si-ming Li and Wing-Shing Tang, (Hong Kong: Chinese University Press, 2000), 133–54.

19. Hsing You-tien, *The Great Urban Transformation: Politics of Land and Property in China* (Oxford: Oxford University Press, 2010).

20. Wang Xinli 王辛莉, "Bi guaidian nongcun zai ying huangjin zengzhang" 避拐点农村再迎黄金增长 [Villages welcome development again at turning point], *Xibu shibao* 西部时报, December 16, 2008, 13. The exchange rate used in this volume for events from 1994 to 2006 is about US$1 to 8.3 Chinese yuan. See appendix for year-by-year rates.

21. Tang Hongkun 唐红坤, "Xibu da kaifa kaishi shishi di jiu ge wunian jihua" 西部大开发开始实施第九个五年计划 (1996年–2000年) [Western China Development Program starts the ninth five-year plan (1996–2000)], *Xibu shibao* 西部时报, September 4, 2009, 8.

22. Yang Yongxian 杨勇先, "Xibu guding zichan touzi qingkuang fenxi" 西部固定资产投资情况分析 [Analysis of investment on fixed assets in West China], *Xibu da kaifa* 西部大开发 6 (2002): 72–73.

23. "Xibu jingji zengzhang fangshi mouqiu zhuanbian" 西部经济增长方式谋求转变 [West China seeks new ways of economic development], *Xibu fazhan bao* 西部发展报, December 16, 2004, 5.

24. Wu Yu 吴宇, "Zhongguo-DongMeng zi mao qu youwang cheng weilai Dongya zi mao rukou" 中国-东盟自贸区有望成未来东亚自贸区入口 [China-ASEAN free trade area (FTA) may become the future East Asia FTA entrance], *Xibu shibao* 西部时报, November 22, 2011, 6.

25. Liu Xuezhi 刘学智, "Kaituo nanya shichang: Sichuan de lishi jiyu" 开拓南亚市场: 四川的历史机遇 [Opening the Southeast Asian market: Sichuan's historical opportunity], September 1, 2005, accessed September 1, 2014, http://sichuan.mofcom.gov.cn/article/sjgongzuody/200509/20050900340468.shtml.

26. Pan Shui 潘水, "Zhongguo-Dong Meng kuangjia xia Guangxi wuliu jingzhengli yanjiu" 中国-东盟框架下广西物流竞争力研究 [Studies on Guangxi's logistic competitiveness under the China-ASEAN framework], *Gaige yu zhanlue* 改革与战略 6 (2004): 4–7.

27. "Economic Zones Said Refueling Development of China's West," *BBC Monitoring Asia Pacific*, December 20, 2009, retrieved from LexisNexis.

28. Yang Chengdong 杨成栋, "Lianhe zou xi kou—wu wei zhongya yanjiu zhuanjia tan xibu kaifa" 联合走西口—五位中亚研究专家谈西部开发 [Going west together: Five central Asian research experts talk about developing the west], *Xibu fazhan bao* 西部发展报, November 8, 2001, 5.

29. Gao Xincai, Guo Aijun, and Wang Ke 高新才 郭爱君 王科, "Xibu jichusheshi zhongda gongcheng pingjia" 西部基础设施重大工程评价 [Evaluation of major infrastructure in western China], *Xibu da kaifa* 西部大开发 8 (2005): 36–38.

30. Lin Ling 林凌, "Da kaifa 5 nian, dongxi bu chaju jixu lada" 大开发5年, 东西部差距继续拉大 [Five years after great development, increased gap between East and West], *Xibu fazhan bao* 西部发展报, July 8, 2004, 5.

31. Dong Jun 董峻 and Zhao Cheng 赵承, "Xibu jichusheshi jianshe de si ge zhongdian" 西部基础设施建设的四个重点 [Four major points in western infrastructure construction], *Xibu fazhan bao* 西部发展报, September 14, 2001, 3.

32. He Zhanjun 贺占军, "Zhongguo tielu jianshe zhongxin zhujian xi yi" 中国铁路建设重心逐渐西移 [China's railway construction shifts emphasis westward], *Xibu shibao* 西部时报, December 9, 2008, 1.

33. Yue-man Yeung, Jin Fengjun, and Zeng Guang, "Infrastructure and the New Economy," in *Developing China's West*, 107, 122.

34. Xiao Dai 肖岱, "Da zao Zhongguo xibu zhongya xinxi jiaoliu xin zuobiao: Wulumuqi quyu xing guoji tongxin yewu churukou ju guapai chengli" 打造中国西部中亚信息交流新坐标—乌鲁木齐区域性国际通信业务出入口局挂牌成立 [Building the new landmark of central Asian information exchange in western China], *Zhongguo dianxinye* 中国电信业 6 (2012): 20–22.

35. Wang Yanlong 王焱龙, "Xibu ruoshi weishi de boyi shengcun" 西部弱势卫视的博弈生存 [Competition and survival of the disadvantaged satellite TV stations in Western China], *Xibu dianshi* 西部电视 3 (2003): 12–13.

36. Wang Song 王松, "Guizhou weishi: dianran dianshi chuanmei ye quyu zhanhuo" 贵州卫视: 点燃电视传媒业区域战火 [Guizhou Television: Igniting the battle fire for television], *Xibu kaifa bao* 西部开发报, August 23, 2002, 3.

37. Barry Naughton, "The Western Development Program," in *Holding China Together: Diversity and National Integration in the Post-Deng Era*, ed. Barry Naughton and Dali L. Yang (Cambridge: Cambridge University Press, 2004), 253–96.

38. Du Ying 杜鹰, 2006 *Zhongguo zhong xibu diqu kaifa nian jian* 2006中国中西部地区开发年鉴 [Yearbook of China's central and western region development, 2006] (Beijing: 中国财政经济出版社, 2006), 431.

39. Cheng Wenchuan 程文全, "1997 nian Sichuan sheng dianzi chanpin shichang zhanwang" 1997年四川省电子产品市场展望 [Prospect of electronic product market in Sichuan province, 1997], *Xibu dianzi xinxi bao* 西部电子信息报, October 16, 1996, 11; Xiao Yi 肖怡 and Leng Xiao 冷筱, "Gaige kaifang zhong xunmeng fazhan de Sichuan dianzi gongye" 改革开放中迅猛发展的四川电子工业 [Sichuan's booming electronic industry in the reform-and-open-up era], *Xibu dianzi xinxi bao* 西部电子信息报, November 8, 1999, 1.

40. Hsing, *Great Urban Transformation*, 2–3.

41. Lin, *Red Capitalism*, 181.

42. Hsing You-tien, *Making Capitalism in China: The Taiwan Connection* (Oxford: Oxford University Press, 1997), 156.

43. Jieh-min Wu, "Launching Satellite: Predatory Land Policy and Forged Industrialization in Interior China," in *China's Regions, Polity, and Economy: A Study of Spatial Transformation in the Post-Reform Era*, ed. Si-ming Li and Wing-Shing Tang (Hong Kong: Chinese University Press, 2000), 309–50.

44. Liu Jiang 刘江, *2002 Zhongguo zhong xibu diqu kaifa nian jian* 2002中国中西部地区开发年鉴 [Yearbook of China's central and western region development, 2002] (Beijing: 中国财经出版社, 2002). Chen Yaobao 陈耀邦, *1997 Zhongguo zhong xibu diqu kaifa nian jian* 1997中国中西部地区开发年鉴 [Yearbook of China's central and western region development, 1997] (Beijing: 改革出版社, 1997), 79.

45. Sichuan Provincial Economic Commission 四川省经济委员会, *2007 Sichuan gongye nian jian* 2007四川工业年鉴 [Yearbook of Sichuan industry 2007] (Chengdu: 成都时代出版社, 2007), 11.

46. Liang Jiang 刘江, *Zhongguo zhong xibu diqu kaifa nian jian 1979–92* 中国中西部地区开发年鉴, 1979–92 [Yearbook of China's central and western region development, 1979–92] (Beijing: 改革出版社, 1992), 144.

47. Mao Haifeng 毛海峰 and Yang Yimiao 杨一苗, "Xi zi dong jin: Chanye ziben de xin liuxiang" 西资东进—产业资本的新流向 [East investing on west: The new industrial capital flow], *Xibu fazhan bao* 西部发展报, May 17, 2007, 2.

48. Hsing, *Making Capitalism*, 115.

49. Chen Xiaowei 陈小玮, "Xi sanjiao: weilai xibu zuida de chengshi qun" 西三角: 未来西部最大的城市群 [Western triangle: The future biggest western city groups], *Xin xibu* 新西部 4 (2009): 25–26.

50. Sichuan Provincial Economic Commission 四川省经济委员会, *2005 Sichuan gongye nian jian* 2005 四川工业年鉴 [Yearbook of Sichuan industry: 2005] (Chengdu: 成都时代出版社, 2005), 112.

51. Liu Jiang 刘江, *1998 Zhongguo zhong xibu diqu kaifa nian jian* 中国中西部地区开发年鉴 [Yearbook of China's central and western region development 1998] (Beijing: 改革出版社, 1998), 357.

52. Chen Ri 陈日, *2006 Sichuan gongye nian jian* 四川工业年鉴 [Yearbook of Sichuan industry 2006] (Chengdu: 四川科技出版社, 2006), 97.

53. Hong, *Labor*, 61.

54. MIIT, "2002 nian dianzi xingxi chanye wancheng qingkuang" 2002年电子信息产业完成情况 [Annual report of electronic information industry 2002], July 19, 2003, accessed May 21, 2016, http://www.miit.gov.cn/n1146312/n1146904/n1648373/c3482991/content.html.

55. "Shangwubu Zhang Ji sizhang tan jiagong maoyi zhuanxing shengji" [Chinese Minister of Commerce Zhang Jisi talks about structure] 商务部张骥司长谈加工贸易转型升级 [Director Zhang Ji from the Ministry of Commerce talks about transformation and upgrading of processing trade], accessed July 15, 2015, http://www.mofcom.gov.cn/fangtan/swgzxlwlat/130816.shtml.
The category of machinery and electronics products overlaps with the category of high-tech products.

56. Dan Breznitz and Michael Murphree, *Run of the Red Queen: Government, Innovation, Globalization, and Economic Growth in China* (New Haven: Yale University Press, 2011), 137.

57. OECD, *OECD Territorial Reviews: Guangdong, China 2010* (Paris: Organization for Economic Cooperation and Development), 2011.

58. Department of Economic System Reform and Economic Operation, MIIT, *Zhongguo dianzi xinxi chanye tongji nian jian (san zi pian) 2005* 中国电子信息产业统计年鉴(三资篇)2005 [Statistical yearbook of Chinese electronic information technology (foreign-funded enterprises) 2005] (Beijing: 电子工业出版社, 2006), 19.

59. Wen Junliang 温均良, "Xibu kaifa Gansu de lu zenme zou" 西部开发甘肃的路怎么走 [Western China development: how to develop Gangsu], *Xibu fazhan bao* 西部发展报, February 21, 2002, 1.

60. Department of Economic System Reform and Economic Operation, *Zhongguo . . . 2005*, 140–42.

61. Sichuan Provincial Economic Commission, *2007 Sichuan gongye nian jian 2007*, 92.

62. Quoted in Walt Custer, "A Flat Global Trajectory," *CircuiTree*, April 1, 2005, cited in Boy Lüthje, Stefanie Hürtgen, Peter Pawlicki, and Martina Sproll, "North America: Network-Based Mass Production in the Age of NAFTA," in *From Silicon Valley to Shenzhen: Global Production and Work in the IT Industry*, ed. Boy Lüthje and Stefanie Hürtgen (Lantham: Rowman and Littlefield, 2013), 95.

63. Jonathan Wright, Manisha Sahni, and Rowena Zamora, "Wage Increases in China: Should Multinationals Rethink Their Manufacturing and Sourcing Strategies," *Accenture*, February 16, 2011, accessed September 1, 2014, http://www.accenture.com/SiteCollectionDocuments/PDF/Accenture_Wage_Increases_in_China.pdf (no longer available).

64. Cheng Ruihua 程瑞华, "Woguo jiang dali fuchi xibu xinxi chanye fazhan" 我国将大力扶持西部信息产业发展 [China to strongly support information industry development in west regions], *Xibu fazhan bao* 西部发展报, September 22, 2005, 1.

65. Department of Industry, Ministry of Commerce, "Guanyu zhichi zhongxibu diqu chengjie jiagong maoyi tidu zhuanyi gongzuo de yijian" 关于支持中西部地区承接加工贸易梯度转移工作的意见 [Suggestions for supporting central and western regions to receive processing trade], November 28, 2007, accessed September 1, 2014, http://cdtb.mofcom.gov.cn/article/tansuosikao/200711/20071105253355.shtml.

66. "Waishang touzi xibu reqing zhunian xiajiang" 外商投资西部热情逐年下降 [Declining enthusiasm of foreign investment in west regions every year], *Xibu fazhan bao* 西部发展报, July 22, 2004, 5.

67. Wu Yiming 吴一明, "Sichuan ruhe chengjie dongbu touzi" 四川如何承接东部投资 [How Sichuan received investment from eastern regions], *Xibu fazhan bao* 西部发展报, May 26, 2005, 8.

68. "Guanyu shenru shishi xibu dakaifa zhanlue youguan qiye suodeshui de gonggao" 关于深入实施西部大开发战略有关企业所得税的公告 [Public decree

regarding corporate income tax for western China development program], State Administration of Taxation, 12 (2012), accessed May 28, 2016, http://www.chinatax.gov.cn/n810341/n810765/n812151/n812421/c1083733/content.html.

69. Guy S. Liu, Sun Pei, and Wing T. Woo, "Chinese Style Privatization: Motives and Constraints," in *Exit the Dragon? Privatization and State Control in China*, ed. Stephen Paul Green and Guy Shaojia Liu (Malden, MA: Wiley-Blackwell, 2005), 60–77.

70. Zhang Yanlong 张延龙, "Xibu zhaoshang anzhan" 西部招商暗战 [West region's hidden battles of attracting investment], *Xibu shibao* 西部时报, March 27, 2009, 5.

71. Yuan Chunqing 袁纯清, "Zai diyi jie dongxi bu hezuo luntan shang de zhici" 在第一届东西部合作论坛上的致辞 [Speaking at the first East-West Cooperation Forum], *Xibu da kaifa* 西部大开发 5 (2010): 5. The exchange rate for 2000 to 2010 is about US$ 1 to Chinese yuan 7.8. See the appendix.

72. Chris Johnston, "When China Says Go West, Young Man, It Means a Fast Train to a Faster-Growing City," *London Times*, December 1, 2012, 83, retrieved from Lexis-Nexis.

73. Jeffrey William Henderson, *The Globalisation of High Technology Production: Society, Space, and Semiconductors in the Restructuring of the Modern World* (London: Routledge, 1991), 70.

74. Kristi Heim, "US Tech Giants Invest in Future Competitor," *San Jose Mercury News*, March 15, 2004, 1A, retrieved from LexisNexis; Jason Dean, "Intel Boosts Role of China with Plans for Chip Plant," *Globe and Mail* (Canada), August 27, 2003, B7, retrieved from LexisNexis.

75. David Christensen, Jim Walker, and Masao Kuniba, "Semiconductor Packaging, Assembly and Test Facilities: Worldwide, 3Q05 Update (Executive Summary)," July 7, 2005, *Gartner*, accessed September 1, 2014, https://www.gartner.com/doc/482190/semiconductor-packaging-assembly-test-facilities.

76. Andrew K. Collier, "Labor Cost, Education Attract Intel; Chipmaker Picks Chengdu Site for Assembly and Test Plant," *South China Morning Post*, August 28, 2003, 3, retrieved from Lexis-Nexis.

77. "Why Intel's Stacking the Chips in Vietnam," *Bloomberg Businessweek*, February 27, 2006, accessed September 1, 2014, http://www.bloomberg.com/bw/stories/2006-02-27/why-intels-stacking-the-chips-in-vietnam.

78. Embrose Evans-Pritchard, "High-Tech Expansion Drives China's Second Boom in the Hinterland: Comment," *Daily Telegraph*, November 26, 2012, 2, retrieved from LexisNexis.

79. Michal Sainsbury, "China's Western Cities on the Rise," *Australian*, April 13, 2009, 17, retrieved from LexisNexis.

80. Li Yu 李昱, "Wuliu chu chuan ji" 物流出川记 [Record of logistics from Sichuan], *Xibu shibao* 西部时报, November 18, 2011, 7.

81. Department of Operation and Testing, MIIT, 工业和信息化部运行检测协调局, *Zhongguo dianzi xinxi chanye tongji nian jian (zonghe pian) 2011* 中国电子信息产业统计年鉴(综合篇)2011 [Statistical yearbook of China's electronic information

industry (general), 2011], ed. 工业和信息化部运行监测协调局 (Beijing: 电子工业出版社, 2012), 125–26.

82. US Department of Commerce, International Trade Administration, "2015 Top Markets Report Semiconductors and Semiconductor Manufacturing Equipment: A Market Assessment Tool for U.S. Exporters," July 2015, accessed May 21, 2016, http://trade.gov/topmarkets/pdf/Semiconductors_Top_Markets_Report.pdf.

83. Yu Zhongyu 俞忠钰, "Zhuoli tuijin IC chanpin chuangxin tigong zhongguo bandaoti chanye jingzhengli" 着力推进IC产品创新提高中国半导体产业竞争力 [Strongly promote innovation of IC product to increase Chinese semiconductor industry's competitiveness], *Zhongguo jichengdianlu* 中国集成电路 82 (2006): 18–20; Yu Zhongyu 俞忠钰, "Dui zhongguo jichengdianlu chanye fazhan de sikao" 对中国集成电路产业发展的思考 [Thoughts on the development of Chinese integrated-circuit industry], *Zhongguo jichengdianlu* 中国集成电路 166 (2013): 12–17.

84. Intel, "Intel Global Manufacturing Facts," December 2011, accessed August 13, 2015, http://www.intel.com/content/www/us/en/silicon-innovations/standards-global-manufacturing-facts.html.

85. Falan Yinug, "Challenges to Foreign Investment in High-Tech Semiconductor Production in China," *Journal of International Commerce and Economics* 2 (2009): 97–126.

86. Li Guo 李果, "Guoji IT Zhanye xian xijing dachao" 国际IT产业掀西进大潮 [International IT industry starts going west], *Xibu shibao* 西部时报, February 2, 2012, 5.

87. Falan Yinug, "Challenges to Foreign Investment," 97–126.

88. Wei Shaojun 魏少军, "Jiaqiang jichu nengli jianshe, zou ke chixu fazhan zhi lu" 加强基础能力建设, 走可持续发展之路 [Strengthen capacity in infrastructure construction for sustainable development], *Zhongguo jichengdianlu* 中国集成电路 164 (2013): 17–22.

89. Li Kunxue 李昆学, "Zai Chengdu gao xin qu dang gongwei guan wei hui gongzuo huiyi shang de jianghua (zhailu)" 在成都高新区党工委管委会工作会议上的讲话(摘录) [Speaking at the party working committee's management division at Chengdu's high-tech zone (excerpt)], in *Chengdu gao xin qu nian jian (2007)* 成都高新区年鉴 (2007) [Chengdu high-tech development zone yearbook 2007], ed. 潭伯祥 (Beijing: 方志出版社, 2008), 2–8.

90. Wang Yuanrang 王远让, "Kaifang dashi ji" 开发大事记 [Chronicle of development], in *Zhongguo zhong xibu diqu kaifa nian jian 1979–92* 中国中西部地区开发年鉴 [Yearbook of China's central and western region development 1979–92], ed. 刘江 (Beijing: 改革出版社, 1992), 162.

91. "Hezuo jiedao banshichu jiben qingkuang" 合作街道办事处基本情况 [Basic facts about the Hezuo district], September 19, 2009, accessed August 12, 2015, http://www.chengdu.gov.cn/GovInfoOpens2/detail_orgInfo.jsp?id=ZKILHpXcRC63N6dnjwi7 (no longer available).

92. Li Mingxue 李岷雪, "Guanzhu minsheng zhu tui hexie: goujian chanye fazhan yu chongfen jiuye shuangying geju" 关注民生助推和谐: 构建产业发展与充分

就业的双赢格局 [Attention to people's livelihood to promote harmony: Construct win-win situation for industry development and full development], *Chengdu gao xin nian jian* 成都高新区年鉴 (2007) [Chengdu high-tech development zone yearbook (2007)], 20–29.

93. Li Yupeng 李瑜鹏, "Laixin laifang" 来信来访 [Letters and visits], *Chengdu gao xin nian jian* 成都高新区年鉴 (2007) [Yearbook of Chengdu high-tech zone (2007)], 61; Taisu Zhang, "The Xinfang Phenomenon: Why the Chinese Prefer Administrative Petitioning over Litigation," Yale Law School Legal Scholarship Repository, paper 68, accessed September 1, 2014, http://digitalcommons.law.yale.edu/student_papers/68.

94. Jianming Cai 蔡建明, Zhenshan Yang 杨振山, Douglas Webster, Tao Song 宋涛, and Andrew Gulbrandson, "Chongqing: Beyond the Latecomer Advantage," *Asia Pacific Viewpoint* 53, 1 (2012): 38–55.

95. Luo Wensheng 罗文胜, "IT xi jing Cheng Yu jing ju" IT洗净的成渝竞局 [IT industry settles the competition between Chengdu and Chongqing], *Xibu da kanfa* 西部大开发 2–3 (2011): 93–95.

96. Yang Weicheng 杨维成 et al., "Chongqing moshi: xibu fazhan dier xuanze zhonggong Chongqing shiwei fu shuji shizhang Huang Qifan fangtanlu" 重庆模式: 西部发展的第二选择—中共重庆市委副书记市长黄奇帆访谈录 [Chongqing model: The second choice of development in west regions—interview with Huang Qifan, Chongqing's deputy secretary of the CPC, mayor], *Sichuan jingji yanjiu* 四川经济研究 5–6 (2010): 36–40.

97. Bernard Levine, "What a Difference 25 Years Makes," *Electronic News* 47, 23 (2001): 1–1, 38.

98. Dennis Normile, "These Slim Margins Are Not by Design," *Electronic Business* 30, 9 (2004): 47–54. According to Normile, the ODM business approach ranges from producing off-the-shelf models for brand-name companies to manufacturing according to specific design requirements.

99. Bill Roberts, "Michael Marks Gets High," *Electronic Business* 29, 15 (2003): 46–51.

100. Dennis Normile, "Why Is Hon Hai So Shy?" *Electronic Business* 30, 4 (2004): 44–52; Bill Roberts, "Beyond the China Mystique," *Electronic Business* 32, 3 (2006): 36–38, 40.

101. Xu Mingtian 徐明天, *Jiemi Fushikang: Taiwan daxiang ye hui tiaowu* 解密富士康: 台湾大象也会跳舞 [Deciphering Foxconn: Taiwanese elephant may also dance] (Beijing: 企业管理出版社, 2011), 22, 12.

102. Pan Yi 潘毅, "Fushikang: quanqiu chanye lian diduan qiye de shengtai huanjing" 富士康: 全球产业链低端企业的生态环境 [Foxconn: Environment of the low-end enterprises in a global industry], *Jingji dao bao* 经济导报 5 (2014), accessed September 1, 2014, http://www.jingjidaokan.com/plus/view.php?aid=188.

103. Zhou Zixue 周子学, comp., *Zhongguo dianzi xinxi chanye tongji nian jian (zonghe pian)* 2005 中国电子信息产业统计年鉴（综合篇）2005 [Statistical yearbook of China's electronic information industry (general), 2005] (Beijing: 电子工业出版社, 2006), 328–30; Zhou Zixue 周子学, comp., *Zhongguo dianzi xinxi chanye tongji nian jian*

(zonghe pian) 2006 中国电子信息产业统计年鉴 (综合篇)2006 [Statistical yearbook of China's electronic information industry (general), 2006] (Beijing: 电子工业出版社, 2007), 248–50.

104. Department of Operation and Testing 工业和信息化部运行检测协调局, *Zhongguo dianzi xinxi chanye tongji nian jian (zonghe pian) 2009* 中国电子信息产业统计年鉴(综合篇)2009 [Statistical yearbook of China's electronic information industry (general), 2009] (Beijing: 电子工业出版社, 2010), 239; *Zhongguo dianzi xinxi chanye tongji nian jian (zonghe pian)* 中国电子信息产业统计年鉴 (综合篇)2011 [Statistical yearbook of China's electronic information industry (general), 2011], ed. 工业和信息化运行监测协调局 (Beijing: 电子工业出版社, 2012), 244.

105. Li Xiuzhong 李秀中, "Zhongxibu waimao piao hong beihou" 中西部外贸飘红背后 [Behind the rising foreign trade in central and western regions], *Xibu shibao* 西部时报, June 19, 2012, 7.

106. Department of Operation and Testing, MIIT, 工业和信息化部运行检测协调局, *Zhongguo dianzi xinxi chanye tongji nian ian (zonghe pian) 2012* 中国电子信息产业统计年鉴 (综合篇)2012 [Statistical yearbook of China's electronic information industry (general), 2012] (Beijing: 电子工业出版社, 2013), 48.

107. Department of Operation and Testing, *Statistical yearbook 2012*, 46; Zhongguo dianzi xinxi chanye tongji nian jian (zonghe pian) 2010 中国电子信息产业统计年鉴 (综合篇)2010 [Statistical yearbook of China's electronic information industry (general), 2010], ed. 工业和信息化部运行监测协调局 (Beijing: 电子工业出版社, 2011), 46; "Jisuanji chanye fazhan baipishu" 计算机产业发展白皮书 (2015版) [White book on PC industry development 2015], China Center for Information Industry Development (hereafter referred to as CCID), a think tank affiliated with MIIT, accessed May 28, 2016, http://www.ccidthinktank.com/uploads/soft/150421/PC.pdf.

108. "Tongxin chanye fei zhang: Ailixin jian quanqiu caigou zhongxin miao shang Chongqing" 通信产业飞涨：爱立信建全球采购中心瞄上重庆 [Skyrocketing telecommunications industry: Ericsson's global purchasing center aims at Chongqing], *Chongqing yu shijie* 重庆与世界 6 (2007): 28–29.

109. Chongqing Statistics Bureau, cited in Cai, Yang, Webster, Song, and Gulbrandson, "Chongqing."

110. Tang Hao 唐浩, "Buju jiuda chanye jiqun IT chanye jinzhang wanyi 5nian zeng jiuye 77 wan" 布局9大产业集群IT产业进账万亿5年增就业77万 [Planning nine industrial clusters: billions of revenue from IT industry and 770,000 new jobs] *Chongqing Shangbao* 重庆商报, A3, August 23, 2012, accessed July 15, 2015, http://e.chinacqsb.com/html/2012-08/23/content_288497.htm.

111. "2015 nian Chongqing zuidi gongzi biaozhun taiozheng zuixin xiaoxi," 2015年重庆最低工资标准调整最新消息 [The latest adjustment of minimum wage standard in Chongqing], Zhikun jiaoyu 智坤教育, April 5, 2015, accessed July 15, 2015, http://www.zhikunedu.com/SheBaoZhengCe/356081.html.

112. Lorraine Luk and Chun Han Wong, "Foxconn Workers Walk off Job at Chinese Plant," *Wall Street Journal*, October 9, 2014, accessed August 18, 2015, http://www.wsj.com/articles/foxconn-workers-walk-off-job-at-chinese-plant-1412854102.

113. Yu Song 于松, "Chongqing dagong diyi xian diaocha" 重庆打工第一县调查 [Investigation on Chongqing's "wage county"], *Xibu shibao* 西部时报, March 1, 2011, 3; Li Xiuzhong 李秀中 and An Zhuo 安卓, "Min gong huang yinfa dongxi bu laodongli zhengduo zhan 民工荒引发东西部劳动力争夺战 [Migrant worker shortage creates battle for labor force between eastern and western regions], *Xibu shibao* 西部时报, February 11, 2011, 5.

114. Sun Xiaofang 孙晓芳, "Yonggong huang: laodongli liudong de zhongguo yangben" 用工荒：劳动力流动的中国样本 [Labor shortage: The Chinese sample of labor mobility], *Zhongguo laodong* 中国劳动 1 (2013): 12.

115. Pan Yi, Lu Huilin, Guo Yuhua, and Chen Yuan 潘毅 卢晖临 郭于华 沈原, eds., *Wo zai fushikang* 我在富士康 [Working at Foxconn] (Beijing: 知识产权出版社, 2012), 131.

116. Li Xiuzhong 李秀中, "Xibu waimao piao hong beihou" 中西部外贸飘红背后 [Behind the rising foreign trade in central and western regions], *Xibu shibao* 西部时报, June 19, 2012, 7.

117. Department of Operation and Testing 工业和信息化部运行检测协调局, *Zhongguo dianzi xinxi chanye tongji nian jian (zonghe pian)* 中国电子信息产业统计年鉴 (综合篇) [Statistical yearbook of China's electronic information industry (general)] (Beijing: 电子工业出版社, 2013), 137; "2014 nian 12 yue chongqing shi waimao jinchukou qingkuang" 2014年12月重庆市外贸进出口情况 [Chongqing's imports and exports in December 2014], Chongqing Customs District, January 27, 2015, accessed May 28, 2016, http://chongqing.customs.gov.cn/publish/portal153/tab60869/module173696/info731052.htm.

118. Tang Song 唐松, "Dianzi xinxi chanye: chengqi chongqing gongye yipian xin lantian" 电子信息产业：撑起重庆工业一片新蓝天 [Electronic information industry: Supporting the industry of Chongqing), *Chongqing yu shijie* 重庆与世界 9 (2012): 16–21.

119. Lin Chun, *China and Global Capitalism*.

120. Lin Chun, *Transformation of Chinese Socialism*.

121. Ying Zhu, *Two billion Eyes: The Story of China Central Television* (New York: New Press, 2012).

Chapter 2. Repurposing Telecoms for Capital

This chapter is adapted from Yu Hong, "Repurposing Telecoms for Capital in China: System Development and Inequality," *Asian Survey* 53, 2 (2013): 319–47.

1. Paul S. N. Lee, "Uneven Development of Telecommunications in China," in *Telecommunications and Development in China*, ed. Paul S. N. Lee (Cresskill, NJ: Hampton, 1997), 113–29, 122.

2. US Congress, House Committee on Energy and Commerce, Special Subcommittee on US Trade with China, *Telecommunications Trade with China, Hearing before the Special Subcommittee on Energy and Commerce House of Representatives*, Serial No. 98-153 (Washington, DC: Government Printing Office, 1984).

3. D. Schiller, *How to Think*, 80–83.

4. "Premier's Report on Sixth Five-Year Plan," *BBC Summary of World Broadcasts*, December 14, 1982, retrieved from LexisNexis. The exchange rate used in this volume for events from 1981 to 1985 is about US$1 to Chinese yuan 2.2.

5. "National Posts and Telecommunications Meeting," *BBC Summary of World Broadcasts*, February 4, 1981, retrieved from LexisNexis.

6. Ding Donghua 丁栋华, "Nuli tansuo xin xingshi xia chouji tongxin jianshe zijin de xin luzi" 努力探索新形势下筹集通信建设资金的新路子 [Explore new ways to raise money for telecom construction in new situation], *C-Enterprise Management* 通信企业管理 3 (1989): 9.

7. S. Lin, "Funding Telecom Expansion," *China Business Review* 20, 2 (1993): 31–33.

8. Zou Jiahua 邹家华, "Tongchou guihua tiaokuai jiehe fenceng fuze lianhe jianshe—guowu weiyuan Zou Jiahua zai quanguo dianxin gongzuo huiyi shang de jianghua zhaiyao" 统筹规划条块结合分层负责联合建设—国务委员邹家华在全国电信工作会议上的讲话摘要 [Coordinated planning, combined central and local *tiao/kuai* administration, layered responsibility, and joint construction—excerpts from state councilor Zou Jiahua's speech at the national telecoms conference], *Youdian qiye guanli* 邮电企业管理 4 (1988): 4–7.

9. Standing Committee of Fujian People's Congress, "Fujiansheng baozhang he fazhan youdian tongxin tiaoli," 福建省保障和发展邮电通信条例 [Fujian provincial ordinance on security and development of posts and telecommunications] (Fujian Science and Technology, 1992).

10. Jiang Zhiwei 蒋志伟, "Youdian bumen xuyao liaojie, youdian bumen xuyao zijin" 邮电部门需要了解，邮电部门需要资金 [The offices of posts and telecommunications need understanding, telecom construction need funding], *Sichuan youdian bao* 四川邮电报, July 24, 1988, 2.

11. Wu Jian and Wang Qing 吴建 王庆, "Xibu jiu shengqu dianxin fazhan qingkuang de diaocha yu fenxi" 西部九省区电信发展情况的调查与分析 [Investigation and analysis of telecom development in western nine provinces], *P&T Enterprise Management* 邮电企业管理 4 (1995): 17.

12. "China: Reform Our Telecom Industry," *China Daily*, June 15, 2001, retrieved from LexisNexis.

13. Zhuang Mingqing 庄明庆, "Guangdong youdian fazhan de zhuyao tedian ji sikao" 广东邮电发展的主要特点及思考 [The main characteristics of telecom development in Guangdong], *C-Enterprise Management* 通信企业管理 6 (1988): 29–30.

14. China Knowledge Resource Integrated Database (CNKI), http://number.cnki.net/cyfd/IndexNaviALL.aspx#15.

15. Alan P. L. Liu, "Communications and Development in Post-Mao Mainland China," *Issues & Studies: Journal of Chinese Studies and International Affairs* 27, 12 (1991): 73–99.

16. Linchuan Qiu, *Working-Class Network Society: Communication Technology and the Information Have-Less in Urban China* (Cambridge: MIT Press, 2009).

17. Wu Jian and Wand Qing, "Investigation and analysis," "Xibu jiu shengqu."

18. Bai Wei 白伟, "Gedi zhengfu lingdao wei youdian fazhan chumou huace" 各地政府领导为邮电发展出谋划策 [Regional leaders gave advice and suggestions for telecom development], *Tongxin* 通信 1 (October 1988): 1; Bai Wei 白伟, "Chengshi zhengfu buzhua tongxin buxing—fang Chongqing shi shizhang Yu Hanqing" 城市政府不抓通信不行—访重庆市市长于汉卿 [City government must grasp communication construction: Interview with the mayor of Chongqing Yu Hanqing], *Sichuan youdian Bao* 四川邮电报, April 7, 1985, 1.

19. Milton Mueller and Zixiang Tan, *China in the Information Age: Telecommunications and the Dilemmas of Reform* (Westport, CT: Praeger, 1997), 33.

20. "Zhuazhu youdian tongxin zhege zhanlue zhongdian" 抓住邮电通信这个战略重点 [Grasp the strategic point of posts and telecommunications], *Sichuan youdian bao* 四川邮电报, November 17, 1985, 1.

21. Qiao Xiaobin 乔晓斌, "Sichuan tongxin fazhan buke zuoshiliangji" 四川通信发展不可坐失良机 [Sichuan telecom development cannot miss the opportunity], *Sichuan tongxin bao* 四川通信报, February 10, 1991, 1.

22. Hang Wen 航文, "Tongxin zhixu hunluan, hangye guanli jixu jiaqiang" 通信秩序混乱,行业管理急需加强 [The disorder of telecommunications needs urgent industry management], *Sichuan tongxin bao* 四川通信报, July 28, 1991, 3. The exchange rate used in this volume for events from 1985 to 1991 is about US$1 to Chinese yuan 4.0.

23. "Youdian tongxin shiye shi jingji fazhan de zhongdian—Sichuan sheng fu shengzhang Ma Lin zai sheng youdian tongxin jianshe huiyi shang de zongjie jianghua" 邮电通信事业是经济发展的重点—四川省副省长马麟在省邮电通信建设会议上的总结讲话 [Posts and telecommunications construction is the focus of economic development—the summary speech of Sichuan deputy governor Ma Lin], *Sichuan tongxin bao* 四川通信报, December 31, 1989, 3.

24. Qiao Xiaobin and Bai Wei 乔晓斌 白伟, "Woguo tongxin wang sanda maodun zhubu huanjie" 我国通信网三大矛盾逐步缓解 [Three big contradictions in telecommunications network have been gradually relieved], *Sichuan tongxin bao* 四川通信报, September 9, 1990, 1.

25. David Zweig, *Internationalizing China: Domestic Interests and Global Linkages* (Ithaca: Cornell University Press, 2002), 68.

26. Liu, "Communications and Development," 83–84.

27. "Guojia jiwei tichu bawo guomin jingji fazhan jiben silu: tongxin ye diwei he touzi jiang tigao" 国家纪委提出把握国民经济发展基本思路：通信地位和投资将提高 [National planning commission proposed the basic idea for the Eighth Five-Year Plan: The position and investment of telecommunications industry will be enhanced], *Sichuan tongxin bao* 四川通信报, November 12, 1989, 1.

28. Zhang Mingbao 张铭宝, "Gaohuo yanhai diqu youdian qiye, wei fazhan waixiang xing jingji fuwu" 搞活沿海地区邮电企业,为发展外向型经济服务 [To revitalize posts and telecommunications enterprises in coastal areas and to serve the

development of export-oriented economy], *C-Enterprise Management* 通信企业管理 4 (1988): 16–17.

29. He Xia 何霞, "Youdian bumen rongzi jiegou fenxi yu zhanwang" 邮电部门融资结构分析与展望 [The analysis and outlook of financing structure in the system of posts and telecommunications], *P&T Enterprise Management* 邮电企业管理 2 (1996): 15–16.

30. He Xia 何霞, "Guanyu xibu dianxin touzi wenti de tantao" 关于西部电信投资问题的探讨 [Discussion about telecom investment in western China], *P&T Enterprise Management* 邮电企业管理 9 (1995): 10.

31. Eric Harwit, "China's Telecommunications Industry: Development Patterns and Policies," *Pacific Affairs* 71, 2 (1998): 175–93.

32. Sichuan Local Annual Editorial Committee, *Sichuan sheng zhi* 四川省志—邮政电信志 [Annals of Sichuan province—Annual of Telecoms and Post] (Chengdu: 四川辞书出版社, 1993), 162.

33. "Zhuazhu youdian tongxin zhege zhanlue zhongdian," 1.

34. Lu Xiangqian 卢向前, "Duocai de kuayue" 多彩的跨越 [A colorful jump], *Sichuan tongxin bao* 四川通信报, January 13, 1991, 3.

35. Lee, "Uneven Development," 125.

36. Li Xuenong, "Expediting Rural Telecom Development by Streamlining the Rural Telephone Mechanism," *World Telecommunications* 12 (2000): 15–18.

37. Email and online video interviews with Zhang Juping, former director of Sichuan Posts and Telecom Administration, November 2011.

38. Lee, "Uneven Development," 124.

39. Mueller and Tan, *China in the Information Age*, 47; Eric Harwit, *China's Telecommunications Revolution* (New York: Oxford University Press, 2008), 163.

40. Interview with Zhang Juping.

41. Sichuan Rural Telephone Bureau, "Gaige, shi nonghua chongman le huoli" 改革使农村充满活力 [Reform revitalized telephone communication in rural areas], *C-Enterprise Management* 通信企业管理, 5 (1988): 18.

42. Liu Du and Song 刘树萍 杜广达 宋军, "Tuidong nongcun tongxin fazhan keburonghuan" 推动农村通信发展刻不容缓 [Telephone development in rural areas permits no delay], *Renmin youdian bao* 人民邮电报, October 29, 2003, 4.

43. Li Xuenong, "Expediting Rural Telecom Development," 15–18.

44. Crothall Geoffey, "Beijing Pledges Reform of Hard-Hit Rural Sector," *South China Morning Post* (Hong Kong), February 17, 1993, 2, retrieved from LexisNexis.

45. Li Xuenong, "Expediting Rural Telecom Development," 15–18.

46. Kong Guoqiang and Yan Xuefeng, "Telecom Development and Countermeasure Research of West China," *Designing Techniques of Posts and Telecommunications* 2 (February 2001): 1–5.

47. Zhou He, "A History of Telecommunications in China: Development and Policy Implications," in Lee, *Telecommunications*, 55–87, 84; Yuezhi Zhao, "Universal Service and China's Telecommunications Miracle: Discourses, Practices, and Post-WTO Accession Challenges," *Info* 9, 2–3 (2007): 108–21.

48. Wang Jianzhou 王建宙, *Yidong shidai shengcun* 移动时代生存 [Mobilizing everything]. (Beijing: 中信出版社, 2014), 5.

49. Xu Fuxin 徐福新, "Cong yaobazi dao dageda de 20 nian youdian ju juzhang qinli" 从摇把子到大哥大的20年有点局长亲历 [Xu Fuxin: A personal experience as the managing director of posts and telecommunications office], November 6, 2008, accessed September 1, 2014, http://tech.sina.com.cn/t/2008-11-06/00592559436.shtml.

50. Data communications was still a small business; in 2001 this business had 13.1 billion yuan (US$1.6 billion) worth of revenue, accounting for 3.7 percent of the total telecom revenue. See CCID Report, "2002 nian diyi jidu zhongguo yidong shuju tongxin fazhan qingkuang" 2002年第一季度中国移动数据通信发展情况 [The development situation of China Mobile's data communication business in the first quarter of 2002], July 30, 2002, accessed July 15, 2015, http://www.ccidnet.com/2002/0730/20933.shtml; MII, "1998 nian tongxin ye fazhan tongji gongbao," 九九八年通信业发展统计公报 [Development report of telecommunications industry in 1998], April 1, 1999, accessed May 21, 2016, http://www.niec.org.cn/gjxxh/tjsjit10.htm.

51. "Ming jiang an sheng de shuofa meiyou yiju" 明降暗升的说法没有依据 [The statement about hidden price increases is ungrounded], *Renmin youdian bao* 人民邮电报, September 6, 2001, 1.

52. D. Schiller, *How to Think*, 186.

53. "Gaige youdian jiage lishun youdian zifei" 改革邮电价格隶属邮电资费 [To reform the posts and telecommunications fare], *Sichuan tongxin bao* 四川通信报, December 4, 1996, 3; Wen Peiyi, "Dianxin zifei tiaozheng jiang dui jingji fazhan qi dao jiji zuoyong" 电信资费调整将对经济发展起到积极作用 [Tariff adjustment in telecommunications plays a positive role in economic development], *Sichuan tongxin bao* 四川通信报, March 21, 2001, 1.

54. "China: Reform Our Telecom Industry," *China Daily*, June 15, 2001, 4, retrieved from LexisNexis.

55. Yuezhi Zhao, "Caught in the Web: The Public Interest and the Battle for Control of China's Information Superhighway," *Info* 2, 1 (2000): 41–66.

56. "China: Telecom Sector Requires Further Reform," *China Daily*, November 25, 1999, retrieved from LexisNexis.

57. Zhang Ying 张英, "Pubian fuwu ruhe maidan?" 普遍服务如何买单? [How to pay the bill for universal service?], *Renmin youdian* 人民邮电, November 8, 2004, 1.

58. Hui Yuk-min, "China Mobile Parent Goes West with $46b," *South China Morning Post* (Hong Kong), June 29, 2002, 3, retrieved from LexisNexis.

59. Gao Chao, "On the Telecom Universal Service in China during the Tenth Five-Year-Plan Period," *High-Speed Router* 4 (2001): 37–39.

60. Wu Jichuan 吴基传, "Tiejin shichang shixian you xiaoyi de fazhan" 贴近市场实现有效益的发展 [Develop telecommunications closely to the market and achieve efficient development], *P&T Enterprise Management* 邮电企业管理, 3 (2002): 8–9.

61. Wu Jichuan et al. 吴基传等, "Da kuayue: zhongguo dianxin ye gaige kaifang sanshi nian huigu zhi fazhan pian" 大跨越: 中国电信业改革开放三十年回顾之发展篇 [Great leapfrog: Chinese telecom reform and opening up in retrospect], *China Communications Trade* 中国电信业 12 (December 2008): 18–23; Wang Guping and Gu Liren 王保平 顾立人, "Ruhe baozhang nongcun tongxin pubian fuwu de shixian" 如何保障农村通信普遍服务的实现 [How to guarantee universal service in rural areas], *Renmin youdian* 人民邮电, June 8, 2004; "2003 nian tongxinye fazhan qingkuang tongji" 2003年通信业发展情况统计 [Statistics about telecoms development in 2003], Zhongguo zhengfu wang 中国政府网, accessed May 29, 2016, http://www.gov.cn/test/2005-07/05/content_12193.htm.

62. H. Schiller, *Information*.

63. Liu Kun 刘坤, "Zuli chongchong dianxin 'fupin jijin' choujian ye jiben tingzhi," 阻力重重电信"扶贫经济"筹建业基本停滞 [Beset by resistance: The poverty alleviation fund for telecommunication is stalled], 2002, accessed September 1, 2014, http://tech.sina.com.cn/it/t/2002-09-20/1047139853.shtml.

64. Zhou Bin 周斌, "Wu Jichuan buzhang zai chuan jiedao diyi hao tousu" 吴基传部长在川街道第一号投诉 [Minster of Posts and Telecommunications Wu Jichuan received the first compliant in Sichuan], *Sichuan tongxin bao* 四川通信报, October 28, 2000, 1.

65. Christopher McNally, "Sichuan: Driving Capitalist Development Westward," in *China's Campaign to "Open Up the West": National, Provincial and Local Perspectives*, ed. David. S. G. Goodman (London: Cambridge, 2004), 112–33.

66. Li Hongrong 李洪戎, "Nongcun tongxin gaobie pinkun shidai" 农村通信告别贫困时代 [Telecommunications in rural areas says good-bye to poverty], *Sichuan tongxin bao* 四川通信报, June 29, 2005, 3.

67. Frederik Balfour, "China Mobile Is Growing Rural; the World's No. 1 Cellular Carrier Is Piling Up Customers by Taking Cheap Handsets and Pricier Add-Ons to Mongolia's Steppes and Tibet's Peaks," *BusinessWeek Online*, December 21, 2006, 19.

68. Dan Schiller, "World Communications in Today's Age of Capital," *Emergences: Journal for the Study of Media and Composite Cultures* 11, 1 (2001): 51–68.

69. Dexter Roberts, "China Mobile's Hot Signal; It's Already the World's Biggest Cellular Carrier: Now It's Planning to Get Even Bigger," *BusinessWeek* 4020 (February 5, 2007), 42–44.

70. Yuezhi Zhao, "Universal Service," 113.

71. National Bureau of Statistics of China, "Shiyiwu jingji shehui fazhan chengjiu xilie baogao zhi shiyi: youdian dianxin ye qude xianzhu chengjiu" 十一五经济社会发展成就系列报告之十一：邮电电信业取得显著成就 [The eleventh report of economic and social achievement during the 'Eleventh Five Year': the achievement in posts and telecommunications industry], 2011, accessed August 11, 2015, http://www.stats.gov.cn/ztjc/ztfx/sywcj/201103/t20110308_71323.html.

72. "Zhongguo yidong leiji tou 195 yi yuan shi 6 wan ge pianyuan cunzhuang yongshang shouji" 中国移动累计投195亿元使6万个偏远村庄用上手机 [China Mobile

cumulatively invested 19.5 billion yuan to enable 60,000 remote villages to have cell-phone service], *People's Daily* 人民日报, 2009, accessed September 1, 2014, http://www.gov.cn/jrzg/2009-02/12/content_1228500.htm. The exchange rate used in this volume for events from 2004 to 2009 is about US$1 to Chinese yuan 7.7. See appendix.

73. MIIT, "2009 nian quanguo dianxinye tongji gongbao" 2009年全国电信业统计公报 [Annual statistical report on national telecommunications sector in 2009], February 3, 2010, accessed May 21, 2016, http://www.cnii.com.cn/tjfx/content/2011-02/20/content_917743.htm.

74. Nicholas Garnham, "Telecommunications Policy in the United Kingdom," in *Capitalism and Communication: Global Culture and the Economics of Information*, ed. Fred Inglis (Newbury Park: Sage, 1999), 136–53.

75. China Internet Network Information Center (hereinafter referred to as CNNIC), "2010 nian zhongguo nongcun hulianwang fazhan zhuangkuang diaocha baogao" 2010年中国农村互联网发展状况调查报告 [Investigative report on internet development in rural China in 2010], August 2011, accessed September 1, 2014, http://www.cnnic.net.cn/research/bgxz/ncbg/201109/t20110906_22721.html.

76. World Bank, "ICT Regulation Toolkit," accessed September 1, 2014, http://www.ictregulationtoolkit.org/en/Index.html; Claire Milne, "Stages of Universal Service Policy," *Telecommunications Policy* 22, 9 (1998): 775–80; Scott Wallsten, "Returning to Victorian Competition, Ownership, and Regulation: An Empirical Study of European Telecommunications at the Turn of the Twentieth Century," *Journal of Economic History* 65, 3 (2005): 693–722.

77. Yuezhi Zhao, "Caught," 43.

Chapter 3. Forging Broadband for the Commanding-Heights Economy

1. Yu Hong, "Reading the Twelfth Five-Year Plan," 1–20.

2. Walter and Howie, *Red Capitalism*.

3. Edward S. Steinfeld, *Playing Our Game: Why China's Economic Rise Doesn't Threaten the West* (Oxford: Oxford University Press, 2010), 51–54.

4. Ibid., 48–63.

5. Gao Dingyi 高定彝, "Woguo xinxi gaosugonglu jihua zhanwang—'xinxi gaosugonglu yu shehui fazhan' taolunhui zong shu" 我国信息高速公路计划—"信息高速公路与社会发展"讨论会综述 [China's prospect for information highway plan: Summation of the symposium on "information highway and social development"], *Renmin ribao* 人民日报, January 4, 1997, 6.

6. Mueller and Tan, *China in the Information Age*, 56.

7. Zhao Qi 张琪, *Wulianwang zai Zhongguo: Tansuo Zhongguo wulianwang zhi lu* 物联网在中国：探索中国物联网之路 [Internet of things in China: Exploring China's journey of internet of things] (Beijing: 电子工业出版社, 2012), 95–96.

8. Evan A. Feigenbaum, *China's Techno-Warriors: National Security and Strategic Competition from the Nuclear to the Information Age* (Stanford: Stanford University Press, 2003), 202.

9. Mueller and Tan, *China in the Information Age*, 48.

10. Feigenbaum, *China's Techno-Warriors*, 198.

11. Hu Qili 胡启立, "Peiyu gongzhong zhichi cujin quanqiu xinxi hua" 培育公众支持促进全球信息化 [Cultivating public support to promote global informationalization], *Zhongguo keji xinxi* 中国科技信息 7 (1996): 47–48. The exchange rate used in this volume for events from 1991 to 1995 is about US$1 to Chinese yuan 6.7. See the appendix.

12. State Council, "Guowuyuan pi zhuan youdianbu guanyu jiaqiang tongxin hangye guanli he renzhen zhengdun tongxin zhixu qingshi de tongzhi" 国务院批转邮电部关于加强通信行业管理和认真整顿通信秩序请示的通知 [Notice of the State Council on approving and forwarding the asking by Ministry of Posts and Communications for instructions on strengthening the management and discipline of the telecommunications industry], 1990, 54, accessed March 6, 2016, http://www.gov.cn/zhengce/content/2012-09/21/content_3595.htm.

13. Mueller and Tan, *China in the Information Age*, 91.

14. Dali Yang, *Remaking the Chinese Leviathan: Market Transition and the Politics of Governance in China* (Stanford: Stanford University Press, 2004).

15. Zhu Rongji 朱镕基, "Zai Xinjiapo jiangzuo shang de yanjiang he dawen" 在新加坡讲座上的演讲和答问 [Presenting the "Singapore Lecture": Premier Zhu's speech on "China and Asia in the New Century"], in *Zhu Rongji da jizhe wen* 朱镕基答记者问 [Zhu Rongji meets the press] (Beijing: 人民出版社, 2009), 298.

16. Shi Cuiming 石萃鸣, "Youdian bu guifan nei zi lianhe touzi de shi yong fanwei" 邮电部规范内资联合投资的适用范围 [Ministry of Posts and Telecommunications standardizes the range of application of domestic joint venture], *Youdian qiyeguanli* 邮电企业管理 2 (1997): 13.

17. John Alden, "Observers Hail Ground-Breaking Telecom Trade Pack; Examination of Fine Print Now Begins," *Telecommunications Reports* 63, 8 (1997): 3, http://search.proquest.com.libproxy1.usc.edu/docview/216935718?accountid=14749.

18. "Bliley Says China Must Open Telecom Market to Enter WTO," *Telecommunications Reports* 63, 45 (November 10, 1997): 32, http://search.proquest.com.libproxy1.usc.edu/docview/216921566?accountid=14749.

19. Irene Wu, *From Iron Fist to Invisible Hand: The Uneven Path of Telecommunications Reform in China* (Stanford: Stanford University Press, 2009), 71.

20. Rongji Zhu 朱镕基, "Zai Meiguo qi tuanti wancan hui shang de yanjiang he dawen" 在美国七团体晚餐会上的演讲和答问 [Premier Zhu's talk at a welcoming dinner in Washington], *Zhu Rongji da jizhe wen*, 257.

21. "China Agrees to Adopt WTO 'Reference Paper,' Lift Some Foreign Restrictions on Telecom Services," *Telecommunications Reports* 65, 47 (1999): 27–28, http://search.proquest.com.libproxy1.usc.edu/docview/749180745?accountid=14749.

22. "Second China Telecom Summit Expands Agenda to IT Products," *Telecommunications Reports* 64, 51 (December 21, 1998): 39, http://search.proquest.com.libproxy2.usc.edu/docview/216947017?accountid=14749.

23. Zou Jiatan 邹家檀, "IP dianhua dui Zhongguo dianxin ye de chongji," IP电话对中国电信业的冲击 [The impact of IP phones on Chinese telecommunication industry], *Youdian shang qing* 邮电商情 1 (2000): 27–30.

24. Steinfeld, *Playing Our Game*, 32.

25. Lisa Endlich, *Optical Illusions: Lucent and the Crash of Telecom* (New York: Simon and Schuster, 2004), 86–87.

26. Dan Schiller, "The Telecom Crisis," *Dissent* 50, 1 (2003): 66–70.

27. Paul Starr, "The Great Telecom Implosion," *The American Prospect* 13, 16 (2002): 20.

28. Endlich, *Optical Illusions*, 240.

29. Yvonne Chan, "Web Wave to Break on Mainland Shores under WTO Membership," *South China Morning Post*, November 18, 1999, 3.

30. Ran Yongping and Wang Hong 冉永平 王宏, "Zhongguo hulianwang bupa ru shi" 中国互联网不怕入世 [China's internet does not fear joining WTO], *Renmin ribao* 人民日报, December 13, 1999, 12.

31. "Chinese Internet Firm Posts Profit after One Year," *Newsbytes*, January 11, 1999, retrieved from LexisNexis.

32. Zhang Chengshuang et al. 张晨霜等, *Da kuayue: Zhongguo dianxinye sanshi chunqiu* 大跨越:中国电信业三十春秋 [Great leap forward: Thirty years of Chinese telecommunications] (Beijing: 人民出版社, 2008).

33. "Daibiao ganyan" 代表感言 [Representatives' comments], July 29, 2004, accessed July 15, 2015, http://www.cnii.com.cn/20040423/ca252317.htm.

34. Dal Yong Jin, "The Telecom Crisis and Beyond: Restructuring of the Global Telecommunications System," *Gazette* 67, 3 (2005): 289–304, 290.

35. See Jiang Qiping 姜奇平, "Hulianwang qimeng yundong shi mo" 互联网启蒙运动始末 [The whole story of internet enlightenment], *Hulianwang zhoukan* 互联网周刊 21 (June 30, 2003): 76–78.

36. "China Netcom's Gateway to the World," *Telecommunications—International Edition* 36, 7 (2002): 20.

37. Gao Hejun 高鹤君, "Wangluo huhuan wushi feng" 网络呼唤务实风 [Web needs pragmatism], *People's Daily*, July 2, 2000, 4.

38. Yang Jian 杨健, "Hulianwang: zenyang jieshu mianfei shidai" 互联网：怎样结束免费时代 [The internet: How to end the free age], *People's Daily*, February 17, 2001, 5.

39. Jin, "Global Telecommunications System," 290; D. Schiller, "Telecom Crisis," 66–70; Michael J. Copps, "From the Desk of a Former FCC Commissioner," *Columbia Journalism Review*, March–April 2014, accessed May 29, 2016, http://www.cjr.org/essay/from_the_desk_of_a_former_fcc.php.

40. "Zhongmei dianxin fenghui huigu: liangguo dianxinye hezuo qianjing meihao" 中美电信峰会回顾：两国电信业合作前景美好 [Sino-US telecom summit review: Prospectus for collaboration is positive], *Renmin youdian* 人民邮电, July 29, 2004, accessed July 15, 2015, http://tech.sina.com.cn/it/t/2004-07-29/1655395158.shtml.

41. International Telecommunications Union, *Birth of Broadband: ITU Internet Reports 2003*, accessed May 29, 2016, http://www.itu.int/osg/spu/publications/sales/birthofbroadband/.

42. Kenji Kushida and Seung-Youn Oh, "The Political Economies of Broadband Development in Korea and Japan," *Asian Survey* 47, 3 (2007): 481–504.

43. Edward Tian, "Wiring China for Its Economic Explosion," *Global Telecoms Business* 63, 26 (February 2002), http://search.proquest.com.libproxy1.usc.edu/docview/218310212?accountid=14749.

44. Ren Jianmin 任建民, "Qidong kuandai jisu zhi lv: Zhongguo Dianxin buzai chi du shi" 启动宽带极速之旅中国电信不再吃独食 [Start the ultrafast journey of broadband, China Telecom no longer enjoys monopoly], *Renmin ribao* 人民日报, Sepember 28, 2002, 11; Gauri Pavate, "Worldwide DSL Equipment Market Shrinks in 3Q02 (Executive Summary)," *Gartner*, December 13, 2002.

45. Zou Jiatan 邹家坛, "Xinxi chanye 'shiwu' fazhan jihua zhixing qingkuang huigu fenxi" 信息产业"十五"发展计划执行情况回顾分析 [Retrospective analysis of the execution of Tenth Five-Year Plan in telecommunication industry], *Youdian guihua* 邮电规划 1 (2004), 17–21.

46. Xu Ming, Zhao Yudong, Ding Shujun, Gongwei, and Zhang Zhenzhuo 许明、赵昱东、丁树军、龚炜、张贞卓, "liaokai dianxin yunyingshang miansha" 撩井电信运营商面纱 [Reveal the character of telecom operators], *Zhongguo zhengquan bao* 中国证券报, October 14, 2002, 15; Lei Zhenzhou 雷震洲, "Fengjing zhebian duhao—zhongguo dianxinye fazhan xianzhuang ji qianjing fenxi" 风景这边独好—中国电信业发展现状及前景分析 [Good prospects here—current and future development analysis of China's telecom sector], *Zhongxing tongxun jishu* 中兴通讯技术, 4 (2004), accessed August 8, 2015, http://www.zte.com.cn/cndata/magazine/zte_communications/2002/4/magazine/200311/t20031126_150021.html; Guo Xiaohong 郭小红, "Dianxin touzi quyu lixing" 电信投资趋于理性 [Telecom investments grow rational], December 10, 2004, accessed August 9, 2015, http://tech.sina.com.cn/t/2004-12-10/1630474452.shtml.

47. Tong Xing 佟醒, "Dianxin qiye li dan kuandai zhanlue zhong jian" 电信企业力担宽带战略中坚 [Telecommunication corporations become the backbone of broadband strategy], *Renmin youdian* 人民邮电, March 1, 2012, 1. The exchange rate used in this volume for events from 2006 to 2010 is about US$1 to Chinese yuan 7.2. See the appendix.

48. Peng Chao 彭超, "Kuandai shijie luntan Yazhou huiyi zai Beijing kaimu," 宽带世界论坛亚洲会议在北京开幕 [Broadband World Forum Asia 2007 opens today in Beijing], *Renmin youdian* 人民邮电, June 6, 2007, 1.

49. Gao Chao 高潮, "Guanyu Zhongguo dianxin ye fuzhai jingying yu rong touzi celve de tantao," 关于中国电信业负债经营与融投资策略的探讨 [Study on the financing strategies in Chinese telecom industry], *Youdian guihua* 邮电规划 3 (2002): 38–41.

50. Hu Yanping 胡延平 and Yu Xiangguo 于向国, "Chongxin kandai dianxin ye de bianqe" 重新看待电信业的变革 [Reconsidering changes in telecom industry], *Hulianwang zhoukan* 互联网周刊 7 (March 11, 2002): 66–70.

51. Zhang Chengshuang et al., *Da kuayu*, 418; Yang Peifang and Shen Jiangyin 杨培芳 申江婴, "Pojie ba da nanti chongqi tongxin zengzhang" 破解八大难题重启通信增长 [Solving eight major puzzles to reinitiate telecommunication growth], *Zhongguo xin tongxing* 中国新通信 14 (2009): 17–21.

52. Kushida and Oh, "Political Economies," 481–504.

53. Kwang-Suk Lee, *IT Development in Korea: A Broadband Nirvana?* (Abingdon, England: Routledge, 2012).

54. Peng Chao 彭超, "Kuandai yinling yeji zengzhang: jiedu Zhongguo Dianxin, Zhongguo Wangtong zhongqi yeji baogao" 宽带引领业绩增长—解读中国电信, 中国网通中期业绩报告 [Broadband leading industry growth: Interpretation of the interim report of China Telecom and China Netcom], *Renmin youdian* 人民邮电, September 13, 2005, 5.

55. "Wu Jichuan buzhang qiangdiao zhengque bawo dianxin guilv, chuli hao si da guanxi," 吴基传部长强调正确把握电信规律,处理好四大关系 [Minister Wu Jihuan stresses: Master the law of telecom, manage well four major relationships], *Zhongguo wang tong nian jian (2002–3)* 中国网通年鉴(2002–3), ed. 文元 等 (Beijing: 中国网络通信集团公司, 2003), 10.

56. He Xia 何霞, "Kuandai zhi lu you duo kuan: weilai Zhongguo kuandai chanye de fazhan yu zhanwang," 宽带之路有多宽—未来中国宽带产业的发展与展望 [How broad is the road of broadband: The development and prospect of China's future broadband industry], *Renmin youdian* 人民邮电, May 14, 2004.

57. Lv Xinjie 吕新杰, "Xin kuandai shinian fazhan huigu ji weilai zhanwang," 新宽带十年发展回顾及未来展望 [Review and prospect of ten-year development of new broadband], *Youdian guihua* 邮电规划 5 (2011): 14–17.

58. Huang Yin 黄莺, "Cong neirong pingjing kan kuandai yule yingyong zhi qianjing," 从内容瓶颈看宽带娱乐应用之前景 [From the bottleneck of content to the future of broadband entertainment applications], *Tongxin qiye guanli* 通信企业管理 5 (2004): 24–26; Hou Daying 候大银, "Bi shi jiu xu" 避虚就实 [Strike the real issues and avoid the abstract] in "Jidang de shinian: Zhongguo shangye hulianwang shinian fazhan baogao" 激荡的十年—中国商业互联网十年发展报告 [A turbulent decade: Report of the ten-year development of China's commercial internet], *Hulianwang zhoukan* 互联网周刊 20 (October 20, 2008): 84–93.

59. Miao Lanbo 苗兰波, "Kuandai xiaofei, yunying shang zhunbei hao le ma?" 宽带消费, 运营商准备好了吗? [Broadband consumption, are the operators ready?], *Tongxin qiyeguanli* 通信企业管理 5 (2004): 27–28.

60. Ma Yun 马芸, "Zheng zhuang dai fa" 整装待发 [Packed and ready], "Jidang de shinian: Zhongguo shangye hulianwang shinian fazhan baogao" 激荡的十年—中国商业互联网十年发展报告 (October 20, 2008): 74–83.

61. Peng Chao 彭超, "Cong yandong zou jin chuntian: 2004 nian kuandai chanye fazhan huimou," 从严冬走进春天—2004年宽带产业发展回眸 [From winter to spring: A review of the development of broadband industry in 2004], *Renmin youdian* 人民邮电, December 15, 2004.

62. "Fragmented Market for $1 Trillion Worth of Telecoms Business Sales," *Global Telecoms Business*, July 2, 2012, retrieved from LexisNexis.

63. Tian, "Wiring China."

64. "China Unicom Looks to the World as Home Market Grows and Grows, Says President Lu Yimin," *Global Telecom Business*, July 2, 2012, retrieved from LexisNexis.

65. Andrew Chetham and Akiyoshi Ishiwata, "Asia/Pacific Midyear Broadband Update: Running with the Wind," *Gartner*, October 3, 2002, 7.

66. Zhongguo Dianxin Bowuguan 中国电信博物馆, *Zhongguo dianxin nian jian* 中国电信年鉴 [2006 yearbook of China Telecom] (Beijing: 北京燕山出版社, 2006), 61.

67. "Dui woguo qiye xinxi hua xianzhuang fenxi" 对我国企业信息化现状分析 [Analysis of the current condition of our nation's enterprise informationalization], *21cn.com*, September 20, 2007, accessed September 1, 2014, http://www.sasac.gov.cn/n87149/n87169/n89570/n89576/c89879/content.html.

68. Zhang Yixuan 张意轩, "Dianzishangwu shengji wuxian" 电子商务生机无限 [Unlimited vitality of e-commerce], *Renmin ribao* 人民日报, March 21, 2009, 14.

69. Zhao Yahui 赵亚辉, "Woguo hai bushi hulianwang qiangguo" 我国还不是互联网强国 [Our country is yet to be a strong internet power], *Renmin ribao* 人民日报, December 8, 2003, 11.

70. CNNIC 中国互联网络信息中心, "2013 nian xiabannian zhongguo qiye hulianwang yingyong zhuangkuang diaocha baogao" 2013年下半年中国企业互联网应用状况调查报告 [Conditions of internet usage among Chinese enterprises in the second half of 2013], January 2014, accessed July 15, 2015, https://www.cnnic.cn/hlwfzyj/hlwxzbg/201409/P020140901331968409803.pdf.

71. Hu Yanping 胡延平, "Cong chunqiu dao zhanguo: wangluo shebei shichang de zhuhou duijue" 从春秋到战国:网络设备市场的诸侯对决 [From the spring and autumn period to warring states period: The warfare of internet equipment market], *Hulianwang zhoukan* 互联网周刊 12 (July 1, 2002): 8.

72. "Tiejin shichang shixian you xiaoyi de fazhan: Wu jichuan buzhang zai quanguo xinxi chanye gongzuo huiyi shang zong lun tongxin qiye de fazhan, gaige, jingying he guanli," 贴近市场实现有效益的发展:吴基传部长在全国信息产业工作会议上纵论通信企业的发展、改革、经营和管理 [Stay close to the market and materialize profitable development: Minister Wu Jichuan discusses the development, reform, operation and management of information industry at the National Information Industry Conference], *Youdian qiyeguanli* 邮电企业管理 3 (2002): 8–9.

73. SASAC 国资委办公厅, "Di er ci zhongyang qiye xinxi huagong zuo huiyi zai jing zhaokai," 二次中央企业信息化工作会议在京召开" [Second state-owned enterprise informatization conference opens in Beijing], October 17, 2008, accessed

September 1, 2014, http://www.sasac.gov.cn/n85881/n85901/c990591/content.html.

74. "Papers Differ on Way to Achieve $100B Broadband Investment," *Telecommunications Reports* 74, 4 (2008): 20–21, http://search.proquest.com.libproxy2.usc.edu/docview/216952030?accountid=14749.

75. Interview with author, May 2014, Beijing. This interviewee wishes to remain anonymous.

76. Zhu Jianhong 朱剑红, "Zhanlve xing xin xing chanye tupokou zai nali (zhengce jiedu: fazhan zhanlve xing xin xing chanye)," 战略性新兴产业 突破口在哪里 (政策解读:发展战略性新兴产业) [Strategic new industry, where is its breakthrough (policy interpretation: Development of strategic new industry)], *Renmin ribao* 人民日报, October 22, 2010, 2; Zhao Yongxin 赵永新, "Zhanlve xing xin xing chanye xuyao xinxin he kuanrong (fazhan xinxing chanye luzi zenme zou shang)—fang quanguo zhengxie jingjiweiyuanhui fu zhuren Chen Yongqing," 战略性新型产业需要信心和宽容(发展新兴产业路子怎么走上)—访全国政协经济委员会副主任陈永清" [Strategic new industry needs confidence and tolerance (how to develop new industry), an interview with Chen Yongqing, the vice director of Subcommittee of Economy, Chinese People's Political Consultative Conference], *Renmin ribao* 人民日报, July 14, 2010, 10.

77. Steinfeld, *Playing Our Game*, 156.

78. Shen Jiangying 申江婴, ed., "*Qushi duihua*," 趋势对话 [Dialogue about trend] (Beijing: 北京邮电大学出版社, 2010), 96.

79. General Office of Bureau of Telecommunication 电信管理局办公厅, "2013 nian shijie dianxin he xinxi shehui ri dahui zai jing zhaokai," 2013年世界电信和信息社会日大会在京召开 [World Information Society Day conference 2013 opens in Beijing], May 17, 2013, accessed May 21, 2016, http://money.163.com/13/0518/10/8V5D7T8V00253B0H.html#from=keyscan; "2015 nian tongxin yunying ye tongji gongbao," 2015年通信运营业统计公报 [2015 telecoms operation statistics], January 21, 2016, accessed March 2, 2016, http://www.miit.gov.cn/n1146312/n1146904/n1648372/c4620679/content.html.

80. Zuo Ya 左娅, "Xinxi xiaofei: kuoda neixu xin yinqing," 信息消费：扩大内需新引擎 [Consumption of information: New engine for boosting domestic demand], *Renmin ribao* 人民日报, October 29, 2011, accessed May 21, 2016, http://cpc.people.com.cn/n/2012/1129/c83083-19735826.html.

81. Chen Jing 陈静, "Kuandai cheng dianxin ye touzi zhongdian," 宽带成电信业投资重点 [Broadband becomes the key point of telecommunication industry], *Zhongguo zhengjuan bao* 中国证券报, January 11, 2011, accessed September 1, 2014, http://tech.hexun.com/2011-01-11/126707073.html.

82. Christine Zhen-Wei Qiang, "Broadband Infrastructure Investment in Stimulus Packages: Relevance for Developing Countries," *Info* 12, 2 (2010): 41–56.

83. Xiao Ya 晓雅, "Zhuizhu kuandai meng ji qing qian li guang" 追逐宽带梦寄情千里光 [Pursue broadband dream and devote to fiber-optic networks], *Renmin youdian*

bao 人民邮电报, February 26, 2016, accessed May 11, 2016, http://www.cnii.com.cn/telecom/2016-02/26/content_1697445.htm.

84. Lu Ling 陆玲, "'Kuandai Zhongguo zhanlve' guizai tichu zhongzai yingyong cheng zai jucuo," "宽带中国"战略贵在提出重在应用成在举措 ["Broadband China" is valuable for proposing application as emphasis and measurements as achievement], *Youdian guihua* 邮电规划 1 (2012): 7–11.

85. "Wei Leping: yunyingshang bupa weiqu jiupa si," 韦乐平：运营商不怕委屈就怕死 [Telecom operators fear death but not misunderstanding], *CWW.Net*, June 4, 2015, accessed July 15, 2015, http://tech.sina.com.cn/t/2015-06-04/doc-icrvvqrf4093827.shtml. The exchange rate used in this volume for events from 2000 to 2014 is about US$1 to Chinese yuan 7.4. See the appendix.

86. Mary Elizabeth Gallagher, *Contagious Capitalism: Globalization and the Politics of Labor in China* (Princeton: Princeton University Press, 2005), 134.

87. Zuo Dongdong 左东东, "Dianxin yunyingshang ying bian laowupaiqian xin gui ton gong ton chou haiyou duoyuan," 电信运营商应变劳务派遣新规 同工同酬还要多远 [Telecom operators react to new labor regulation; how far from equal job and equal pay], August 27, 2013, accessed September 1, 2014, http://market.c114.net/220/a789309.html; Jintou Wuxian 尽头无限, "Zhong yidong dafanwei tiaozheng laowugong bufen ke huo zhuanzheng," 中移动大范围调整劳务工部分可获转正 [China Mobile reforms the dispatch of labor; many expect formal employment], November 19, 2014, accessed July 15, 2015, http://www.580114.com/u/Infinite.

88. Yu Hong and Wei Wang, "Embracing Communication: China's Post-2008 Economic Restructuring and Labor," in *The Routledge Companion to Labor and Media*, ed. Richard Maxwell (London: Routledge, 2016), 107–18.

89. MII, "Guanyu kaifang yonghu zhu di wang yunying shi dian gongzuo de tongzhi," 关于开放用户驻地网运营市场试点工作的通知 [Notice of carrying out pilot work of the operating market of customer premises network], *Sina Laws*, August 15, 2001, accessed March 11, 2016, http://review.jcrb.com.cn/ournews/asp/readNews.asp?id=49585.

90. Huang Sha 黄沙, "Dianxin yunyingshang zhu di wang luan xiang: chanquan wenti cheng zuida banjiaoshi" 电信运营商驻地网乱相:产权问题成最大绊脚石 [The chaos in customer-premises network for telecom operators: Property issue becomes the biggest stumbling block], *Finance and Economics Times* 财经时报, March 3, 2007, accessed May 21, 2016, http://www.c114.net/market/181/a176406.html; "Shui zu'ai kuandai tisu jiang fei: you wu ye kaikou yao jinchangfei 80 wan" 谁在阻碍宽带提速降费:有物业开口要进场费80万 [Who is hindering the faster and more affordable broadband connection: Some property-management company asks a 800 thousand yuan entrance fee], *National Business Daily*, 每日经济报道, June 5, 2015, accessed March 6, 2016, http://finance.sina.com.cn/chanjing/cyxw/20150605/010922351941.shtml.

91. Zhang Lina 张丽娜, "San wang ronghe gei hulianwang dailai de yingxiang," 三网融合给互联网带来的影响 [The impact of unification of three webs on internet], *Youdian guihua* 邮电规划 2 (2011): 23–26.

92. Zhou Qi 周旗, "San wang ronghe xianzhuang fenxi yu fazhan celue yanjiu" 三网融合"现状分析与发展策略研究 [Analysis of the current condition and development strategy of "unification of three webs"], *Youdian guihua* 邮电规划 3 (2011): 6–8.

93. Chuan Fu 船夫, "Zhongguo dianxin fali 20M guangxian kuandai," 中国电信发力20M光纤宽带 [China Telecom fights for 20M optical broadband], *People's Post and Telecommunication*, 人民邮电报, July 10, 2014, accessed March 6, 2016, http://www.chinatelecom.com.cn/m/newm/t20140710_117938.html.

94. CNNIC, "2010 nian Zhongguo nongcun hulianwang fazhan zhuangkuang diaocha baogao" 2010年中国农村互联网发展状况调查报告 [China research report on internet development in rural area 2010], August 2011, accessed July 15, 2015, http://www.cnnic.net.cn/hlwfzyj/hlwxzbg/201109/P020120709345273379676.pdf; CNNIC, "Zhongguo hulianwangluo fazhan zhuangkuang tongji baogao" 中国互联网络发展状况统计报告 [China's statistical report on internet development], January 2016, accessed March 4, 2016, https://www.cnnic.net.cn/hlwfzyj/hlwxzbg/201601/P020160122469130059846.pdf.

95. "Interview: Kevin Zhang of Huawei," *Global Telecoms Business*, December 1, 2009, http://search.proquest.com.libproxy1.usc.edu/docview/218309883?accountid=14749.

96. Min Tan and Yishi Zhu, "China Broadband Bulls Lean on National Strategy," *Caixin Online*, June 1, 2012, retrieved from LexisNexis.

97. Ya Xiao 晓雅, "Zhuizhu kuandai meng ji qing qian li guang zhongguo dianxin 'kuandai zhongguo guangwang chengshi' wu zhounian xilie (yi)," 追逐宽带梦 寄情千里光 中国电信"宽带中国·光网城市" 五周年系(一) [Chasing the dream of broadband and optical cable, China Telecom "broadband China· Optical network city" five-year series (a)], *China Information Industry Net*, 中国信息产业网, February 26, accessed March 11, 2016, http://www.cnii.com.cn/telecom/2016-02/26/content_1697445.htm. The exchange rate used in this volume for events from 2001 to 2015 is about US$1 to Chinese yuan 7.3. See appendix.

98. Breznitz and Murphree, *Run of the Red Queen*, 91.

99. MIIT, "Jiedu: gongxinbu jiedu tisu jiang fei zhi dao yi jian," 解读:工信部解读提速降费指导意见 [MIIT interprets state council instruction on raising speed and reducing price], May 20, 2015, accessed July 13, 2015, http://money.163.com/15/0520/12/AQ2DCK5J00253B0H.html.

100. "Yuan gongxinbu zhang Li Yizhong pilu si wan yi chutai guocheng" 原工信部长李毅中披露四万亿出台过程 [Former minister of industry and information technology Li Yizhong revealed the process of introducing the 4 trillion yuan package], *International Business Times*, March 8, 2013, accessed September 1, 2014, http://www.ibtimes.com.cn/articles/23050/20130308/li-yizhong-siwanyi-financial-crisis.htm.

101. Wei Jie, [China's economic transition], 68.

102. Wang Shaoguang and Hu Angang 王绍光 胡鞍钢, "Chongxin renshi guojia de zuoyong" 重新认识国家的作用 [Reconsidering the values of the state], in *Zhefu yu shichang* 政府与市场 [The state and the market], ed. Hu Angang and Wang Shaoguang (Beijing: 中国计划出版社, 1999), 3–7.

103. Yang, *Remaking the Chinese Leviathan*, 2004.

104. Li Guangrong and Liu jian 李光荣 刘健, "Jianguan bumen de ganga" 监管部门的尴尬 [The embarrassment of supervision departments], *Xibu kaifa bao* 西部开发报, July 11, 2003, 4.

105. Su Wen 素文, "Wu Hequan: tisu jiang fei wangmin qing duo xie naixin yunyingshang yao shou de zhu weiqu" 邬贺铨：提速降费网民请多些耐心运营商要受得住委屈 [Wu Hequan: Improve speed and lower price, netizens should be patient and operators hold on], *Renmin youdian* 人民邮电报, June 4, 2015, accessed July 15, 2015, http://www.cnii.com.cn/telecom/2015-06/04/content_1581830.htm; Zhengwei Li, Xiaohui Zhang, and Jing Zhou 李峥巍 孙晓辉 周竟, "San wen 'wang fei gao wangsu man' xianxiang: weihe man? gui bu gui? neng xiatiao ma?" 三问"网费高网速慢"现象:为何慢?贵不贵?能下调吗? [Three inquiries of the 'expensive but slow internet': Why is it slow? Is it expensive? Can the price be reduced?], *Xinhua Net*, 新华网, April 17, 2015, accessed March 12, 2016, http://politics.people.com.cn/n/2015/0417/c1001-26860994.html.

106. Yan Ni and Chen Yuyan 闫妮 陈予燕, "'Dianxin' kuandai fan longduan: dianxin liantong qian yi yingshou shou weixie" 典型宽带反垄断:电信联通千亿营收受威胁 ["Exemplary" broadband encounters antimonopoly, China Telecom and China Unicom's revenue threatened to lose hundreds of billions], November 28, 2011, accessed September 14, 2014, http://www.antimonopolylaw.org/article/default.asp?id=3541.

107. Tan and Zhu, "China Broadband."

108. "Investing in Broadband in the Access Market," *Global Telecoms Business* 1 (July 2007), http://search.proquest.com.libproxy1.usc.edu/docview/218312435?accountid=14749.

109. Tan and Zhu, "China Broadband."

110. "Yunyingshang qian jin tuolei kuandai zhongguo jincheng wangluo jianshe chengben liao da wan yi" 运营商钱紧拖累宽带中国进程 网络建设成本料达万亿 [Operators' tight budgets burden broadband in China, internet infrastructure construction costs estimated to reach trillion], *Jinji cankao bao* 经济参考报, November 6, 2013, accessed September 1, 2014, http://news.xinhuanet.com/finance/2013-11/06/c_125657120.htm.

111. Victor Pickard, "Social Democracy or Corporate Libertarianism? Conflicting Media Policy Narratives in the Wake of Market Failure," *Communication Theory* 23 (2013): 336–55.

112. Gallagher, *Contagious Capitalism*, 7.

113. Samuel S. Kim, "China and Globalization: Confronting Myriad Challenges and Opportunities," *Asian Perspectives* 33, 3 (2009): 41–80.

114. OECD, *OECD Reviews of Regulatory Reform: China 2009: Defining the Boundary between the Market and the State* (Paris: OECD, 2009), doi: 10.1787/9789264059429-en.

Chapter 4. Making a Home-Base Strategy

This chapter is adapted from Yu Hong, François Bar, and Zheng An, "Chinese Telecommunications on the Threshold of Convergence: Contexts, Possibilities, and

Limitations of a Domestic Demand-Based Growth Model," *Telecommunications Policy* 36, 10–11 (2012): 914–28.

1. Yuezhi Zhao, "China's Pursuits of Indigenous Innovations in Information Technology Developments: Hopes, Follies and Uncertainties," *Chinese Journal of Communication* 3, 3 (2010): 266–89, 270.

2. Xie Wei and Richard Li-Hua, "Evolving Learning Strategies for Latecomers," *Journal of Technology Management* 3, 2 (2008): 154–67; Breznitz and Murphree, *Run of the Red Queen*.

3. Yuezhi Zhao, "China's Pursuits," 267.

4. Jack Linchuan Qiu, "Chinese Techno-Nationalism and Global WiFi Policy," in *Reorienting Global Communication: Indian and Chinese Media beyond Borders*, ed. Michael Curtin and Hemant Shah (Urbana: University of Illinois Press, 2010), 284–304; Jiang Yu and Richard Li-Hua, *China's Highway of Information and Communication Technology* (New York: Palgrave Macmillan, 2010).

5. "Xiao Hua: Jiakuai fazhan yidong tongxin zhongduan tuidong tongxin chanye maishang xintaijie," 肖华:加快发展移动通信终端 推动通信产业迈上新台阶 [Xiao Hua: Accelerate the development of mobile communication devices and push the telecommunications industry to a new stage], May 24, 2010, accessed September 1, 2014, http://www.miit.gov.cn/n11293472/n11293877/n13218055/13218089.html.

6. Yuezhi Zhao, "China's Pursuits," 282.

7. See Fu Hanlong and Yi Mou, "An Assessment of the 2008 Telecommunications Restructuring in China," *Telecommunications Policy* 34, 10 (2010): 649–58; Nir Kshetri, Prashant Palvia, and Hua Dai, "Chinese Institutions and Standardization: The Case of Government Support to Domestic Third-Generation Cellular Standard," *Telecommunications Policy* 35, 5 (2011): 399–412; Xia Jun, "The Third-Generation-Mobile (3G) Policy and Deployment in China: Current Status, Challenges, and Prospects," *Telecommunications Policy* 35, 1 (2011): 51–63.

8. Samuel S. Kim, "China and Globalization"; Hsueh Roselyn, "Nations or Sectors in the Age of Globalization: China's Policy toward Foreign Direct Investment in Telecommunications," *Review of Policy Research* 32, 6 (2015): 627–48.

9. Sun Lin, "Funding Telecom Expansion," *China Business Review* 20 (1993): 31–33.

10. Editorial Board of China Yearbook of Electronics Industry, *Zhongguo dianzi gongye nian jian 1995* 中国电子工业年鉴—1995 [China yearbook of the electronic industry 1995] (Beijing: 电子工业出版社, 1995).

11. Eric Harwit, "Building China's Telecommunications Network: Industrial Policy and the Role of Chinese State-Owned, Foreign, and Private Domestic Enterprises," *China Quarterly* 190 (2007): 311–32; Yuezhi Zhao, "China's Pursuits."

12. Harwit, "Building China's Telecommunications."

13. Zixiang Alex Tan, "Product Cycle Theory and Telecommunications Industry—Foreign Direct Investment, Government Policy, and Indigenous Manufacturing in China," *Telecommunications Policy* 26, 1 (2002): 17–30.

14. Chen Zhongxun 陈仲旭, "Minzu tongxin gongye renzhongdaoyuan," 民族通信工业任重道远 [The national communications industry—a long way to go], *China Infoworld* 中国计算机报, June 19, 1998, D3.

15. Dan Steinbock, *The Wireless Horizons: Strategy and Competition in the Worldwide Mobile Marketplace* (New York: AMACOM, 2003), 195–98.

16. Tan, "Product Cycle Theory."

17. Harwit, "Building China's Telecommunications."

18. Chen, "National Communications Industry."

19. Yan Junping 闫俊平 and Yao Chuanfu 姚传富, "Shixian woguo tongxin zhizaoye kuayue shi fazhan" 实现我国通信制造业跨越式发展 [Leap-forward development of China's mobile communications industry—an interview with Qu Weizhi, the vice minister of Ministry of Information Industry], *China Electronics News* 中国电子报, March 20, 2001, 1.

20. Yan and Yao, "Leap-forward."

21. Harwit, "Building China's Telecommunications."

22. Tan, "Product Cycle Theory."

23. Mi Zhou 米周 and Yin Sheng 尹生, Zhonxing tongxun: Quanmian fensan qiye fengxian de zhongyongzhidao, 中兴通讯:全面分散企业风险的中庸之道 [ZTE: The strategies of comprehensively reducing enterprise risk] (Beijing: 当代中国出版社, 2005).

24. Evelyn Iritani, "China's WTO Challenge; Telecoms Key Test of China's Accessibility," *Los Angeles Times*, August 5, 2001, C1.

25. Steinbock, *Wireless Horizons*.

26. Iritani, "China's WTO Challenge."

27. Mi and Yin, "Zhonxing tongxun" [*ZTE*: The strategies].

28. Ibid.

29. Kathryn Balint, "The Battle over 3G Technology Is Creating Bitter Rivals," *San Diego (CA) Union-Tribune*, July 30, 2006, H 1.

30. Loretta Chao, "China's Telecom-Gear Makers, Once Laggards at Home, Pass Foreign Rivals," *Wall Street Journal*, April 10, 2009, B1.

31. Mi and Yin, "Zhonxing tongxun" [*ZTE*: The strategies].

32. Roman Boutellier, Oliver Gassmann, and Maximilian von Zedtwitz, "Huawei: Globalizing through Innovation," in *Managing Global Innovation: Uncovering the Secrets of Future Competitiveness*, 3rd ed. (New York: Springer, 2008), 507–22.

33. "Up, Up, and Huawei," *Economist* 392, 8650 (2009): 13.

34. Gang Qiu, Xu Liyan, and Sun Xiaofei, "Assessment of Chinese Companies' Competitiveness," *SERI Quarterly* 2, 3 (2009): 40–51.

35. "Up, Up and Huawei," 13.

36. Tao Wang 王涛, "Cong Huawei nian bao kan 2009 tongxin shebei shichang geju," 从华为年报看2009通信设备市场格局 [Assessment of market structure of telecom equipment in 2009 via Huawei's annual report], May 4, 2009, accessed May 21, 2016, http://labs.chinamobile.com/mblog/2168_18222.

37. Boutellier, Gassmann, and Zedtwitz, "Huawei."

38. "China GSM Industry Supply Chain and Competition Analysis," *Cellular News*, July 9, 2006, accessed September 1, 2014, http://www.cellular-news.com/story/18167.php.

39. Mike Clendenin, "Local Companies Win Big as China Mobile Hands Out 3G Contracts," *Electronic Engineering Times*, April 16, 2007, 28.

40. Wang Jianjun 王健君, "Shui jiang kongzhi zhongguo shouji," 谁将控制中国手机 [Who to control Chinese handset market], *Lifeweek* 三联生活周刊 22 (2000), accessed August 1, 2015, http://www.chinanews.com/zhonghuawenzhai/2001-02-01/new/13.html.

41. Hui Yuk-min, "Mainland in No Great Hurry to Give Vendors Green Light," *South China Morning Post*, November 16, 2004, technology post, 1.

42. US Information Technology Office, *Written Comments to the US Government Interagency Trade Policy Staff Committee in Response to Federal Register Notice regarding China's Compliance with Its Accession Commitments to the World Trade Organization (WTO)*, September 20, 2013, accessed May 29, 2016, http://www.tiaonline.org/sites/default/files/pages/2013%20USITO%20China%20WTO%20Compliance%20Filing%20-%20Final.pdf.

43. Brian Low, "Huawei Technologies Corporation: From Local Dominance to Global Challenge?" *Journal of Business and Industrial Marketing* 22, 2 (2007): 138–44.

44. "Xinxi tongxin lingyu quanqiu biaozhun hezuo dahui juxing Xi Guohua chuxi bing jianghua," 信息通信领域全球标准合作大会举行 奚国华出席并讲话 [The collaboration Conference for Global Standards of Information and Telecommunications is held; Xi Guohua attends and gives speech], August 31, 2010, accessed May 21, 2016, http://finance.ifeng.com/roll/20100831/2571261.shtml.

45. Yu Jiang and Richard Li-Hua, *China's Highway of Information and Communication Technology* (New York: Palgrave, 2010).

46. Yuezhi Zhao, "China's Pursuits."

47. Wang Jenn-hwan and Tsai Ching-jung, "How Does China Restructure Global Production Networks?" paper presented at the Industry Studies Conference, Chicago, Illinois, May 6–7, 2010.

48. Richard P. Suttmeier, Xiangkui Yao, and Alex Zixiang Tan, "Standards of Power? Technology, Institutions, and Politics in the Development of China's National Standards Strategy," *National Bureau of Asian Research (NBR) Special Report* 10 (June 2006).

49. Karl J. Weaver, "Developing Business with Greater China Handset Vendors," *Newport Technologies*, accessed September 1, 2014, http://www.newporttechnologies.biz/GreaterChinaHandsetmarket.pdf; Chuan-Kai Lee and Annalee Saxenian, "Coevolution and Coordination: A Systemic Analysis of the Taiwanese Information Technology Industry," *Journal of Economic Geography* 8 (2008): 157–80.

50. National Development and Reform Commission (NDRC), "Shouji shengchan kuaisu fazhan touzi fengxian burong hushi" 手机生产快速发展 投资风险不容忽视 [Rapid development of mobile phone production, investment risk cannot be

ignored], February 2, 2005, accessed May 21, 2016, http://news.xinhuanet.com/fortune/2005-02/19/content_2593091.htm.

51. Jan Krikke, "Fortunes Changing in Asia," *Wireless Week* 8, 31 (August 19, 2002): 1.

52. Editorial Board of China Yearbook of Electronics Industry, *Zhongguo dianzi gongye nian jian 2005* 中国电子工业年鉴2005 [China yearbook of the electronics industry 2005] (Beijing: China City, 2005); MIIT, "2013 nian shouji hangye fazhan qingkuang huigu yu zhanwang," 2013年手机行业发展情况回顾与展望 [Review and prospect of the developmental conditions of handset industry in 2013], March 7, 2014, accessed May 21, 2017, http://www.c114.net/market/186/a825050.html.

53. Sina, "Xinwen"; Jamie P. Horsley, "PRC Regulation of Foreign Telecom Equipment and the WTO," *China Business Review* 28, 5 (2001): 66–68.

54. Liu Xiaoming 刘晓明, "Xinxi chanye bu queding jinnian shouji tiaokong mubiao" 信息产业部确定今年手机调控目标 [Ministry of Information Industry to determine this year's mobile phone control objectives], *China Electronics News* 中国电子报, March 20, 2001, A1.

55. Yu Chen, "Licensing Restrictions to Remain for Handset Makers," *China Daily*, July 24, 2004, accessed September 1, 2014, http://www.chinadaily.com.cn/english/doc/2004-07/24/content_351207.htm.

56. Yan and Yao, "Leap-forward."

57. Faith Hung, "Taiwan Seeks Open Door to China-Delegation Hopes to Tap Mainland's Burgeoning Cell Phone Market," *EBN* 1264 (2001): 10.

58. "Xinwen bei jing: xin chan bu wu hao wen jian dianding shouji geju" 新闻背景:信产部'五号文件'奠定手机格局 [Backgrounder: The Ministry of Information Industry issued the fifth document to establish the setup of mobile-phone production], June 16, 2004, accessed September 1, 2014, http://tech.sina.com.cn/it/t/2004-06-20/1356377822.shtml.

59. Susan Myers and Lin Yuan, "China's Mobile Phone Market: Market Barriers for Japanese Vendors," *THT Research*, accessed May 21, 2016, http://www.chinadmd.com/file/pr6xsrrwv3ow0oove3sutvoc_1.html.

60. MIIT, "2008 nian woguo shouji hangye fazhan huigu he 2009 nian zhanwang," 2008年我国手机行业发展回顾和2009年展望 [Review of the development of China's mobile phone industry in 2008 and the prospects for 2009], February 23, 2009, accessed May 21, 2016, http://www.c114.net/market/598/a393483.html.

61. "Communication Equipment Manufacturing in China: Market Research Report," *IBISWorld*, July 2013, accessed September 1, 2013, http://www.ibisworld.com/industry/china/communication-equipment-manufacturing.html.

62. Krikke, "Fortunes Changing in Asia."

63. Zixiang Alex Tan, "Product Cycle, Wintelism, and Cross-National Production Networks for Developing Countries," *Info* 4, 3 (2002): 57–65, 57.

64. Yu Zhou, "Synchronizing Export Orientation with Import Substitution: Creating Competitive Indigenous High-Tech Companies in China," *World Development* 36, 11 (2008): 2353–70, 2359.

65. Kevin Wang, "China's Gray Market Handset Shipments Continue Expanding in 2011," *iSuppli Corporation*, December 16, 2010, accessed September 1, 2014, https://technology.ihs.com/388766/china-gray-market-cell-phone-shipments-slow-in-2011.

66. MIIT, "The Economic Analysis of the Electronic Information Industry in January–April 2003," 2004, accessed July 1, 2010, http://dw.miit.gov.cn/n11293472/n11293832/n11294132/n11302737/11825412.html (no longer available).

67. Zero2IPO Research Center, "2010 nian Zhongguo zaixian yingyong shangdian shichang touzi yanjiubaogao," 2010年中国在线应用商店市场投资研究报告 [Investment report of China's online application stores in 2010], August 2010, accessed September 1, 2014, http://tech.qq.com/a/20100908/000445_3.htm.

68. MIIT, "2014 nian shouji hangye fazhan huigu yu zhanwang" 2014年手机行业发展与展望 [Hanset industry development and outlook in 2014], February 27, 2015, accessed May 22, 2016, http://www.miit.gov.cn/n1146312/n1146904/n1648373/c3337297/content.html.

69. David Tilson and Kalle Lyytimen, "The 3G Transition: Changes in the US Wireless Industry," *Telecommunications Policy* 30, 10–11 (2006): 569–86, 579.

70. "Xiao Hua," 2010.

71. Ibid.

72. Xia Jinghui 夏竞辉 and Chen Peng 陈鹏, "TD: Cong aoyun caichang zouxiang dazhong shenghuo," TD:从奥运赛场走向大众生活" [TD: From Olympic game to daily life], *China Telecommunications Trade* 中国电信业 10 (2008): 15–21.

73. Wang and Tsai, "How Does China Restructure."

74. MIIT, "Prospect for 2009."

75. Wang and Tsai, "How Does China Restructure."

76. K. Wang, "China's Gray Market."

77. Ibid.

78. China Telecommunications Newswire, "Interview with Chen Haofei, Secretary-General of the TD-SCDMA Forum," July 19, 2007, retrieved from LexisNexis.

79. K. Wang, "China's Gray Market," and "Zhongguo 3G shouji shichang fenxi," 中国3G手机市场分析 [China 3G mobile phone market analysis], *iSuppli Corporation*, February 23, 2011, accessed September 1, 2014, http://www.zte.com.cn/cndata/magazine/zte_technologies/2011/2_11/magazine/201102/t20110223_221063.html.

80. Dan Schiller, "Power under Pressure: Digital Capitalism in Crisis," *International Journal of Communication* 5 (2011): 924–41.

81. Ronald Deibert, John Palfrey, Rafal Rohozinski, and Jonathan Zittrain, eds., *Access Controlled: The Shaping of Power, Rights, and Rule in Cyberspace* (Cambridge: MIT Press, 2010).

82. MIIT, "2009 nian 8 yue tongxinye yunxing zhuangkuang," 2009年8月通信业运行状况 [Operational condition of telecommunications in August 2009], October 13, 2009, accessed May 21, 2016, http://data.acmr.com.cn/freesource/zixunshow.asp?id=15641.

83. CNNIC, "Zhongguo hulianwangluo fazhan zhuangkuang tongji baogao," 中国互联网络发展状况统计报告 [Statistical report of China's internet development], January 2010, accessed September 1, 2014, http://tech.qq.com/zt/2010/cnnic25/.

84. CNNIC, "Statistical report . . . January 2016."

85. Dan Schiller and Christian Sandvig, "Google v. China: Principled, Brave, or Business as Usual?" June 5, 2010, http://www.huffingtonpost.com/dan-schiller/google-v-china-principled_b_524727.html.

86. Jiang Yu and Kim Hua Tan, "The Evolution of China's Mobile Telecommunications Industry: Past, Present and Future," *International Journal of Mobile Communication* 3, 2 (2005): 114–26.

87. Yang Guoqiang 杨国强, "Duli WAP gongkai zhi yi zhong yidong baquan xin chan bu mimi diaoyan" 独立WAP公开质疑中移动霸权信产部秘密调研 [Independent WAP sites contested monopoly of China Mobile and MII made secret investigation], *China Business News* 第一财经日报, March 30, 2007, accessed August 3, 2015, http://tech.sina.com.cn/t/2007-03-30/02581440351.shtml.

88. Anita Davis, "Mobile Applications," *Media*, November 27, 2008: 11, http://search.proquest.com.libproxy2.usc.edu/docview/206318853?accountid=14749.

89. D. Schiller, "Power under Pressure," 928.

90. "Zhongguo Liantong cheng iPhone yonghu yue zhan zong yonghu shu 10 percent," 中国联通称iPhone用户约占3G总用户数10 percent [China Unicom said iPhone users account for about 10 percent of 3G users], *China Business News* 第一财经日报, November 22, 2010, accessed February 12, 2015, http://finance.jrj.com.cn/tech/2010/11/2219078619837.shtml.

91. He Jianhua 何建华, "Zhongguo yidong 3G yonghu jiejin 2700 wan" 中国移动3G用户接近2700万 [China Mobile has nearly 27 million 3G users], *Cien.com.cn* 中国产经新闻, April 25, 2011, accessed September 1, 2014, http://tech.hexun.com/2011-04-25/129006022.html; Su Wen 素文, "Zhong yidong TD-SCDMA yonghushu tupo 2 yi," 中移动TD-SCDMA用户数突破2亿 [China Mobile's TD-SCDMA subscribers surpassed 200 million], February 1, 2014, accessed May 22, 2016, http://www.cnii.com.cn/statistics/2014-02/21/content_1308734.htm; Mao Qiying 毛启盈, "Liantong dianxin shangyue 3G yonghu zengzhang fanghuan, shi 4G zaocheng de ma?" 联通电信上月3G用户增长放缓，是4G造成的吗？ [3G subscription slowed down last month, and is the cause 4G?], January 20, 2014, http://it.sohu.com/20140120/n393841232.shtml.

92. Davis, "Mobile Applications."

93. Trisha C. T. Lin, "Prospect of Mobile Broadcasting TV in China: Socio-technical Analysis of CMMB Development," *Chinese Journal of Communication* 5 (2012): 1–21.

94. D. Schiller, "Power under Pressure," 933.

95. Jerry Harris, "Statist Globalization in China, Russia, and the Gulf States," *Perspectives on Global Development and Technology* 8, 2–3 (2009): 139–63, 149.

96. Jan Nederveen Pieterse, "Globalization the Next Round: Sociological Perspective," *Future* 40, 8 (2008): 707–20, 717.

97. Wang Jianzhou, [Mobilizing everything], 101.

98. Robert Clark, "Lost in 3G: Celebrating Its Tenth Birthday, TD-SCDMA May Be Too Old for 3G; China's Wireless Champ May Be Better Suited to 4G—If It Can Beat Wimax to the Spectrum," *Telecom Asia* 19, 11 (2008): 20.

99. Wang Jianzhou, [Mobilizing everything], 194.

100. Chen Baoliang 陈宝亮, "Qian yi guojia xinpian jijin tou xiang zheng yi: fuchi zhuanli, tian 4G duan ceng" 千亿国家芯片基金投向争议：扶持专利，填4G断层 [Controversy over the state chip foundation's hundreds of billion yuan investment: Support patents, fill the 4G gap], *21st Century Business Herald*, September 17, 2014, accessed July 15, 2015, http://it.sohu.com/20140917/n404378526.shtml.

101. "Woguo zhineng zhongduan xinpian fazhan taishi fenxi" 我国智能终端芯片发展态势分析 [Analysis of China's smart-device chip development], *China Academy of Telecommunications Research*, April 18, 2016, accessed May 27, 2016, http://www.catr.cn/kxyj/qwfb/zdyj/201604/P020160418575550363334.docx.

102. Liu Yufang 刘育芳, "Fagaiwei hongguan yuan zhuanjia: yunyingshang duanyashi jiang fei bukequ ying jianjin youhua," 发改委宏观院专家：运营商断崖式降费不可取应渐进优化 [NDRC expert: Telecom operators should not make abrupt price cuts but gradual improvement], *Chinanews*, June 12, 2015, accessed July 15, 2015, http://www.chinanews.com/cj/2015/06-11/7337487.shtml. The exchange rate for events from 2009 to 2015 is about US$1 to Chinese yuan 6.4. See appendix.

103. Liu Xiaofeng and Tan Xin 刘晓峰 谭辛, "Tisu jiang fei bushi yunyingshang yijia de shi" 提速降费不是运营商一家的事 [Improve speed and lower price: An issue not just of telecom operators], *Jingji ribao* 经济日报, 7, June 17, 2015, accessed July 15, 2015, http://paper.ce.cn/jjrb/html/2015-06/17/content_244535.htm.

Chapter 5. Recasting the Media System

The first two sections were adapted from Yu Hong, "Between Corporate Development and Public Service: The Cultural System Reform in the Media Sector," *Media, Culture, and Society* 36 (2014): 610–27.

1. Li Ruigang 黎瑞刚, "Chuanmei gaige shi jian de diandi sikao" 传媒改革实践的点滴思考 [Thoughts on media-reform practice], *Xinwen jizhe* 新闻记者 11 (2007): 15–16.

2. Michael Keane, *Created in China: The Great Leap Forward* (London: Routledge, 2007), 82.

3. Joseph Man Chan, "Commercialization without Independence: Trends and Tensions of Media Development in China," in *China Review 1993*, ed. J. C. Yu-shek and M. Brosseau (Hong Kong: Chinese University Press of Hong Kong, 1993), 25.1–.21.

4. Richard Curt Kraus, *The Party and the Arty in China: The New Politics of Culture* (Oxford: Rowman and Littlefield, 2004), 22.

5. Michael Curtin, *Playing to the World's Biggest Audience: The Globalization of Chinese Film and TV* (Berkeley: University of California Press, 2007).

6. He Sen 何森, ed., "Minzu linghun—zhongguo wenhua tizhi gaige zhengshi qidong" 民族灵魂—中国文化体制改革正式启动 [Soul of the nation—Chinese cultural reform was officially launched] (Changchun: 吉林出版集团有限责任公司, 2010).

7. "China Rules Out Full Commercialization of Culture Sector—Official," *Xinhua Economic News*, February 28, 2011, retrieved from LexisNexis Academic Database.

8. Christine Wong, "Rebuilding Government for the Twenty-First Century: Can China Incrementally Reform the Public Sector," *China Quarterly* 200 (2009): 929–52; Kraus, *Party*, 192.

9. Licai Wu and Qian Wang 吴理财 王前, "Wenhua quan li daoxiang de guojia jiben gonggong wenhuafuwu baozhang fanwei yanjiu" 文化权利导向的国家基本公共文化服务保障范围研究 [Cover study of the cultural rights–oriented national basic public cultural services], *Academic Journal of Hubei University* 5 (2015), 湖北大学学报 201505, accessed February 20, 2016, http://www.cssn.cn/zzx/xsdj_zzx/wlc/201511/t20151103_2556706.shtml.

10. In 2013, the General Administration of Press and Publications and the State Administration of Radio, Film, and Television announced their merger into a new body, the State Administration of Press, Publications, Radio, Film, and Television as part of the restructuring of State Council ministries and departments.

11. Yuezhi Zhao, *Communication in China: Political Economy, Power, and Conflict* (Lanham: Rowman and Littlefield, 2008), 109.

12. Yuezhi Zhao, "From Commercialization to Conglomeration: The Transformation of the Chinese Press within the Orbit of the Party State," *Journal of Communication* 50, 2 (2000): 3–26; Chengju Huang, "Trace the Stones in Crossing the River: Media Structural Changes in Post-WTO China," *International Communication Gazette* 69 (2007): 413–30.

13. World Bank and Development Research Center of State Council, the People's Republic of China, "China 2030: Building a Modern, Harmonious, and Creative High-Income Society," 2012, accessed September 1, 2014, http://www.worldbank.org/content/dam/Worldbank/document/China-2030-complete.pdf.

14. Linda Yueh, "The Chinese Box: The Opaque Economic Borders of the Chinese State," *Oxford Review of Economic Policy* 27, 4 (2011): 658–79, 674.

15. Yuezhi Zhao, *Communication in China*, 109.

16. Yik Chan Chin, "Public Service Broadcasting, Public Interest, and Individual Rights in China," *Media, Culture, and Society* 34, 7 (2012): 898–912.

17. State Administration of Radio Film and Television (hereinafter referred to as SARFT) and China Radio and Television Yearbook Editorial Committee, *China Radio and Television Yearbook* (Beijing: China Radio and Television Yearbook Press, 2007), 7. The exchange rate used for events from 1998 to 2005 is about US$1 to Chinese yuan 8.3.

18. SARFT, "Quanguo 'shi yi wu' guangbo dianshi cun cun tong gongcheng jianshe renwu quanmian wancheng" 全国"十一五"广播电视村村通工程建设任务全面

完成 [The completion of the Eleventh Five-Year Plan of national television to every village project], January 5, 2011, accessed May 22, 2016, http://www.sarft.gov.cn/art/2011/1/5/art_135_17373.html. The exchange rate used for events from 2006 to 2010 is about US$1 to Chinese yuan 7.2.

19. Department of Financial Management of the MOC, "Jin ji nian woguo wenhua touru qingkuang ji duice jianyi" 近几年我国文化投入情况及对策建议 [Conditions of cultural investment in recent years and proposed solutions], August 23, 2011, accessed May 11, 2012, http://zwgk.mcprc.gov.cn/auto255/201108/t20110823_20110.html.

20. Brett Caraway, "Audience Labor in the New Media Environment: A Marxian Revisiting of the Audience Commodity," *Media, Culture, and Society* 33, 5 (2011): 693–708, 696.

21. Chengju Huang, "The Development of a Semi-Independent Press in Post-Mao China: An Overview and a Case Study of Chengdu Business News," *Journalism Studies* 1, 4 (2000): 649–64, 650.

22. Geng Xiao, "Clarification of SOE Property Rights," background paper for the World Bank project on the state asset management in China, November 1996, accessed May 22, 2016, http://www.econ.hku.hk/~xiaogeng/research/Paper/Clarification%20of%20SOE%20Property%20Rights.pdf.

23. Chin-Chuan Lee, Zhou He, and Yu Huang, "Chinese Party Publicity Inc. Conglomerated: The Case of the Shenzhen Press Group," *Media, Culture, and Society* 28, 4 (2006): 581–602, 599.

24. Nailene Wiest Chou, "Mainland Media Market Ripening to Foreign Products and Investments; Experts Warn the Industry's Liberalization Won't Happen Fast," *South China Morning Post*, August 29, 2003, retrieved from LexisNexis Academic Database.

25. Michael Sainsbury, "China's Censors Ban Foreign TV," *Australian*, February 20, 2012, retrieved from LexisNexis Academic Database.

26. Lilian Lin, "China to Limit Foreign TV Shows on Video-Streaming Sites," *Wall Street Journal*, September 3, 2014, accessed August 1, 2015, http://www.wsj.com/articles/china-to-limit-foreign-tv-shows-on-chinese-video-streaming-sites-1409744165.

27. Craig Stephen, "China's Online-Video Market Goes Legit," *Wall Street Journal*, October 31, 2010, accessed July 1, 2015, http://www.marketwatch.com/story/chinas-online-video-market-goes-legit-2010-10-31.

28. Ibid.

29. Xinhua News Agency, "Jueding jiedu: zhichi zhuangda guoyou huo guoyou konggu wenhua qiye"《决定》解读：支持壮大国有或国有控股文化企业 [Interpretation of government policy: Support and expanse of state-owned or state-controlled cultural enterprise], January 1, 2012, accessed October 1, 2014, http://www.gov.cn/jrzg/2012-01/01/content_2035317.htm.

30. Nicolai Volland, "From Control to Management: The CCP's 'Reform of the Cultural Structure,'" in *China's Thought Management*, ed. Anne-Marie Brady (London: Routledge, 2012), 107–22.

31. Yuming Zhao, *China Radio & TV Yearbook 2005* (Beijing: China Radio and TV Yearbook Press, 2005), 53.

32. Zhao Huayong 赵化勇, "Zhuazhu jiyu yingjie tiaozhan zengqiang Zhongguo dianshi meiti shili he yingxiangli" 抓住机遇 迎接挑战 增强中国电视媒体实力和影响力 [Seize the opportunity, meet the challenge, strengthen China's media and expand its influence], *TV Research* 电视研究 6 (2004): 5–10.

33. "Tongjiju: 08 nian woguo wenhua chanye fazhan qingkuang de baogao (zhaiyao)" 统计局:08年我国文化产业发展情况的报告(摘要) [Bureau of Statistics: 2008 Report of China's cultural industry development (summary)], May 14, 2010, accessed October 1, 2014, http://www.gov.cn/gzdt/2010-05/14/content_1606451.htm.

34. Interview with author, May 2014.

35. SARFT and China Radio and Television Yearbook Editorial Committee, *Zhongguo guangbo dianshi nian jian* 中国广播电视年鉴—2004 [China Radio and Television Yearbook—2004] (Beijing: 中国广播电视年鉴社, 2004), 17.

36. Dwayne Winseck, "Netscapes of Power: Convergence, Consolidation and Power in the Canadian Mediascape," *Media, Culture & Society* 24, 6 (2002): 795–819.

37. Ibid.

38. SARFT and China Radio and Television Yearbook Editorial Committee, "Zhongguo guangbo dianshi nian jian," 中国广播电视年鉴—2003 [China Radio and Television Yearbook—2003] (Beijing: China Radio and Television Yearbook Press, 2003), 7.

39. The subheading "Claiming Cable's Digital Future" is borrowed from François Bar and Jonathan Taplin, "Cable's Digital Future," in *Cable Visions: Television beyond Broadcasting*, ed. Sarah Banet-Weiser, Cynthia Chris, and Anthony Freitas (New York: New York University Press, 2007), 66–84.

40. Yuezhi Zhao, "Caught in the Web: The Public Interest and the Battle for Control of China's Information Superhighway," *Info* 2, 1 (2000): 41–66.

41. SARFT, "Guangdian gaige kaifang he shuzi dianshi fazhan bi huo chenggong—guojia guangdian zongju xinwen fayanren Zhu Hong da jinrong shibao jizhe wen" 广电改革开放和数字电视发展必获成功—国家广电总局新闻发言人朱虹答《金融时报》记者问 [The media reform and development of digital television will surely succeed: Zhu Hong, SARFT spokesperson, People's Republic China, talks to journalist from *Financial Times*], November 11, 2004, accessed May 22, 2016, http://shexun.cn/www/book/196908/00055.html, http://shexun.cn/www/book/196908/00056.html.

42. Yuezhi Zhao, "Caught Web," 41–66.

43. Zheng Zhong 郑重, "Zhang Haitao hao mai guangdian" 张海涛号脉广电 [Zhang Haitao feels the pulse of the SARFT], Hulianwang zhoukan 互联网周刊 8 (March 28, 2005): 12–14.

44. Wang Yun 汪云 and Bao Ran 包冉, "Shuzi dianshi: zhongxibu jueqi" 数字电视：中西部崛起 [Digital TV: The rise of central and western regions], *Zhongguo shuzi dianshi* 中国数字电视 20 (March 2006): 31–36; Liu Yigong 刘亦功, "Bian yaowo zhuanhuan wei woyao zhuanhuan" 变要我转换为我要转换 [Transform from forced transition to willing transition], *Zhongguo shuzi dianshi* 中国数字电视 36 (July 2007): 22–24; "Kan dianshi cheng shechipin shuzi dianshi xiangbobo weihe re minyuan" 看

电视成奢侈品数字电视香饽饽为何惹民怨 [TV watching became a luxury, digital TV aroused complaint], *Ban yue tan* 半月谈, February 28, 2007, accessed July 15, 2015, http://news.xinhuanet.com/fortune/2007-02/28/content_5783094.htm.

45. Chao Liming 巢立明, "Fufei dianshi yu zhongguo dianshi de jingzheng you shi," 付费电视与中国电视的竞争优势 [Pay TV and comparative advantage of Chinese TV], *TV Research* 电视研究 9 (2004): 31–32.

46. Zheng Zhong, "Zhang Haitao."

47. Vivian Wu, "CCTV Lifeline to Ailing Cable Network," *South China Morning Post*, July 25, 2005, retrieved from LexisNexis.

48. Wang Yun 汪云 and Bao Ran 包冉, "Hangzhou Qishilu" 杭州启示录 [Inspiration from Hangzhou], *Zhongguo shuzi dianshi* 中国数字电视 37 (September 2007): 34–41.

49. Wang Yun 汪云, "You xian 2009–2010 neiwaijiaokun zhong tansuo qianxing" 有线2009–2010内外交困中探索前行 [Cable television is struggling through internal and external difficulties during 2009–2010], *Zhongguo shuzi dianshi* 中国数字电视 63 (January 2010): 43–45.

50. Yuezhi Zhao, "Caught," 41–66.

51. Li Ruigang 黎瑞刚, "Zhongguo dianshi de chanye sikao" 中国电视的产业思考 [Thoughts on Chinese television industries], *Zhongguo dianshi* 中国电视 1 (2009): 11–13.

52. Shen Yun and Zhang Yonghua 沈芸 张咏华, "Chonggou zuzhi jiegou he jiazhilian yi chuangzao jingzheng you shi—fang Shanghai wen guang xinwen chuanmei jituan zongcai Li Rui gang" 重构组织结构和价值链以创造竞争优势—访上海文广新闻传媒集团总裁黎瑞刚 [Reconstruct organization structure and value chain to create competitive advantage—interview with Li Ruigang, president of Shanghai Wen Guang Xinwen Chuanmei Group], *Zhongguo guangbo dianshi xue kan* 中国广播电视学刊 5 (2006): 22–25.

53. Ying Zhu, *Two billion Eyes*, 206.

54. Zhang Xin and Yu Tao 张欣 于涛, "Xiju lanhai-tansuo Guizhou weishi dianshiju fazhan zhi lu" 喜剧蓝海-探索贵州卫视电视剧发展之路 [The blue sea of comedies: Exploring the development of Guizhou television station], *Guizhou dianshi* 贵州电视, 32–35.

55. Li Xinmin 李新民, "Yi shuzi hua daidong chanye shixian Guizhou guangbo dianshi de xin kuayue—zai sheng guangdian ju wenhua tizhi gaige he wenhua chanye fazhan dongyuan hui shang baogao" 以数字化带动产业化实现贵州广播电视的新跨越—在省广电局文化体制改革和文化产业发展动员会上的报告 [Promote industrialization through digitalization in order to materialize the new leap of Guizhou radio and television—report on mobilization conference for institutionally reforming the Provincial Administration of Broadcast and Culture], *Guizhou ribao* 贵州日报, September 21, 2006, 007.

56. Bai Fangqin 白芳芹, "Ju'ansiwei fenfatuqiang wei shixian qiang tai zhi meng bu xie nuli—zai Guizhou dianshitai 2009 nian gongzuo zongjie huiyi shang de jianghua" 居安思危奋发图强为实现强台之梦不懈努力—在贵州电视台2009年工作总结

会议上的讲话 [Thinking of adversity in prosperity, working with stamina and diligence, for realizing the dream of a stronger television station—address on the closing meeting of Guizhou television station in 2009], *Xinwen chang* 新闻窗 2 (2010): 4–9.

57. Zhao Huayong 赵化勇, "Zai zhongyang dianshitai 2005 nian gongzuo huiyi shang de baogao" 在中央电视台2005年工作会议上的报告 [Summary of the speech on CCTV Work Conference in mid-2005], *TV Research* 电视研究 8 (2005): 5–10.

58. Haitao Zhang 张海涛, "Zhongguo guangbo dianshi shuzihua de fazhan zhi lu" 中国广播电视数字化的发展之路 [The development road of digital broadcasting in China], *TV Research* 电视研究 10 (2004): 6–8.

59. Huang Yan, Chen Guang, and Peng Zhenyi 黄燕, 陈钢, 彭祯艺, "Shuzi dianshi meiyou shijianbiao," 数字电视没有时间表 [Digital TV has no timeline], *Hulianwang zhoukan* 互联网周刊 44 (December 22, 2003): 25–33.

60. Interview by author, May 2014. This person requested anonymity.

61. Xu Xiaoqing 许晓青, "Dazao Zhongguo tese guoji shiye de chuanmei pinpai" 打造中国特色国际视野的传媒品牌 [Build a media brand with Chinese characteristics and international vision], *Xinhua News*, August 9, 2010, accessed May 22, 2016, http://www.smg.cn/review/201008/0163011.shtml.

62. Li Ruigang 黎瑞刚, "Cong xinwen guancha kan dianshi xinwen lanmu zhipianren zhi," 从《新闻观察》看电视新闻栏目制片人制 [Review the system of column producer in television news from "News Observation"], *Xinwen jizhe* 新闻记者 9 (1998): 17–20.

63. Follow-up interview by author, July 2, 2015.

64. Wang Xiaoxi 王小溪, "Qianjing kanhao rencai nanqiu zhong shu chuanmei shou bian fufei dianshi rencai," 前景看好人才难求中数传媒收编付费电视人才 [Positive prospect, difficult head-hunting, China DTV Media takes in talent from pay TV], *Beijing qingnian bao* 北京青年报, May 10, 2004, accessed July 1, 2015, http://news.xinhuanet.com/newmedia/2004-05/10/content_1460222.htm.

65. Zheng Na 郑娜, "Dianshi de 'zi mao qu gaige'" 电视的"自贸区改革" [The "free trade area reform" of television], *Renmin ribao haiwai ban* 人民日报海外版, 8, April 11, 2014, accessed July 15, 2015, http://paper.people.com.cn/rmrbhwb/html/2014-04/11/content_1413877.htm; follow-up interview by author, July 2, 2015.

66. Yuezhi Zhao, *Communication in China*, 84.

67. "Ni bu zhidao de yangshi xinchou tixi" 你不知道的央视薪酬体系 [CCTV's salary system that you do not know], *Sohu*, August 13, 2014, accessed October 1, 2014, http://news.sohu.com/s2014/dianji-1469/.

68. Zhang Rui 张锐, "2012 nian Zhongguo chuanmei ye rongzi shangshi baogao" 2012年中国传媒业融资上市报告 [Report on Chinese media industry's financing and listing: 2012], *Xue li shenshi* 学理审视 2 (2013): 39–42.

69. Gabriel Wildau, "China Kicks Off Second Round of Privatisations," *Financial Times*, August 10, 2014.

70. Yuezhi Zhao, "Caught," 41–66.

71. Lin Chun, *China and Global Capitalism*.

72. Ai Huang, "A Study of the Conceptual Framework of Policies for China's Public Service Based on New Media," paper presented at the International Conference on Communication and Global Power Shifts, Communication University of China, Beijing, October 12–13, 2012.

73. Bao Ran and Wang Yun 包冉 汪云, "Guizhou de zhi yu xing" 贵州的知与行 [Guizhou's knowledge and practice], *Zhongguo shuzi dianshi* 中国数字电视 50 (November 2008): 47–50.

74. Wang and Bao, "Hangzhou," 34–41; Lu Chen 鲁晨, "Hua shu chuanmei 2014 zhongqi jing li 1.67 yi tong bi zeng 23 percent" 华数传媒2014中期净利1.67亿同比增23 percent [Wasu Media's interim net profit in 2014 reaches 167,000,000 RMB, up by 23 percent over last year], *Zongyijia* 综艺+ August 30, 2014, accessed October 1, 2014, http://www.zongyijia.com/News/News_info?id=25132; "Hua shu fu zongcai Qiao Xiaoyan: guangdian yunyingshang ruhe yingdui OTT tiaozhan" 华数副总裁乔小燕:广电运营商如何应对OTT挑战 [Wasu's vice president Qiao Xiaoyan: How broadcast operators deal with OTT challenges], *Meijie zazhi* 媒介杂志 August 25, 2014, accessed October 1, 2014, http://www.zongyijia.com/News/News_info?id=24882.

75. Zhou Ting 周婷, "Fufei dianshi pindao xin shangye moshi" 付费电视频道新商业模式 [Pay-TV channels as the new business model], *Zhongguo zhengquan bao* 中国证券报 January 31, 2007, accessed October 1, 2014, http://it.sohu.com/20070131/n247956500.shtml.

76. Luo Weilan 罗伟兰, "Guonei fufei pindao de shangye moshi tan xi" 国内付费频道的商业模式探析 [Exploring and evaluating domestic pay-TV channels' business model], *Zhongguo shuzi dianshi* 中国数字电视 19 (January–February, 2006): 98–101.

77. Mure Dickie, "Problems Threaten Success of China's Digital Pay TV," *Financial Times*, August 27, 2004.

78. Gao Mian 高棉, "Guanyu fufei dianshi fazhan de jidian sikao" 关于付费电视发展的几点思考 [Some thoughts on the Pay TV development], *TV Research* 电视研究 11 (2004): 39–40.

79. Cao Qian 曹倩, "Dianshi chuanmei chanye fazhan qian xi" 电视传媒产业发展浅析 [Analyses of TV media industry development], *TV Research* 电视研究 8 (2004): 28–29.

80. Zhang Haitao 张海涛, "Jiakuai shishi shuzihua gongcheng dali tuidong xiandaihua zhuanbian" 加快实施数字化工程 大力推动现代化转变 [Accelerate the implementation of digitalization project and vigorously to promote the change of modernization], *TV Research* 电视研究 7 (2007): 5–6.

81. Shen Rui and Huang Meiruan 申睿 黄梦阮, "Goujian xibu chengshi shuzi dianshi chanyelian" 构建西部城市数字电视产业链 [Construct digital television industry chain in western cities], *Xibu dianshi* 西部电视 3 (2006): 52–53.

82. Guideline Research, "2013 nian 2 yue de Zhongguo youxian shuzi dianshi yonghu dadao 14236.9 wan hu" 2013年2月底中国有线数字电视用户达到14236.9万户 [At the end of February 2013, China's digital television reaches 142,369,000 households], *Zhongguo shuzi* dianshi 中国数字电视 99 (April 2013): 27.

83. Shen and Huang, "Gou jian," 52–53.

84. Li Xinmin 李新民, "Yi xinxihua shuzihua shixian Guizhou youxiandianshi chanyehua de xin kuayue" 以信息化数字化实现贵州有线电视产业化的新跨越 [Promote industrialization through digitalization in order to materialize the new leap of Guizhou radio and television], *Qin qian zaixian—Guizhou ribao* 金黔在线—贵州日报, October 9, 2006, accessed October 1, 2014, http://info.broadcast.hc360.com/2006/10/09172794614.shtml.

85. Xinhua Net 新华网, "Guangdian 'he wang' beihou de liyi boyi" 广电"合网"背后的利益博弈 [Benefit game behind the "network integration" of radio and cable TV], *Time Message* 时代信报, July 24, 2008, accessed February 20, 2016, http://www.cq.xinhuanet.com/2008-07/24/content_13916985.htm.

86. Xinhua Net 新华网, "Yuan jiaoqu xian shuzi dianshi zhengti zhuanhuan huanhuan tuikai damen" 远郊区县数字电视整体转换缓缓推开大门 [The overall conversion of digital TV has gradually started in the remote suburbs], *Chongqing Evening Post* 重庆晚, July 28, 2008, accessed February 20, 2016, http://www.cq.xinhuanet.com/news/2008-07/28/content_13947881_1.htm.

87. Zuo Shuguang and Zhang Yi 左曙光张一, "Wangluo zhenghe tuijin Chongqing guangdian chanyehua" 网络整合推进重庆广电产业化 [Integrated network promotes the industrialization of Chongqing's broadcasting industry], *Xibu dianshi* 西部电视 5 (2008): 23–26.

88. Jia Yuntao and Zhao Qiang 贾云涛 赵强, "IPTV OTT TV dui youxian dianshi yunying fenxi ji yingdui celue de sikao" IPTV OTT TV 对有线电视运营影响分析及应对策略的思考 [Analysis of the impact of IPTV, OTT, TV on cable TV, and strategic thinking], *Zhongguo shuzi dianshi* 中国数字电视 102–3 (July–August 2013): 30–35.

89. Chen Jinlong 陈金龙, "Qian yi xianji dianshitai xianzhuang ji fazhan celue" 浅议县级电视台现状及发展策略 [A brief discussion on the status quo and developmental strategy of county television stations], *Xibu guangbo dianshi* 西部广播电视 2 (2014): 105–6; Tingde Yang 杨廷德, "Qian xi xian tai jiemu zai xiangzhen tongbu bochu he kuoda fugai" 浅析县台节目在乡镇同步播出和扩大覆盖 [Analysis of the township simulcast and coverage expansion of programs of county-level television stations], *People's Daily Online*, December 29, 2011, accessed March 6, 2016, http://media.people.com.cn/GB/22114/157392/237097/16753733.html.

90. Wu Xingchen and Wang Yihe 吴星晨 王一赫, "Xianji dianshitai fazhan xianzhuang yanjiu—yi Hebei Shanxi wu jia xianji dianshitai wei li," 县级电视台发展现状研究—以河北山西五家县级电视台为例 [Study on the development of county television stations—five cases from Hebei and Shanxi], *Xinwen tiandi* 新闻天地 6 (2011): 72–73.

91. Ministry of Finance, "Zhongyang caizheng 2014 nian anpai zijin 208 yi yuan zhichi goujian xiandai gonggong wenhua fuwu tixi" 中央财政2014年安排资金208亿元支持构建现代公共文化服务体系 [State central budgets to spend 20.8 billion yuan to support modern public cultural service systems], February 11, 2015, accessed August 10, 2015, http://jkw.mof.gov.cn/zhengwuxinxi/tourudongtai/201502/

t20150210_1191020.html; SARFT, "Tian Jin chuxi goujian xiandai gonggong wenhua fuwu tixi jianshe zuotanhui" 田进出席构建现代公共文化服务体系建设座谈会 [Tian Jin attends the conference on building modern public cultural service systems], May 7, 2015, accessed August 10, 2015, http://www.sarft.gov.cn/art/2015/5/7/art_112_26453.html.

92. Winseck, "Netscapes of Power," 2002.

93. Henry L. Hu, "The Political Economy of Governing ISPs in China: Perspectives of Net Neutrality and Vertical Integration," *China Quarterly* 207 (2011): 523–40.

94. Aihwa Ong, *Neoliberalism as Exception: Mutations in Citizenship and Sovereignty* (Durham: Duke University Press, 2006).

95. Angang Hu, "Government Transition and Public Finance in China," in *30 Years of Economic Transition in China*, ed. Fang Cai (Beijing: Social Science Academic Press, 2009), 151–92; Ling Li, Qiulin Chen, and Dillon Powers, "Chinese Healthcare Reform: A Shift toward Social Development," *Modern China* 38, 6 (2012): 630–45.

Chapter 6. Building Network Nation

The title of this chapter is borrowed from Richard R. John, *Network Nation: Inventing American Telecommunications* (Cambridge: Belknap Press of Harvard University Press, 2010).

1. "Guojia xinwen chuban guangdian zongju fabu 2014 nian guangdian lanpishu" 国家新闻出版广电总局发布2014年广电蓝皮书 [State Administration of Press, Publication, Radio, Film, and Television of the PRC issued the 2014 blue book of radio and television], July 9, 2014, accessed October 1, 2014, http://tv.sohu.com/20140709/n402007288.shtml; MIIT, "2014 nian 9 yuefen tongxin ye jingji yunxing qingkuang" 2014年9月份通信业经济运行情况 [Economic conditions and operations of telecom industry in September 2014], October 21, 2014, accessed May 22, 2016, http://www.miit.gov.cn/n1146312/n1146904/n1648372/c3336963/content.html; CNNIC, "Zhongguo hulianwang fazhan zhuangkuang tongji baogao" 中国互联网发展状况统计报告 [Statistical report on internet development in China], July 2014, accessed July 15, 2015, http://www.cnnic.cn/hlwfzyj/hlwxzbg/hlwtjbg/201407/P020140721507223212132.pdf.

2. Martin Hart-Landsberg, *Capitalist Globalization: Consequences, Resistance, and Alternatives* (New York: Monthly Review, 2013).

3. Bao Zhengbin 鲍政斌, "Jianli shiying xiandai tongxin fazhan de xin jizhi" 建立适应现代通信发展的新机制 [Establish new mechanism to adapt to modern telecommunication development], *Youdian qiye guanli* 邮电企业管理 4 (1998): 14–15.

4. Li Na 丽娜, "Nei yuan rongzi: buying hushi zijin qudao" 内源融资:不应忽视的资金渠道 [Internal financing, a capital channel ought not to be neglected], *Tongxin qiye guanli* 通信企业管理 10 (2003): 13–16; He Wei 何伟, "Zhongguo kuandai zhanlue ji zhengce sikao" 中国宽带战略及政策思考 [Some thoughts on China's broadband strategies and policies], *Xinxi tongxin jishu* 信息通信技术 1 (2011): 12–17.

5. Margaret M. Pearson, "Governing the Chinese Economy: Regulatory Reform in the Service of the State," *Public Administration Review* 67, 4 (2007): 718–30.

6. Shi Zhiliang 施智梁, "Guo zi wei yanjiu zhongxin zhuren: guo qi buneng tuichu jingzheng xing lingyu" 国资委研究中心主任: 国企不能退出竞争性领域 [Chairman of State-Owned Assets Supervision and Administration Commission: State enterprises will not withdraw from competitive fields], *Caijing* 财经网, August 27, 2014, accessed January 1, 2015, http://column.caijing.com.cn/20140827/3675674.shtml.

7. Barry Naughton, "SASAC and Rising Corporate Power in China," *China Leadership Monitor* 24, 2 (2008), accessed July 15, 2015, http://www.hoover.org/research/sasac-and-rising-corporate-power-china.

8. Dan Schiller, *Digital Depression: Information Technology and Economic Crisis* (Urbana: University of Illinois Press, 2014), 92.

9. Su Deyue 苏德悦, "Gongxinbu jiakuai tuijin guojia xinxi xiaofei shi dian gongzuo" 工信部加快推进国家信息消费试点工作 [MIIT promotes state point-specific experiment on information consumption], *Renmin youdian bao* 人民邮电 1, September 22, 2014, accessed July 15, 2015, http://news.xinhuanet.com/info/2014-09/22/c_133661756.htm.

10. "Li Yanhong: jiaoyu ziyuan ying mianfei shangwang" 李彦宏: 教育资源应免费上网 [Li Yanhong: Education resources will go online free], *Zhongguo guangbo wang* 中国广播网, March 10, 2014, accessed July 1, 2015, http://news.cnr.cn/special/2014lh/ljr/q11/zy/201403/t20140310_515041615.shtml; "Li Yining Chen Xiwen Li Yanhong deng jizhehui zhibo" 厉以宁陈锡文李彦宏等记者会直播 [Live broadcast of Li Yining, Chen Xiwen, and Li Yanhong's press conference], *People.com.cn* 人民, March 6, 2014, accessed July 15, 2015, http://topics.caixin.com/2014-03-06/100647661.html.

11. Scott Roxborough, "MIPCOM: Chinese Online Video Pioneer Charles Zhang Tells TV Broadcasters to Quit," *The Hollywood Reporter*, October 14, 2014, accessed July 15, 2015, http://www.hollywoodreporter.com/news/mipcom-chinese-online-video-pioneer-740653.

12. Clifford Coonan, "China's Youku Tudou Launches Film Division," *The Hollywood Reporter*, August 28, 2014, accessed July 15, 2015, http://www.hollywoodreporter.com/news/chinas-youku-tudou-launches-film-728794; "Busan: China's Online Movie Revenues Forecast to Match Box Office in Five Years," *The Hollywood Reporter*, October 6, 2014, accessed July 15, 2015, http://www.hollywoodreporter.com/news/busan-chinas-online-movie-revenues-738274; "China's Alibaba Pictures, Hengdian Studios to Form Film, TV Joint Ventures," *The Hollywood Reporter*, October 14, 2014, accessed July 15, 2015, http://www.hollywoodreporter.com/news/chinas-alibaba-pictures-hengdian-studios-740601.

13. Clifford Coonan, "China's Radio, Film, TV Industries Hit $60 billion in Revenue in 2013," *The Hollywood Reporter*, July 11, 2014, accessed July 15, 2015, http://www.hollywoodreporter.com/news/china-s-radio-film-tv-717941.

14. Lin Chun, *China and Global Capitalism*.

15. D. Schiller, *Digital Depression*.

16. Zhou Liwen 周丽雯, "Guanyu ru shi yilai Zhongguo duiwai maoyi yi cun du de tantao" 关于入世以来中国对外贸易依存度的探讨 [Discussion about China's

dependence on export since its entry into WTO], *Jinrong jingji* 金融经济, March 21, 2014, accessed July 11, 2015, http://125.71.236.88:81/show.asp?id=2786.

17. "2009 nian Zhongguo dianzi xinxi chanye huigu yu zhanwang" 2009年中国电子信息产业回顾与展望 [Review of and outlook from the mobile phone industry development in 2009], *CCIDNET*, January 19, 2010, accessed July 1, 2015, http://it.sohu.com/20100119/n269693753.shtml.

18. "2008 nian renli ziyuan he shehui baozhang shiye fazhan tongji gongbao" 2008年人力资源和社会保障事业发展统计公报 [Statistics report on the development of human resources and social security: 2008], National Bureau of Statistics, July 23, 2011, accessed July 1, 2015, http://www.stats.gov.cn/tjsj/tjgb/qttjgb/qgqttjgb/200905/t20090519_30639.html.

19. Zhang Qianqian and Li Enping 张倩倩 李恩平, "Zuidi gongzi biaozhun de xianzhuang fenxi yu quyu bijiao" 最低工资标准的现状分析与区域比较 [Analysis of minimum wages and regional comparison], *Zhongguo laodong* 中国劳动 7 (2013): 12.

20. "Guojia tongji ju juzhang Ma Jiantang jiu 2013 nian quannian guo min jingji yunxing qingkuang da jizhe wen" 国家统计局局长马建堂就2013年全年国民经济运行情况答记者问 [Ma Jiantang, commissioner of National Bureau of Statistics, answered journalists' questions concerning the national economy in 2013], *National Bureau of Statistics*, January 20, 2014, accessed October 1, 2014, http://www.stats.gov.cn/tjgz/tjdt/201401/t20140120_502414.html; "2014 nian quanguo nongmingong jiance diaocha baogao" 2014年全国农民工监测调查报告 [2014 monitoring and research report of national migrant workers], *National Bureau of Statistics*, April 29, 2015, accessed March 6, 2016, http://www.stats.gov.cn/tjsj/zxfb/201504/t20150429_797821.html; Bai Tianliang 白天亮, "Quanguo jumin renjun ke zhipei shouru zengsu lianxu liangnian pao ying GDP nongmingong yuejun shouru tupo 3000 yuan" 全国居民人均可支配收入增速连续两年跑赢GDP农民工月均收入突破3000元 [Growth of per capita disposable income of national residents has outpaced the GDP growth for two years: The average monthly income of migrant workers exceeds 3,000 yuan], *People's Daily Online*, January 20, 2016, accessed March 6, 2016, http://society.people.com.cn/n1/2016/0120/c1008-28068399.html.

21. "Monthly Analysis of U.S.-China Trade Data," *U.S.-China Economic and Security Review Commission*, November 4, 2015, accessed March 6, 2016, http://origin.www.uscc.gov/sites/default/files/Research/December%202015%20Trade%20Bulletin.pdf.

22. Wang Baobing 王宝滨, "Zhongguo touzi gao su zengzhang buke chixu" 中国投资高速增长不可持续 [China's fast-speed increase of investment is unsustainable], *National Bureau of Statistics*, February 20, 2014, accessed July 15, 2015, http://www.stats.gov.cn/tjzs/tjsj/tjcb/dysj/201402/t20140220_513673.html; "2011 nian guomin jingji yunxing qingkuang xinwen fabu hui da jizhe wen" 2011年国民经济运行情况新闻发布会答记者问 [Answering journalists' questions at press conference concerning the national economy in year 2011], *National Bureau of Statistics*, January 17, 2012, accessed October 1, 2014, http://www.stats.gov.cn/tjgz/tjdt/201201/t20120117_17639.html.

23. "Guojia tongji ju juzhang Ma Jiantang jiu 2013 nian quannian guomin jingji yunxing qingkuang da jizhe wen" 国家统计局局长马建堂就2013年全年国民经济运行情况答记者问, National Bureau of Statistics; Ren Xiao 任晓, "2015 nian GDP zengzhang 6.9% hongguan zhengce renyou kuansong kongjian" 2015年GDP增长6.9% 宏观政策任由宽松空间 [GDP grew at 6.9 percent in 2015, and macroeconomic policy has space for more liberalization], *Zhongguo zhengquan bao* 中国证券报, *People.cn*, January 20, 2016 accessed May 22, 2016, http://finance.people.com.cn/n1/2016/0120/c1004-28068600.html.

24. Li Deshui 李德水, "Zhongguo 'chaozhong' jingji zheng guo kaner" 中国 "超重"经济正过坎儿 [China's "overweighed" economy is trying to get through], *China Economy and Informatization* 中国经济和信息化 15, August 13, 2014, accessed July 1, 2015, http://www.chinaeinet.com/article/detail.aspx?id=9023.

25. Li Hong 李宏, "Chanye jiegou tiaozheng yao kaolv jiuye zengzhangdian" 产业结构调整要考虑就业增长点 [Taking employment increase into consideration in the industrial restructuring], *Zhongguo laodong* 中国劳动 8 (2011): 8.

26. Jiang Zhifeng 姜学霞, "Gao jineng rencai chengzhang huanjing yingzao fanglue" 高技能人才成长环境营造方略 [Thoughts on promoting the employment of college students in an economic transformation period], *Zhongguo laodong* 中国劳动 12 (2011): 27.

27. D. Schiller, *Digital Depression*, 240.

28. Wang Yunhui 王运辉, "Yunyingshang jiceng yuangong diaocha: xianshi yu xiwang" 运营商基层员工调查：现实与希望 [Research on grassroots employees in telecom operation: Reality and hope], *Baijia.baidu.com* 百家, *Baijia*, August 14, 2014, accessed September 1, 2014, http://wyh.baijia.baidu.com/article/25963.

29. Lin Fen, "A Survey Report on Chinese Journalists in China," *The China Quarterly* 202, (2010): 421–34.

30. Zhao Baohua et al., 周葆华等 "Zhongguo wangluo xinwen congyezhe shengcun zhuangkuang diaocha baogao" 中国网络新闻从业者生存状况调查报告 [Research report on Chinese internet journalists' conditions], *Yiben zhengjing* 一本政经, September 16, 2014, accessed October 1, 2014, http://chuansong.me/n/678347.

31. "Woguo jinming liangnian dianxin ye touzi youwang da xingao" 我国今明两年电信业投资有望达新高 [China expects a new peak of investment in telecommunication industry in the coming two years], *ICCSZ*, January 27, 2014, accessed September 1, 2014, http://www.iccsz.com/site/cn/News/2014/01/27/20140127012853047600.htm; "'Shi yi wu' qijian dianxinye guding zichan touzi nianjun jin 3000 yi yuan" 十一五期间电信业固定资产投资年均近3000亿元 [Annual investment in fixed assets of telecom industry approximated 300 billion yuan during "the eleventh five-year plan"], *China Association of Communications Enterprises*, April 2, 2011, accessed May 22, 2016, http://www.cace.org.cn/2011-03/30/content_865703.htm. The exchange rate used in this volume for events from 2006 to 2010 is about US$1 to Chinese yuan 7.2 and from 2011 to 2013, 6.3.

32. "China Mobile: Base Stations Amounts to 1.8 million by End of 2014, with Huge Power Consumption," *C114*, June 26, 2014, accessed September 1, 2014, http://www

.cn-c114.net/576/a844124.html; Zhang Peng 张鹏, "Jujiao yunyingshang zhuanxing zhi kun: OTT yewu tuwei yu guoyou zhidu jiesuo" 聚焦运营商转型之困: OTT业务突围与国有制度解锁 [Focus on the difficulty of transforming operations: OTT's business breakthrough and the unlocking of state ownership], *Tongxin shijie* 通信世界 26 (October 16, 2014).

33. Wang Zheng and Xin Miao 王政 辛苗, "Zhongguo yidong xuanbu 4G yonghu tupo 1 yi hu" 中国移动宣布4G用户突破一亿户 [China Mobile announced 4G subscribers passed 1 million], *People's Daily*, February 16, 2015, accessed May 22, 2016, http://media.people.com.cn/n/2015/0216/c40606-26573466.html.

34. "2015 naan guo min jingji he shehui fazhan tongji gongbao" 2015年国民经济和社会发展统计公报 [2015 statistics bulletin of national economic and social development], *National Bureau of Statistics*, February 29, 2016, accessed March 11, 2016, http://www.stats.gov.cn/tjsj/zxfb/201602/t20160229_1323991.html.

35. Hu Hu 胡虎, "Fazhan jingji xinxi yao cong wangshang lai! Wang xin ban dianshang tan hui huhang shuang 11" 发展经济信息要从网上来！网信办电商谈会护航双11 [Information for developing economy comes from the internet!], *Renmin youdian* 人民邮电, November 10, 2014, accessed October 1, 2014, http://www.cnii.com.cn/informatization/2014-11/10/content_1475484_2.htm; "2015 nian shuang 11 jieshu alibaba xiaoshoue wei guo qian yi" 2015年双11结束 阿里巴巴销售额未过千亿 [Double 11 ends for 2015, Alibaba's sales do not exceed 100 billion yuan], *Tencent Finance*, November 12, 2015, accessed March 6, 2016, http://finance.qq.com/a/20151112/000722.htm.

36. Sophia Yan, "China Spend billions in World's Biggest Online Shopping Day," *CNN*, November 11, 2014, accessed September 1, 2015, http://money.cnn.com/2014/11/10/investing/alibaba-singles-day-china//.

37. Su, "MIIT."

38. Li Xiaotong 李小彤, "Kuaidiyuan quanyi weihu duanban yin he er sheng" 快递员权益维护短板因何而生 [Why the rights and interests of delivery staff become the weak link?], *Zhongguo laodong baozhang bao* 中国劳动保障报, October 28, 2014, accessed January 1, 2015, http://www.clssn.com/html1/report/10/7982-1.htm.

39. "2013 nian dianzi xinxi chanye tongji gongbao" 2013年电子信息产业统计公报 [Public report on electronic information industry 2013], *MIIT*, March 4, 2014, accessed May 22, 2016, http://www.miit.gov.cn/n1146312/n1146904/n1648355/c3335511/content.html.

40. Qu Weiping 屈伟平, "Dianzi zhizao chanye jing qi du xiahua bing chengxian jiegou xing fazhan jihui" 电子制造产业景气度下滑并呈现结构性发展机会 [Electronics manufacturing falls yet encounters structural development opportunities], *Zhongguo jichengdianlu* 中国集成电路 112 (2008): 67–73.

41. "Zhongguo dianxin fu zongjingli Yang Xiaowei: tuidong zishen hulianwang hua" 中国电信副总经理杨小伟:推动自身互联网化 [Vice president of China Mobile Yang Xiaowei: Internetize China Mobile] *Renmin youdian* 人民邮电, September 23, 2014, accessed October 1, 2014, http://www.c114.net/news/117/a859955.html.

42. Charles Babcock, "IBM Building 'Smarter City' Cloud in China," *Information Week*, September 25, 2009, retrieved from LexisNexis.

43. "China Sees Future in Cloud Computing Technology," *BBC Monitoring Asia Pacific*, 2011.

44. Lin Jing and Su Zhou, "Looking towards the Clouds," *China Daily European Edition*, September 1, 2012, retrieved from LexisNexis.

45. Wang Chunhui 王春晖, "Jingti shuju zhongxin channeng guosheng xianxiang" 警惕数据中心产能过剩现象 [Be cautious about oversupply of data-center capacity], *Xinhua News*, April 15, 2016, accessed May 27, 2016, http://news.xinhuanet.com/info/2016-04/15/c_135280482.htm.

46. Leigh Ann Ragland, Joseph McReynolds, Matthew Southerland, and James Mulvenon, "Red Cloud Rising: Cloud Computing in China," *U.S.-China Economic and Security Review Commission*, September 5, 2013, accessed September 1, 2014, http://www.uscc.gov/sites/default/files/Research/DGI_Red%20Cloud%20Rising_2014.pdf.

47. Su Deyue 苏德悦, "Gongxinbu dianxin yanjiuyuan yuanzhang Cao Shumin: Hulianwang yu gongye ronghe yinfa xinyilun chanye biange" 工信部电信研究院院长曹淑敏：互联网与工业融合引发新一轮产业变革 [Director of China Academy of Telecommunications Research under MII Cao Shumin: Convergence between internet and industry triggers industrial revolution], *Renmin youdian bao* 人民邮电, August 28, 2014, accessed July 15, 2015, http://www.chinatelecom.com.cn/tech/hot/sd/yj/t20140828_120218.html.

48. "2013 nian zhongguo gongye tongxin ye yunxing baogao" 2013年中国工业通信业运行报告 [Operation report on China's industry and telecom industry 2013], *MIIT*, December 30, 2013, accessed May 23, 2016, http://big5.gov.cn/gate/big5/www.gov.cn/banshi/2014-01/09/content_2563156.htm.

49. Ibid.

50. National Development and Reform Commission, "Nongcun kuandai pujilv jin 6.3% 2020 nian 98% xingzhengcun tong kuandai" 农村宽带普及率仅6.3% 2020年98%行政村通宽带 [Broadband penetration rate in villages is only 6.3 percent; 98% of villages will have broadband by 2020], *Chinanews* 中国新闻网, August 19, 2013, accessed October 1, 2014, http://www.chinanews.com/gn/2013/08-19/5176301.shtml.

51. Montnets 梦网科技, "Kuandai zhongguo zhanlue zijin jiang luodi nongcun shichang; nan duanqi jianxiao" 宽带中国战略资金将落地农村市场 难短期见效 ["Broadband China" beginning to serve the rural market; hardly effective in the short run], September 5, 2014, accessed March 12, 2016, http://www.montnets.com/cn/article-details-106.html.

52. D. Schiller, *Digital Depression*, 73.

53. David L. Shambaugh, *China Goes Global: The Partial Power* (New York: Oxford University Press, 2013).

54. Hart-Landsberg, *Capitalist Globalization*.

55. "2013 nian jisuanji hangye niandu baogao," 2013年计算机行业年度报告 [Annual report on computer industry 2013], MIIT, March 11, 2014, accessed July 1,

2015, http://www.miit.gov.cn/n11293472/n11293832/n11294132/n12858387/15918275.html.

56. China Academy of Telecommunication Research, MIIT, "Tongxin shebei chanye baipishu," 通信设备产业白皮书 (2014) [White book on telecommunication equipment industry], *MIIT*, May 2014, accessed May 23, 2016, http://www.miit.gov.cn/n1146312/n1146909/n1146991/n1648536/c3489509/part/3489510.pdf.

57. Ibid., 3.

58. Ibid., 23.

59. "Enterprise Router Market's Strong Q4 in China Not Enough to Offset Global Declines," *Infonetics Research*, April 1, 2015, accessed March 6, 2016, http://www.infonetics.com/pr/2015/4Q14-Enterprise-Routers-Market-Highlights.asp.

60. MIIT, "2013 nian shouji hangye fazhan qingkuang huigu yu zhanwang" 2013年手机行业发展情况回顾与展望 [Review of and outlook from the mobile phone industry development in 2013], *C114.com* 中国通信网, March 7, 2013, accessed May 23, 2016, http://www.c114.net/market/186/a825050.html.

61. Chen Baoliang, "Controversy."

62. MIIT, "2013 nian jisuanji hangye niandu baogao" 2013年计算机行业年度报告 [Annual report on computer industry 2013], *gmw.com* 光明网, May 23, 2016, accessed July 1, 2015, http://tech.gmw.cn/2014-03/11/content_10646210.htm.

63. Liu Juhua and Zheng Shuyang 刘菊花郑舒杨, "Gongxinbu: yuzhuang zhengban caozuoxitong ruanjian shuliang bili zhunian tigao" 工信部:预装正版操作系统软件数量比例逐年提高 [MIIT: Proportion of preinstalled legitimate copies of operation systems increases each year], *Xinhua News* 17, August 2012, accessed May 23, 2016, http://www.cctime.com/html/2012-7-19/2012719911489362.htm.

64. Jin Kai, "Why China Banned Windows 8," *The Diplomat*, May 28, 2014, accessed September 1, 2014, http://thediplomat.com/2014/05/why-china-banned-windows-8/.

65. Wang Feng 王峰, "Zhongguo wangluo anquan chanye yingtouganshang" 中国网络安全产业正迎头赶上 [Chinese internet security industry is catching up], *21st Century Business Herald* 21世纪财经报道, September 11, 2014, accessed May 23, 2016, http://m.21jingji.com/article/20140911/herald/7923f746dc9b37a9667615445eab04d5.html.

66. *Asian Development Outlook Update: Asia in Global Value Chains* (Mandaluyong City, Philippines: 2014), *Asian Development Bank*, 68, 42, accessed September 1, 2014, http://www.adb.org/publications/asian-development-outlook-2014-update-asia-global-value-chains.

67. Stephen J. Ezell and Robert D. Atkins, "How ITA Expansion Benefits the Chinese and Global Economies," *Information Technology & Innovation Foundation*, April 2014, accessed July 30, 2105, http://www2.itif.org/2014-ita-expansion-benefits-chinese-global-economies.pdf.

68. Iacob Koch-Weser, "Should China Join the WTO's Services Agreement," *USCC Economic Issue Brief* 1 (March 11, 2014), *U.S.-China Economic and Security Review Commission*, accessed July 30, 2015, http://www.uscc.gov/Research/should-china-join-wto's-services-agreement.

69. Faqin Lin, Hsiao Chink Tang, and Lin Wang, "The Nexus between Antidumping Petitions and Exports during the Global Financial Crisis: Evidence on the People's Republic of China," *Asian Development Bank Working Paper Series on Regional Economic Integration* 131 (May 2014), accessed September 1, 2014, http://aric.adb.org/pdf/workingpaper/WP131_Lin_Tang_Wang_Nexus_Between_Antidumping.pdf.

70. "Monthly Summary of U.S.-China Trade Data," *U.S.-China Economic and Security Review Commission*, January 8, 2014, accessed September 1, 2014, http://origin.www.uscc.gov/sites/default/files/trade_bulletins/January%202014%20Trade%20Bulletin.pdf; "Monthly Analysis of U.S.-China Trade Data," *U.S.-China Economic and Security Review Commission*, November 4, 2015, accessed May 23, 2016, http://origin.www.uscc.gov/sites/default/files/trade_bulletins/November%20Trade%20Bulletin%202015.pdf.

71. "2014 nian Zhongguo duiwai maoyi fazhan huanjing fenxi" 2014年中国对外贸易发展环境分析 [Analysis on the developmental environment of China foreign trade 2014], *Ministry of Commerce*, October 30, 2013, accessed July 1, 2015, http://zhs.mofcom.gov.cn/article/Nocategory/201405/20140500570707.shtml.

72. Shambaugh, *China Goes Global*.

73. Yuezhi Zhao, "China's Quest for 'Soft Power': Imperatives, Impediments and Irreconcilable Tensions?" *Javnost—the Public* 20, 4 (2013): 17–29.

74. Zhang Xiaoming et al. 张晓明 等, "Tiaowang wenhua chanye xia yige fazhan zhouqi" 眺望文化产业下一个发展周期 [Look out to the next development cycle of cultural industry], *Zhongguo wenhua bao* 中国文化报, July 3, 2009, 5.

75. Liu Wei, "IMAX Expands China Operation," *China Daily*, April 22, 2014, retrieved from LexisNexis.

76. Ha Mai 哈麦, "Quanqiu 3D dianying baogao: zhiyou Zhongguo guanzhong ai bei keng" 全球3D电影报告:只有中国观众爱被坑 [Global 3D movie report: Only Chinese audiences are easy dupes], *yule.sohu* 搜狐娱乐, November 10, 2014, accessed July 15, 2015, http://yule.sohu.com/20141110/n405913193.shtml.

77. "2013–2014 Zhongguo dianying chanye yanjiu baogao (jian ban)" 2013–2014中国电影产业研究报告 (简版) [China Film Industry Report 2013–2014 (summary)], *Entgroup* 艺恩咨询, March 3, 2014, accessed July 15, 2015, http://www.entgroup.cn/report/f/0318120.shtml.

78. "Guojia xinwen chuban guangdian zongju fabu 2014 nian guangdian lanpishu" 国家新闻出版广电总局发布2014年广电蓝皮书.

79. Kyodo, "TV Program Exports Lag South Korea's," *The Japan Times*, April 23, 2014, accessed September 1, 2014, http://www.japantimes.co.jp/news/2014/04/23/business/economy-business/tv-program-exports-lag-south-koreas/#.VY2fQ1adLwI; "Korean Film Industry Logs Record Revenue in 2013," *BusinessKorea*, January 28, 2014, accessed September 4, 2015, http://www.businesskorea.co.kr/article/3096/movie-industry-korean-film-industry-logs-record-revenue-2013.

80. Xinhua Insight, "Film Industry Eyes More Success after Record Holiday Box Office," *China Daily Online*, February 22, 2016, accessed March 11, 2016, http://m.chinadaily.com.cn/en/2016-02/22/content_23584497.htm.

81. "Analysis: Global TV Industry on a Roll—MIPCOM Trade Show," *BBC Monitoring World Media*, October 13, 2006, retrieved from LexisNexis.

82. Andrew Jacobs, "Chinese TV Rules Limit Foreign Shows," *The International Herald Tribune*, February 15, 2012, retrieved from LexisNexis.

83. Chris Dodd, "Protect Intellectual Property Rights, Ingenuity," *Roll Call*, May 10, 2012, accessed October 1, 2014, http://www.rollcall.com/issues/57_133/Dodd-Protect-Intellectual-Property-Rights-Ingenuity-214390-1.html.

84. mtime, "Zhang Chaoyang cheng daoban zai Zhongguo yi si" 张朝阳称盗版在中国已死 [Zhang Chaoyang claimed that privacy had died in China], *cnBeta.com* 中文业界咨询站, October 15, 2014, accessed July 1, 2015, http://m.cnbeta.com/view_337089.htm.

85. "China Film Industry Report 2013–2014."

86. "2012–2013 nian Zhongguo wangmin wangluo shipin yingyong yanjiu baogao," 2012–2013年中国网民网络视频应用研究报告 [Chinese internet users' online video application use research report: 2013–14], *CNNIC*, June 2014, accessed September 1, 2014, http://www.cnnic.cn/hlwfzyj/hlwxzbg/spbg/201406/P020140609392906022556.pdf.

87. See also Shawn M. Powers and Michael Jablonski, *The Real Cyber War: The Political Economy of Internet Freedom* (Urbana: University of Illinois Press, 2015).

88. D. Schiller, *Digital Depression*.

89. Li Yuxiao 李欲晓, "Yi wangluo xin zhanlue di zhi baquan chouxing" 以网络新战略抵制霸权丑行 [Resist hegemony through new cyber strategy], *People's Daily* 人民日报, May 25, 2014, 5, http://data.people.com.cn.

90. Hong Shen, "Beyond Cyber-Sovereignty? China and Global Internet Governance, 1987–2012," paper presented at the International Communication Conference, Seattle, 2014.

91. Milton L. Mueller, *Networks and States: The Global Politics of Internet Governance* (Cambridge: MIT Press, 2010), Kindle edition.

92. Ibid.

93. National Telecommunications and Information Administration, "US Principles on the Internet's Domain Name and Addressing System," *US Department of Commerce*, June 30, 2005, accessed May 23, 2016, https://www.ntia.doc.gov/other-publication/2005/us-principles-internets-domain-name-and-addressing-system, cited in Mueller, *Networks and States*, 70.

94. Hong Shen, "Beyond Cyber-Sovereignty?"

95. "Zhao Houlin gaopiao dangxuan dianlian mishuzhang" 赵厚麟高票当选电联秘书长 [Zhao Houlin elected as secretary of International Telecommunication Union with a majority of votes], *Renmin youdian* 人民邮电, October 23, 2014, 1.

96. Houlin Zhao, "Internet Governance: A Personal Perspective," *Information Polity* 12, 1–2 (2007): 39–47.

97. "Jingti leng jing men cuisheng gelie" 警惕棱镜门催生割裂 [Be aware that the prism gate feeds fragmentation], *People's Daily* 人民日报, September 25, 2013, 3, http://data.people.com.cn.

98. "CNNIC zhuren Mao Wei: CN yuming shuliang dao 1000 wan cai heli," CNNIC 主任毛伟: CN域名数量到1000万才合理 [CNNIC director Mao Wei: It is only sensible when CN domain names reach 10 million], *CNNIC*, March 7, 2007, http://tech.sina.com.cn/i/2007-03-07/17331405744.shtml.

99. CNNIC, "China's statistical report . . . January 2016."

100. The State Council Information Office of the People's Republic of China 国务院新闻办公室, "Zhongguo hulianwang zhuangkuang" 中国互联网状况 [The internet in China (white paper)], June 9, 2010, 14, *Xinhuanet*, http://news.xinhuanet.com/politics/2010-06/08/c_12195221.htm. The exchange rate used in this volume for events from 1995 to 2009 is about US$1 to Chinese yuan 8.0.

101. Zuo An 左岸, "BT diaocha xianshi: IT sheshi kuifa zu'ai qiye zouchuqu" BT调查现实:IT设施匮乏阻碍企业走出去 [BT investigating reality: Lack of IT infrastructure prevents enterprises from "going out"], *CWW* 通信世界网, September 19, 2014, http://www.cww.net.cn/news/html/2014/9/18/2014918188406963.htm.

102. Qi Ming 齐鸣, "Zhongguo dianxin guoji gongsi qi sannian hou bi jian dingji yunyingshang" 中国电信国际公司期三年后比肩顶级运营商 [China Mobile international corporations will stand at par with top-notched operators three years later], *C114* 中国通信网, February 21, 2014, accessed July 1, 2015, http://www.c114.net/news/117/a821576.html.

103. Wayne Arnold, "Asians Take Tentative Steps towards Cloud Computing," *The International Herald Tribune*, October 12, 2010, 21, retrieved from LexisNexis; Bert Verschelde, "The Impact of Data Localization on China's Economy," *European Center for International Political Economy Bulletin*, July 2014, accessed September 1, 2014, http://www.ecipe.org/app/uploads/2014/12/ECIPE_bulletin714_dataloc_china.pdf.

104. "Promoting Cross-Border Information and Data Flows in the TPP: Building a Lasting Framework for Economic Growth and Jobs," *Business Roundtable*, accessed September 1, 2014, http://businessroundtable.org/sites/default/files/TPP_Promoting_Cross-Border_Information_Flows_Statement_0.pdf.

105. "China Unicom Looks to the World."

106. Hong Shen, "Beyond Cyber-Sovereignty?"

107. Tang Lan 唐岚, "Wangluo kongjian ji xu yizhang zhi xu zhi wang" 网络空间亟须一张秩序之网 [Cyberspace needs a network of order], *People's Daily*, July 26, 2013, 23, http://data.people.com.cn.

108. Mueller, *Networks and States*; Phillip Hallam-Baker, "The Geo-Politics of ICANN vs. ITU," *CircleID*, July 20, 2010, http://www.circleid.com/posts/the_geo_politics_of_icann_vs_itu/.

109. State Council Information Office, "Internet in China," 14.

110. "Zhongyang wang xin ban xian qi wangluo jiangguo tounao fengbao" 中央网信办掀起"网络强国"头脑风暴 [Cyberspace administration of China initiates the brainstorm on "strengthening the nation through internet"], *Zhongguo dianzi bao* 电子信息产业网, September 9, 2014, accessed July 1, 2015, http://yjs.cena.com.cn/2014-09/09/content_241853.htm.

111. Meng Jing, "'Made in China' Online Enterprises on Global Mission," *China Daily*, September 16, 2014.

112. "Jack Ma, Founder of Alibaba, Elected Co-chairman of Global Internet Governance Alliance," *Xinhua News*, July 1, 2015, accessed May 23, 2016, http://news.xinhuanet.com/english/2015-07/01/c_134373596.htm.

113. Homi Kharas and Geoffrey Gertz, "The New Global Middle Class: A Cross-Over from West to East," *Brookings*, March 2010, accessed July 15, 2015, http://www.brookings.edu/research/papers/2010/03/china-middle-class-kharas.

114. "Lu Wei zai diqijie zhongmei hulianwang luntan fabiao yanjiang" 鲁炜在第七届中美互联网论坛发表演讲 [Lu Wei spoke at the seventh US-China Internet Forum], *Xinhua News*, December 3, 2014, accessed September 1, 2015, http://news.xinhuanet.com/world/2014-12/03/c_1113493513.htm.

Conclusion

1. Walter and Howie, *Red Capitalism*.
2. Yuezhi Zhao, "Caught in the Web."
3. You-Tien Tsing, "Development as Culture: Human Development and Information Development in China," in *Reconceptualizing Development in the Global Information Age*, ed. Manuel Castells and Pekka Himanen (Oxford: Oxford University Press, 2014), 116–39.
4. Liu Ting 刘婷, "Wenhua lanpishu: wenhua xiaofei xuqiu zengzhang zhi hou yu jingjifazhan" 文化蓝皮书:文化消费需求增长滞后于经济发展 [Cultural blue book: The increase in cultural consumption demand lags behind economic development], *Beijing Morning Post*, April 10, 2014, accessed May 23, 2016, http://culture.people.com.cn/n/2014/0410/c22219-24870274.html.
5. Wang Yanan 王亚南, "Zhongguo renjun wenhua xiaofei wei 753.36 yuan zengzhang kongjian hezai" 中国人均文化消费为753.36元 增长空间何在? [Chinese per capita cultural consumption is 753.36 yuan; where is the room for growth?], *Guoming Daily* 光明日报, November 29, 2012, accessed May 23, 2016, http://www.chinanews.com/cul/2012/11-29/4370243.shtml.
6. D. Schiller, *Digital Capitalism*.
7. Jerry Harris, "To Be or Not to Be: The Nation-Centric World Order under Globalization," *Science & Society* 69, 3 (2005): 329–40.
8. Milton L. Mueller, "China and Global Internet Governance: A Tiger by the Tail," in *Access Contested: Security, Identity, and Resistance in Asian Cyberspace Information Revolution and Global Politics*, ed. Ronald Deibert (Cambridge: MIT Press, 2012), 177–94.
9. D. Schiller, *Digital Depression*.

Index

Accenture, 25
access technology, 71–74, 76–77
accumulation, 5, 151–52; cultural industry and, 107; digital capitalism and, 140; economic restructuring and, 129–30; geopolitics and, 145; low-wage model of, 149; mobile communications and, 88, 98; network convergence and, 114, 121; production and, 138; transnational corporations and, 146; western China and, 19–21. *See also* capital
Acer, 29
advertising, 103, 105, 109, 112, 118
Africa, 20, 137
agriculture, 22
Alcatel, 58, 86
Alibaba Group, 64, 144, 147; communication networks and, 127; economic restructuring and, 131; network convergence and, 116
All China Sports Federation, 64
Amazon, 144
Android operating system, 93–96, 135
antidumping investigations, 137. *See also* monopolies
antinetwork convergence policy, 109. *See also* network convergence
Apple, 93–94; handset manufacturing and, 91; transnational accumulation and, 145; vertical reintegration and, 31–32
applications, 64, 92–97; wireless and, 93–97
Asia, 2, 20–21, 134; broadband and, 59; China-only standard and, 87; communication networks and, 124; transnational accumulation and, 145; WTO and, 56
Asian Development Bank, 25, 136
Asian financial crisis (1997), 9, 19, 55, 60, 124
Asian Infrastructure Investment Bank, 138
Asia-Pacific Economic Cooperation meetings (2014), 137
Asia-Pacific region, 137, 143
assembly-and-processing capacities, 17, 67, 69, 124
Asus, 29
AT&T, 57
austerity, 100
Australia, 71

Baidu, 127, 144–45
Bai Fangquin, 114
Barrett, Craig, 67
Basic Telecommunications Service Agreement (WTO), 56
Beijing, 16, 21, 31, 114, 123; decentralization and, 40; economic restructuring and, 71
Beijing Media Corporation LTD., 106
Beijing Municipal Bureau of Radio, Film and Television, 110
Berlin Wall, 52
"best practices" reform, 45–49
BesTV, 112–13, 126; network convergence and, 116–17, 120
Blackberry, 94
Black Friday, 131
Blue Ocean Strategy, 48
brand names, 24, 90–91, 134–35
Brazil, 144–45
Britain, 11, 143
British Telecom, 143
broadband, 4, 13, 50–52, 71–74, 77; commanding-heights economy and, 69–71; e-commerce and, 65–69; economic restructuring and, 130, 133; markets for, 60–65; neoliberalism and, 58–60; state development and, 74–76; state policy and, 51–55; WTO entry and, 55–58
broadcasting, 96, 104, 106, 126; network convergence and, 101, 114–16; SARFT and, 111–12
Bureau of Letters and Visits, 29
Bush, George W., 59
business-to-business (B2B), 67

cable, 72, 126, 152; cultural industry and, 106; network convergence and, 101, 119, 121; SARFT and, 109–11, 117–18
Caixin Media, 75
Canada, 108, 119
capital, 5, 125–28, 148; corporate reforms and, 46–49; cultural industry and, 106; decentralization and, 36–41; domestic markets and, 151; economic restructuring and, 129; fixed-asset investment and, 150; industrialization and, 23; inequality and, 35, 49–50; neoliberalism and, 58; network convergence and, 114, 116, 121; rural networks and, 41–45; semiconductor chips and, 27; spatial rebalancing and, 50; state policy and, 9; switches and, 84; taxes and, 33; telephone networks and, 41, 43; transnational accumulation and, 146; western China and, 20. *See also* accumulation; foreign direct investment (FDI); transnational capital
capitalism, 3–5, 13, 125, 128; China model and, 33; Chinese-style of, 7; decentralization and, 36; expansionist logic of, 15; exports and, 24–26; industry and, 21–23; infrastructure and, 19–21; Intel and, 26–29; internet governance and, 141; network convergence and, 120; US hegemony and, 53; vertical reintegration and, 29–33; western China and, 14–18, 32–34; WTO and, 55–58. *See also* digital capitalism; globalization; transnational capital
Cavite, 27
CDMA (code division multiple access) standard, 82–83, 85, 89; CDMA2000 and, 80, 85, 88
censorship, 6, 102, 141
centralization, 10, 26; handset manufacturing and, 89; mobile communications and, 99. *See also* decentralization; regulation; state policy
Central Leading Group for Cyber Security and Informatization, 144
Changhong Electric Corporation, 22
Chen, Yang, 6
Chengdu, 25, 31–32, 42; Intel and, 26–27
Chengdu High-Tech Industrial Development Zone, 29
Chen Haofei, 92
China Academy of Social Sciences, 150
China Academy of Telecommunications Research, 87
China Broadcasting Network (CBN), 110
China Cable Television Network, 110–11
China Central Television (CCTV), 114–16, 118, 123
China Daily (newspaper), 145
China Development Bank, 110
China DTV Media, 115

China Electronics Corporation, 136
China Information Economic Society, 76
China Internet Network Information Center (CNNIC), 143
China Media Capital, 139–40
China Mobile, 46–49, 64; China-only standard and, 87; domestic markets and, 86; economic restructuring and, 130, 132; handset manufacturing and, 91–92; mobile communications and, 80, 99–100; Multimedia Broadcasting and, 97; production and, 135–36; Tietong and, 75; wireless applications and, 93, 95, 97
ChinaNet, 55
China Netcom, 46, 62, 66; neoliberalism and, 59; WTO and, 57
China Next-Generation Internet, 143
China-only standard, 86–88, 91
China Radio and Television Network Ltd, 111
China Railcom, 46
China Satellite Mobile Broadcasting Corporation, 97
China Telecom, 45–48, 64; development and, 75; domestic markets and, 82; e-commerce and, 66–67; economic restructuring and, 71, 73, 132; global subsidiary of, 143; markets and, 61–62; mobile communications and, 80; state policy and, 55; WTO and, 57
China Unicom, 66, 80, 82–83, 85–86; corporate reform and, 45, 47; development and, 75; internet governance and, 144; Research Institute of, 76; wireless applications and, 94–95
Chinese Academy of Science, 136
Chinese Communist Party (CCP), 16, 102, 104, 144. *See also* state policy
Chinese People's Political Consultative Conference, 127
Chiu, Willy, 132
Chongqing, 16, 23–26, 39, 71; telephone networks and, 42; vertical reintegration and, 29–33
Chongqing Cable Network, 119
Cisco Systems, 57–58, 135
Clarent, 57
class, 4–5, 9, 11

Clinton, Bill, 53
cloud computing, 4, 131–32
coastal regions, 14–15, 17, 19–21, 149; bias towards, 36–41; broadband and, 59; export-processing regime and, 24–26; markets and, 62; mobile communications and, 81; spatial rebalancing and, 50; state policy and, 53–54; telephone networks and, 43, 45; vertical reintegration and, 31
commanding heights economy, 51, 69–71, 151; communication networks and, 128; development and, 74; economic restructuring and, 77–78
commercialization, 110, 114
Commission of Foreign Trade and Economic Cooperation, 68
commodification, 115–16
communes, 42
communication networks, 2, 8, 13, 100–101, 147–48; cultural industry and, 105–8; cultural-system reform and, 102–5; digital capitalism and, 138–41; digital television and, 113–16, 119–22; economic restructuring and, 123–24, 128–33; production and, 134–38; SARFT and, 109–12, 116–18, 120–21. *See also* network convergence
Compal, 27–28
competition, 75–76, 149; broadband and, 52; corporate reform and, 45; economic restructuring and, 72–73, 77; network convergence and, 115; SARFT and, 112
consumers, 2–3, 5, 8, 150, 152; broadband and, 60–65; commanding-heights economy and, 70; communication networks and, 125–27; consumers of last resort and, 145; cultural industry and, 107; cultural-system reform and, 105; e-commerce and, 66; economic restructuring and, 50, 77, 129–31; industrialization and, 18; information hotspots for, 151; mobile communications and, 100; network convergence and, 101; production and, 134–38; spatial rebalancing and, 33; state policy and, 9; structural power of, 6; wages and, 34; western China and, 15; WTO and, 56

content, 92–97, 102, 114–15, 121, 149; aggregation platforms and, 97; communication networks and, 127; digital capitalism and, 139–40; entertainment and, 141; proprietary forms of, 150; SARFT and, 109–12. *See also* media
contract manufacturers, 29–33. *See also* manufacturing
Coolpad, 92
Copps, Michael J., 69
corporate reform, 101, 121, 149–50; "best practices" and, 45–49; communication networks and, 125; cultural industry and, 108; digital capitalism and, 138; economic restructuring and, 71–72; SARFT and, 110
corporations, 105–8, 148; communication networks and, 126–27; cultural-system reform and, 103–4; development and, 151; economic restructuring and, 129–30; internet governance and, 144; mixed-ownership structure and, 153; network convergence and, 102, 114–16, 119–20, 122; SARFT and, 109, 111, 117; state policy and, 10
costs, 31, 115, 149
CSM Media Research, 114
Cultural Revolution, 16. *See also* Maoist era
culture, 101–2, 116, 119; communication networks and, 126; industry of, 104–8, 138; reform of, 102–5; transnational accumulation and, 146; wireless applications and, 93
Cyber Monday, 131

Dalian, 28
data capacity, 62
data centers, 143–44
Datang, 87, 99
Davos, Switzerland, 1
decentralization, 33, 53, 56, 82, 109; telephone networks and, 36–41. *See also* centralization; local policy; neoliberalism
"Decision of the CCP Central Committee on Major Issues Pertaining to Deepening Reform of the Cultural System and Promoting the Great Development and Flourishing of Socialist Culture" (2012), 108
delinking strategy, 36, 86–88, 91–92, 98
demand, 6, 62, 75, 77, 102, 120, 150; cultural-system reform and, 104–5; overproduction and, 12; production and, 136; state policy and, 68
dependent development, 79, 81–82, 88
development, 3, 79, 97, 149–50; China model and, 33; communication networks and, 124; corporations and, 151; decentralization and, 36; dependent form of, 81–82; digital capitalism and, 12; economic restructuring and, 78; internet governance and, 144; markets and, 61; national champions and, 98; nationalism and, 152; network convergence and, 120; SARFT and, 109; state policy and, 10, 74–76; telephone networks and, 41–45; 2008 global economic criss and, 50; western China and, 14–15
development zones, 22–23
digital capitalism, 2, 5–7, 11–13, 138–41, 147, 150–51; communication networks and, 124; economic restructuring and, 134; SARFT and, 117; transnational accumulation and, 145. *See also* capitalism; globalization; transnational capital
Digital Capitalism (Schiller), 8
Digital Depression (Schiller), 3
digital television, 13, 100–101, 126; cultural industry and, 105–8; cultural-system reform and, 102–5; network convergence and, 113–16, 119–22; SARFT and, 109–12, 116–18, 120–21
Direct-to-home satellite, 21, 117, 119; cultural industry and, 106
distribution, 92–97, 138; cultural industry and, 106–7
domain names, 143
domestic markets, 13, 147, 150; capital and, 151; China model and, 33; China-only standard and, 87–88; commanding-heights economy and, 70; communication networks and, 125; cultural-system reform and, 104–5;

economic restructuring and, 129, 134; globalization and, 86; handset manufacturing and, 90, 92; mobile communications and, 81–85, 100; network convergence and, 114, 120; overproduction and, 12; policy and, 6; production and, 134–38; state policy and, 9; transnational accumulation and, 146; western China and, 15–16
Double 11, 130
downstream manufacturing, 2–3, 151
Dragon TV, 115
DreamWorks, 140

East Asia, 17, 20, 51, 76. *See also* Asian financial crisis
Eastern Europe, 52
e-commerce, 64–69, 145; commanding-heights economy and, 70; economic restructuring and, 130–31
economic restructuring, 1–4, 8, 13, 147–50, 152; broadband and, 51–52, 69–73, 77–78; communication networks and, 123–25, 128–34; consumption and, 50; cultural-system reform and, 104; development and, 74–76; e-commerce and, 69; export-processing regime and, 26; geopolitics and, 145; industrialization and, 18; markets and, 64; mobile communications and, 80–81, 98, 100; network convergence and, 101–2; vertical reintegration and, 31–32; western China and, 15; WTO and, 56. *See also* 2008 global economic criss
Electronic Business, 30
employment, 18, 129, 132, 149. *See also* labor
enclosure movement, 60
energy, 20–21
Enlight Media Group, 115
entertainment, 13, 64, 124, 138–39. *See also* media
environment, 132, 148
equity, 4–5
equity incentive plan, 116–17
Ericsson, 82–83, 85–86; Chongqing Ericsson and, 31; handset manufacturing and, 89
Eurasian continental railway, 20

Europe, 20, 124, 135, 137; broadband and, 59; China-only standard and, 87; economic restructuring and, 128–29; internet governance and, 143; state policy and, 53
exceptionalism, 6
export-processing regime, 5, 8, 13, 24–26, 148–49; broadband and, 51, 59; commanding-heights economy and, 69; communication networks and, 124–25; corporate reform and, 49–50; decentralization and, 38, 40; development and, 74; domestic markets and, 85; e-commerce and, 67; economic restructuring and, 76–77, 128–29; handset manufacturing and, 89; industry and, 21–23; inequality and, 35; infrastructure and, 19–21; Intel and, 26–29; markets and, 3; nationalism and, 152; state policy and, 9, 53; telephone networks and, 43; transnational accumulation and, 146; vertical reintegration and, 29–33; western China and, 14–18, 32–34; WTO and, 55–56

Federal Communications Commission (FCC), 56, 59, 69
fee-based gateways, 64, 93. *See also* pay sites; subscription services
feudalism, 16
fiber-optic cable, 45, 54, 72; broadband and, 59–60; commanding-heights economy and, 71; corporate reform and, 47; development and, 74, 76; domestic markets and, 85; markets and, 60; neoliberalism and, 58
film, 139–40; cultural industry and, 107–8; cultural-system reform and, 105; digital capitalism and, 139; SARFT and, 112
financialization, 3, 61, 116, 126, 128, 136
FITx (fiber to the x) scheme, 60
Five Year Plans, 152; Eighth (1991–1995) of, 41, 43, 82; Eleventh (2006–2010) of, 49, 61, 79, 104, 118; First (1953–1957) of, 16; Ninth (1996–2000) of, 18, 45; Second (1958–1962) of, 16; Seventh (1986–90) of, 82; Sixth (1981–1985) of, 37; Tenth (2001–2005) of, 45; Twelfth (2011–2015) of, 68, 71, 108

fixed-assets investment, 74, 77, 100
flat tax, 25
Flextronics, 25, 30
foreign direct investment (FDI), 22–23, 152; broadband and, 51; corporate reform and, 45–46, 48; decentralization and, 36, 40; domestic markets and, 82–83; economic restructuring and, 76; export-processing regime and, 24–25; handset manufacturing and, 88–89; industrialization and, 17–19; network convergence and, 115; state policy and, 53; transnational accumulation and, 146; vertical reintegration and, 33; wireless applications and, 93; WTO and, 55, 57. *See also* capital; transnational capital
Fortune 500, 26, 66
4G mobile communications, 13, 79–81, 99–100; China-only standard and, 88; development and, 75; economic restructuring and, 130; production and, 135
Foxconn, 27–28; Chongqing and, 26; suicides at, 25; vertical reintegration and, 29–33
free services, 59, 64
free-trade agreements, 137–38
frequency-division long-term evolution (FD-LTE), 99
Fujian, 38, 40, 43

gaming, 64
Gansu, 16, 118
General Administration of Press and Publications (GAPP), 103, 107
General Administration of Press, Publications, Radio, Film and Television, 126
General Electric, 132
geopolitics, 8, 11, 13; central Asia and, 21; mobile communications and, 97; transnational accumulation and, 145
Global Internet Governance Alliance, 145
globalization, 2, 7, 24, 148, 150–53; "best practices" and, 45–49; broadband and, 52; China model and, 33; Chinese entry into, 16; commanding-heights economy and, 70–71; communication networks and, 127; decentralization and, 36, 40; de-Westernizing of, 6; digital capitalism and, 11; domestic markets and, 86; e-commerce and, 66; economic restructuring and, 76–77, 133; handset manufacturing and, 88–92, 97–100; industrialization and, 17; internet governance and, 145; mobile communications and, 81; network convergence and, 120; production and, 136; spatial rebalancing and, 50; transnational accumulation and, 145–46; US domination and, 147; US hegemony and, 52–53; western China and, 20; wireless applications and, 92–96; WTO and, 55–58. *See also* capitalism; digital capitalism; network convergence; transnational capital
Global North, 20, 127, 134, 136; WTO and, 56
Global South, 20
global system for mobile communications (GSM), 45–49; domestic markets and, 82–83, 85–86; handset manufacturing and, 89–90. *See also* mobile communications
Golden Bridge Information Network, 54–55
Golden Customs, 54
Golden Projects, 54
Google, 143–44; wireless applications and, 94–96
go-out strategy, 85, 97, 124, 138, 143
"Government Guidelines for Foreign Investment in Telecommunications" (1995), 83
Government Procurement Center, 136
Great Firewall, 141
G20 Leader's Summit (2009), 3
Guangdong, 20, 37–40; e-commerce and, 67; export-processing regime and, 24–25; mobile communications and, 47; vertical reintegration and, 31
Guangxi, 20
"Guiding Opinion for the Converged Development of Traditional and New Media" (2014), 116

"Guiding Opinions on Deepening Reform of the Cultural System" (2005), 104
Guiyang, 20
Guizhou, 111, 114
Guizhou Satellite TV, 21, 114

Haidan District, 123
Hai'er, 90
handset manufacturing, 88–92, 97–100; wireless applications and, 93–96
Hart-Landsberg, Martin, 2, 134
Harvey, David, 7, 50
Harwit, Eric, 41
Henan, 31, 119
Hewlett-Packard, 29, 135
Hohhot, 20
Hollywood system, 138–41
home-base strategy, 81–85, 97; mobile communications and, 98; production and, 137–38. *See also* domestic markets
Hong Kong, 22–23, 26; communication networks and, 124; corporate reform and, 46; digital capitalism and, 140
household income, 145
Hu, Henry L., 120
Huang, Philip, 5
Huawei, 66, 100, 135, 137; China-only standard and, 87–88; domestic markets and, 83, 85–86; handset manufacturing and, 91–92
Hunan, 38
Hunan Satellite TV, 114
Hundt, Reed E., 56

IBM, 66, 131–32, 143
IMAX, 139
import-substitution policy, 82–83, 135; China-only standard and, 87; mobile communications and, 98; production and, 136; wireless applications and, 93
Industrial Revolution, 132
industry, 17–19, 148, 153; communication networks and, 125; cultural industry and, 108; development of, 150; economic restructuring and, 76; expansionist logic of, 15; export-processing regime and, 24; home-base strategy and, 81; internet governance and, 143; neo-industrialization strategy and, 68; telephone networks and, 41; western China and, 16, 21–23. *See also* manufacturing; production
inequality, 35, 51, 102, 125–27; corporate reform and, 47, 49–50; decentralization and, 40; economic restructuring and, 73, 130; markets and, 62
inflation, 127
information age, 68, 71; commanding-heights economy and, 70; superhighway concept and, 53
Information and the Crisis Economy (Schiller), 7
"Information Consumption: A New Expansion Engine of Domestic Demand" *(People's Daily)*, 70
Information Technology Agreement (ITA), 136–37
infrastructure, 13, 74, 76; Asian Infrastructure Investment Bank and, 138; economic restructuring and, 77; industrialization and, 23; internet governance and, 143; overproduction and, 12; state policy and, 9; western China and, 14, 19, 21. *See also* development; production
initial public ownership (IPOs), 105–6, 116
Inspur, 136
Intel, 26–29, 67, 143
intellectual property, 137
interactive TV, 140
International Market of Communication Programs, 141
International Telecommunications Union (ITU), 60, 109, 142; markets and, 61
internet, 13, 141–45; disruptive force of, 119–20. *See also* broadband; communication networks; network convergence
Internet Age, The (film), 123
internet bubble (2001), 24, 29–30, 64; broadband and, 60; China-only standard and, 87; corporate reform and, 47; neoliberalism and, 58
Internet Corporation for Assigned Names and Numbers (ICANN), 142, 144–45
Internet Governance Forum, 142

internet of things, 4, 131–32
Internet Plus, 1, 144; economic restructuring and, 133; production and, 136
internet-protocol networks (IP), 57, 59; communication networks and, 126; e-commerce and, 66; markets and, 62; SARFT and, 110
internet protocol television (IPTV), 112, 119, 121, 126
internet service providers (ISPs), 72; development and, 75
iPads, 31
iPhones, 31–32, 95
IPv6 routers, 143
iQiyi, 106, 127, 140
Ireland, 28
Israel, 28

Japan, 20, 51, 60, 70; economic restructuring and, 129; handset manufacturing and, 90; internet governance and, 143–44; production and, 135, 137; state policy and, 53
Jiangsu, 31, 37, 40, 71
Jin Bingliang, 116
Jingdong Mall, 131
Jinpeng, 87
Ji Zhengkun, 87
joint operating agreements, 106

Kazakhstan, 21
Kluver, Randolph, 6
Kumming, 20
Kupai, 135

labor, 5, 148–49, 153; capital and, 150; commodification of, 115; communication networks and, 127; decentralization and, 40; economic restructuring and, 72, 77, 128, 130–31; export-processing regime and, 25; global division of, 3; personnel-system reform and, 116; spatial rebalancing and, 33; vertical reintegration and, 30–32; western China and, 15. *See also* peasants
laissez-faire, 10
land speculation, 23
"last mile" connection, 43

Latin America, 20, 137
Leadcore Technology, 100
Lenovo, 90–92, 135–36
Lhasa, 21
Li, Robin, 127, 144
Liaoning, 40
liberalism, 10, 119, 148; broadband and, 52; internet governance and, 141
liberalization, 17, 19; corporate reform and, 47; economic restructuring and, 76; market reform and, 143; mobile communications and, 98; production and, 135; state policy and, 54; telephone networks and, 41; transnational accumulation and, 146; WTO and, 56–57. *See also* neoliberalism
libertarianism, 144
licensing, 87, 97
Li Deshui, 129
Li Keqiang, 1, 130, 133
Lin Chun, 16, 33, 127
Linux operating system, 94, 136
Liu Zhongyi, 43
Li Yiquing, 111
local policy, 149, 151–52; coastal regions, 36–41; communication networks and, 126, 128; development and, 74; digital capitalism and, 138; economic restructuring and, 73; export-processing regime and, 25; handset manufacturing and, 89; mobile communications and, 97; network convergence and, 114; SARFT and, 111; telephone networks and, 41–45; western China and, 21–22. *See also* western China
Loongson central processing unit, 136
Lou Qinjian, 87
LTE standard, 99
Lucent, 58, 85–86
Lu Yimin, 66

Ma, Jack, 144–45
Macao, 124
"made for China" strategy, 134–38
Malaysia, 25, 27
Mansell, Robin, 6
manufacturing, 2, 8, 13, 134–38, 151; broadband and, 51; capital and, 84;

China-only standard and, 88; Chinese-style capitalism and, 7; digital capitalism and, 138–41; e-commerce and, 67–68; economic restructuring and, 76, 123–24, 128–33; export-processing regime and, 25; handsets and, 88–92, 97–100; industrialization and, 18; overproduction and, 12; vertical reintegration and, 29–33; western China and, 15; wireless applications and, 92–96. *See also* industry; production

Maoist era, 16–17, 37; cultural-system reform and, 102; decentralization and, 36; technonationalism and, 54; telephone networks and, 41–42

market reform, 8, 13, 147–48, 151; "best practices" and, 45–49; communication networks and, 123; cultural-system reform and, 102–3; liberalization and, 143; mobile communications and, 81; SARFT and, 111; telephone networks and, 42; WTO and, 57

markets, 4, 6, 51–52, 59, 149; broadband and, 60–65; China-only standard and, 86; commanding-heights economy and, 71; communication networks and, 126, 128; cultural industry and, 106–7; cultural-system reform and, 103, 105; decentralization and, 40; digital capitalism and, 139–40; e-commerce and, 67; economic restructuring and, 77, 130, 133; entertainment and, 141; export and, 3; failure of, 74, 76, 78; handset manufacturing and, 90–91; mobile communications and, 97; network convergence and, 114, 116; regulation and, 150; SARFT and, 109, 117; state policy and, 9–11, 53; transnational accumulation and, 146; wireless applications and, 96; WTO and, 56

Marks, Michael, 25

media, 13, 100–101, 126–28; cultural industry and, 105–8; cultural-system reform and, 102–5; digital capitalism and, 138–41; digital TV and, 113–16, 119–22; economic restructuring and, 123–24, 128–34; entertainment and, 141; production and, 134–38; SARFT and, 109–12, 116–18, 120–21; state system of, 21

MediaTek, 90, 92

Mianyang, 119

Miao Wei, 70

Microsoft, 136, 143–44

Middle East, 137

migrant workers, 38–39

military, 22

minimum-wage standard, 31, 128

Ministry of Commerce, 25, 89

Ministry of Culture (MOC), 103–4, 108

Ministry of Electronics Industry (MEI), 22, 45, 54–55

Ministry of Finance (MOF), 75

Ministry of Foreign Trade and Cooperation, 57

Ministry of Industry and Information (MIIT), 74–75, 127, 135; commanding-heights economy and, 70; corporate reform and, 45; economic restructuring and, 71, 73; handset manufacturing and, 91; internet governance and, 142; mobile communications and, 80, 99; SARFT and, 111

Ministry of Information Industry (MII), 25, 45, 47–48, 83; China-only standard and, 87; e-commerce and, 68; handset manufacturing and, 89; neoliberalism and, 58; SARFT and, 109; state policy and, 55

Ministry of Posts and Communications (MPT), 37–39, 45; communication networks and, 125; corporate reform and, 45, 47, 49; decentralization and, 40; domestic markets and, 82; state policy and, 54–55; telephone networks and, 42–43; WTO and, 56–57

Ministry of Science and Technology (MOST), 68, 73; SARFT and, 109, 111

mixed-ownership reform, 116

mobile communications, 97–100; branding and, 90–91; China-only standard and, 86–88; domestic markets and, 81–85; next generation of, 79–80; production chain and, 88–90; wireless applications and, 92–96. *See also* 2G; 3G; 4G; global system for mobile communications (GSM)

Mobile Market app store, 95–96
monopolies, 9, 55, 75, 149; antidumping investigations and, 137; corporate reform and, 45, 47; cultural industry and, 106; economic restructuring and, 131; WTO and, 56
Monternet, 64, 93
Motorola, 58, 83, 85, 89–90
Mueller, Milton L., 142, 152

Nanhai County, 47
Nanning, 20
National Bureau of Statistics, 129
national champions, 52, 57, 68, 83, 97, 152; development and, 98; mobile communications and, 99; network convergence and, 102; production and, 136. *See also* pillar industries
National Development and Reform Commission (NDRC), 57, 75–76, 125, 139; economic restructuring and, 73, 133; handset manufacturing and, 89; SARFT and, 109
National Development Bank, 25
National High Technology Research and Development Program, 64
nationalism, 80, 136, 149, 152; transnational accumulation and, 146. *See also* techno-economic nationalism
National Joint Conference on State Economic Informatization, 54
National Security Agency (NSA), 135
Naughton, Barry, 21
neoclassical economics, 10, 74, 150
neo-industrialization strategy, 68
neoliberalism, 2, 52, 58–60, 148; cultural-system reform and, 103; economic restructuring and, 71, 77; industrialization and, 17; network convergence and, 121; spatial rebalancing and, 50; WTO and, 55–56. *See also* decentralization; regulation
Netease, 93
Netflix, 140
network convergence, 6, 100–101, 151; communication networks and, 126; cultural industry and, 105–8; cultural-system reform and, 102–5; digital television and, 113–16, 119–22; internet governance and, 141–45; SARFT and, 109–12, 116–18, 120–21. *See also* communication networks; globalization; networks
new-media, 6, 106, 126, 140, 150. *See also* digital capitalism
newspapers, 107, 116
New York Stock Exchange, 58, 147
New Zealand, 71
1989 student movement, 52
Nokia, 82–83, 86, 93–95; China-only standard and, 87; handset manufacturing and, 89–90
nonstate actors, 12, 106–7, 127; domestic markets and, 82–83; network convergence and, 116; proprietary content and, 98
Normile, Dennis, 30
Nortel, 58, 83, 85–86
North America, 20, 59, 128
Number 1 Project, 118

oligopoly, 130
One Hundred Electronics Enterprises, 68
online video, 106, 112, 141
operating system market, 93–95
operational assets, 104
Organization for Economic Co-operation and Development (OECD), 7, 134
original design manufacturers (ODM), 30. *See also* manufacturing
outward looking economy, 17, 19, 21–22
overseas markets, 85–86
over-the-top technology (OTT), 120, 140
Ovi Store, 93–95. *See also* Nokia
ownership structure, 41–42, 148. *See also* corporate reform

paperless economy, 54
parallel economy, 51
Party Congresses, 68, 109, 116, 125; commanding-heights economy and, 70; cultural-system reform and, 103–4; SARFT and, 109
pay TV, 118, 121, 127
Pearl River delta, 26
peasants, 149, 153; Intel and, 29; network convergence and, 114; telephone

networks and, 43; vertical reintegration and, 31. *See also* labor
Penang, 27
People's Congresses, 75, 133, 144
People's Daily (newspaper), 59, 70, 142, 144
personal computers, 27–28; vertical reintegration and, 29–33. *See also* manufacturing
personnel-system reform, 116
Philippines, 27
Philips, 89–90
pillar industries, 2–4, 99, 108, 119, 152, 152. *See also* national champions
piracy, 140–41
planning economy, 51, 53, 71, 77. *See also* state policy
Plenary Sessions, 105, 108, 125
Political Consultative Congress, 144
postcolonialism, 12
Post & Telephone administration (PTAs), 37–38, 40–41, 43; telephone networks and, 42
Posts and Telecommunications bureaus (P&T bureaus), 36–38; decentralization and, 40; domestic markets and, 82
Powerleader, 136
predatory behavior, 74
privatization, 126, 136, 146, 148
production, 2–3, 5, 134–38, 151; cultural-system reform and, 104–5; digital capitalism and, 138–41; domestic demand, 12; economic restructuring and, 123–24, 128–33; export-processing regime and, 24; fixed-asset investment and, 150; globalization and, 16, 149; handset manufacturing and, 88–92, 97–100; industrialization and, 18; military orientation of, 22; network convergence and, 114–16, 121; structural power of, 6, 8; transnational accumulation and, 145–46; western China and, 14, 21; wireless applications and, 92–96. *See also* industry; manufacturing
propaganda, 10, 117, 120, 138; Department of, 112
proprietary commerce, 79, 93, 98, 150
protectionism, 86, 138
public institutions, 104, 115, 121, 148; broadcasting and, 126; cultural industry and, 105–8; cultural-system reform and, 103–4; SARFT and, 110
public-interest concept, 102, 104, 117
public service, 74, 76, 126, 128, 150; corporate reform and, 47; cultural-system reform and, 104–5; economic restructuring and, 77; network convergence and, 114, 120–22; SARFT and, 111, 117–18
publishing houses, 107, 116
Pudong District, 57
Pun Ngai, 30–31

Qingdao, 110
Qing dynasty, 15
Qinzhou, 20
Qualcomm, 28, 82–83, 85, 135, 145; mobile communications and, 80, 100
Quanta, 30
quotas, 43

radio, 107, 110, 112
Radio and Television Shanghai, 108
regulation, 8, 74, 101, 150; corporate reform and, 45–47; counter-deregulation approach and, 59; cultural-system reform and, 102; decentralization and, 33; digital capitalism and, 139; e-commerce and, 67–68; economic restructuring and, 78; entertainment and, 141; mobile communications and, 99; re-regulation and, 10, 81; SARFT and, 111–12; western China and, 15. *See also* state policy
robot strategy, 32
router markets, 135
rural areas, 73, 75, 77, 125, 133; corporate reform and, 47, 49; cultural-system reform and, 104; inequality and, 35; markets and, 62; network convergence and, 119; spatial rebalancing and, 50; telephone networks and, 41–45

Samsung, 85, 134; handset manufacturing and, 90–91; wireless applications and, 95–96
Schiller, Dan, 3, 8, 48, 133; digital capitalism and, 11; internet governance and, 141

Schiller, Herbert, 7
security, 81, 116, 120–21, 126, 135; SARFT and, 117
semiconductor chips, 27, 90–92, 99–100; commanding-heights economy and, 69; production and, 135–36
Semiconductor Manufacturing International Corporation (SMIC), 28
"Several Instructional Opinions about Accelerating the Development of Mobile Communications Industries" (1998), 89
Shambaugh, David L., 134
Shandong, 71
Shanghai, 21, 24, 27–28, 115; IP networks and, 57; vertical reintegration and, 31
Shanghai Media and Entertainment Group (SMEG), 108
Shanghai Media Group (SMG), 108, 112, 115–17, 120, 139
Shanghai Oriental DreamWorks Film, 140
Shanxi, 16, 22–23
Shekou Industrial Zone, 36
Shenzhen, 25, 38; Special Economic Zone of, 36
Sichuan, 16, 20, 22–23; corporate reform and, 48; decentralization and, 40; economic restructuring and, 133; export-processing regime and, 24; Intel and, 26–29; network convergence and, 119; telephone networks and, 42; vertical reintegration and, 31
Siemens, 86–87, 89–90
Silicon Valley, 27
Silk Road Fund, 138
Sina, 93
Singapore, 51, 71
Singles Day, 131
small- and medium-size enterprises (SMEs), 66–67, 75, 77
smart technology, 66, 92–97, 126, 131–32, 135; commanding-heights economy and, 70; replacement of, 100; smart-cities and, 66
Snowden, Edward, 135, 141
social-engineering campaign, 62
social interests, 9, 75–76; redistribution projects and, 150

socialism, 4–5, 16, 52; communication networks and, 128; decentralization and, 36; democracy and, 152; digital capitalism and, 12; economic restructuring and, 72; international socialist movement and, 52; market economy of, 53; SARFT and, 109, 117
soft power, 138–39
software development, 7, 135
Sohu, 93, 140
Sony, 89
Southern Publishing and Media Corporation, 116
South Korea, 20, 62, 135, 140, 144; broadband and, 51, 60; handset manufacturing and, 90
Soviet Union, 16, 52, 101
spatial rebalancing, 15, 19, 21, 149; China model and, 33; corporate reform and, 50; export-processing regime and, 26; Intel and, 29; vertical reintegration and, 32. *See also* economic restructuring
special economic zones, 17, 19, 36–37, 40, 53
Spreadtrum, 100
Standardization Administration, 87
State Administration of Radio, Film and Television (SARFT), 96–97, 126; digital TV and, 109–12, 116–18, 120–21
State Council, 37, 54, 74, 76, 106, 108; cultural-system reform and, 104; decentralization and, 40; e-commerce and, 68; economic restructuring and, 131; mobile communications and, 80; production and, 136; SARFT and, 109, 111
State Council Information Office, 143
State Development and Planning Commission, 17, 19
State-Owned Assets Supervision and Administration Commission (SASAC), 62, 68, 73–74, 116, 125
state-owned enterprises (SOE) reform, 23
State Planning Commission, 17
State Planning Committee, 41
state policy, 3, 5–6, 8, 147–49, 151; broadband and, 52; China-only standard and, 86–88; communication networks

and, 124, 127; cultural industry and, 107; cultural-system reform and, 102–3; demand, 68; dependent development and, 81–82; development and, 74–76; digital capitalism and, 11–12, 139; domestic markets and, 83–86; economic restructuring and, 73, 77, 132; handset manufacturing and, 88–92; internet governance and, 141–45; markets and, 9–11, 62; media and, 21; mobile communications and, 79–81, 97–100; neoliberalism and, 58–60; network convergence and, 101–2, 114–16, 119–20; planning economy and, 51; western China and, 15; wireless applications and, 92–96; WTO and, 55–58. *See also* economic restructuring

Steinfeld, Edward S., 53
stimulus packages, 71, 74
subscription services, 100, 106, 110, 127
subsidiaries, 103, 105–7, 114
suicide, 25
Sun Yusheng, 115, 118
supply, 88, 98–99, 150
Sweden, 143
switch technology, 43, 45, 54–55; capital and, 84; domestic markets and, 82–83; WTO and, 57
Symbian operating system, 94–95

Taiwan, 25–26, 51, 124, 134, 140; handset manufacturing and, 89–92; semiconductor chips and, 27; vertical reintegration and, 29
Tang Xiaoyan, 76
tariffs, 43, 46, 53
taxes, 33
TCL corporation, 90, 139
TD-SCDMA standard, 80, 86–88, 91–92, 99–100; economic restructuring and, 130; production and, 135; wireless applications and, 95
techno-economic nationalism, 12, 52, 80–81, 97, 136, 149; economic restructuring and, 77. *See also* nationalism
Telecommunications Act of 1996 (US), 56, 58
Telecommunications Decree (2000), 48

telephone networks, 36–41, 53, 62, 77; local development of, 41–45
"telephone to every township" campaign, 42, 48–49, 117; SARFT and, 117
television, 96–97, 107, 119, 121; cultural-system reform and, 105; digital capitalism and, 140; SARFT and, 110, 112, 118. *See also* digital television
Television Technology Corporation, 140
Tencent, 93
Texas Instruments, 28
Third Front project, 16, 22–23
3rd Generation Partnership Project (3GPP), 99
Third Industrial Revolution, 132
3-D films, 139
3G mobile communications, 13, 49, 79–81, 91, 97, 99–100; China-only standard and, 87–88; development and, 74–75; economic restructuring and, 130; handset manufacturing and, 92; production and, 135; wireless applications and, 95
Tian, Edward, 59
Tianyu, 92
Tibet, 119
Tietong, 75
time-division long-term evolution (TD-LTE), 99
ToonMax Media, 115
tourism, 105
transnational capital, 2–3, 5, 7–8, 12, 147–50; accumulation and, 146; broadband and, 51; commanding-heights economy and, 71; communication networks and, 124, 128; consumption and, 34; corporate reform and, 48–49; decentralization and, 40; development and, 74; de-Westernizing and, 6; digital capitalism and, 140; domestic markets and, 82; e-commerce and, 66, 68; export-processing regime and, 25; foreign ownership ban and, 81; geopolitics and, 145; handset manufacturing and, 91; homegrown origin of, 152; industrialization and, 17–18; inequality and, 35; internet governance and, 143–44; mobile communications and, 97, 99;

transnational capital (*continued*):
production and, 135, 138; state policy and, 9, 54; telephone networks and, 43; vertical reintegration and, 29, 32; western China and, 15; WTO and, 55–58. *See also* capitalism; digital capitalism; globalization

Trans-Pacific Partnership (TPP), 143

transportation, 20

"trickle down" theory, 42

2G mobile communications, 81–82, 97; China-only standard and, 87; domestic markets and, 86; handset manufacturing and, 92

2008 global economic crisis, 1–3, 12–13, 147–48; broadband and, 51; China-only standard and, 87; communication networks and, 125; development and, 50; economic restructuring and, 69, 128; export-processing regime and, 25; mobile communications and, 79–80; network convergence and, 101, 121; production and, 134; SARFT and, 111; spatial rebalancing and, 33; state policy and, 9; vertical reintegration and, 30; western China and, 14. *See also* economic restructuring

United Kingdom, 11, 143

United Nations, 142

United States, 2, 7, 60, 83, 123–24; Chinese markets and, 85; commanding-heights economy and, 69–70; corporate reform and, 46; decentralization and, 36; digital capitalism and, 140; domination by, 52–53, 147, 150; economic restructuring and, 71, 129, 131–33; export-processing regime and, 24; handset manufacturing and, 88; internet governance and, 141–45; mobile communications and, 80; neoliberalism and, 58–59; production and, 134–35, 137; SARFT and, 108; semiconductor chips and, 27–28; state policy and, 10, 53–54; Trade Representative of, 140; transnational accumulation and, 145; wireless applications and, 93; WTO and, 56–57

universal service fund, 47–50, 75, 133

urban areas, 22–23, 37–38, 72–73, 77; communication networks and, 125; corporate reform and, 47–49; decentralization and, 36, 40; development and, 74–75; inequality and, 35; markets and, 62; open cities and, 17; SARFT and, 109; spatial rebalancing and, 50; state policy and, 9, 55; telephone networks and, 41–44; WTO and, 56

US-China Telecommunications Summit (1999), 57

utilities, 73, 76

value-added services, 48, 50, 92–97; communication networks and, 126; network convergence and, 121; SARFT and, 117; WTO and, 56

venture capital, 58, 93

vertical integration, 29–33, 93

Vietnam, 27, 134

Vnet, 64

Vocaltso, 57

wages, 2, 5, 72, 130, 133; accumulation and, 149; consumption and, 34; minimum-wage and, 31–32; vertical reintegration and, 31

Wang Zinzhou, 99

Wasu, 111, 113, 116, 118, 120, 126; digital capitalism and, 139

WCDMA standard, 80, 87–88

web-enabled enterprises. *See* e-commerce

Web 2.0, 127, 136

western China, 13–18, 32–34; communication networks and, 125; corporate reform and, 49; decentralization and, 40; industry and, 21–26; infrastructure and, 19–21; Intel and, 26–29; mobile communications and, 47; network convergence and, 119; SARFT and, 110; telephone networks and, 41; vertical reintegration and, 29–33

Western China Development Program (WCDP), 14, 19–21, 23, 25, 31; corporate reform and, 47–48; vertical reintegration and, 31

Western society, 20, 53, 100, 149; capitalist crises and, 7
Windows operating system, 94–95
Winseck, Dwayne, 119
wireless networks, 69, 92–96; applications for, 93–97; mobile communications and, 98
World Economic Forum, 1
World Summit on the Information Society (WSIS), 142
World Trade Organization (WTO), 26, 66, 85, 125, 137; corporate reform and, 45; entry to, 55–58; industrialization and, 18; neoliberalism and, 58; semiconductor chips and, 28; state policy and, 9; western China and, 24
Wostore, 95. *See also* China Unicom
Wuhan, 71
Wu Jichuan, 47, 58

Xi'an, 25
Xiang Huaicheng, 68
Xiao Hua, 91
Xiaomi, 91, 135
Xi Jinping, 144
Xinjiang, 20–21, 111
Xu Guangchan, 109
Xu Yu, 87

Yang Peifang, 76
Yangtze River, 20
Youku-Tudou, 106, 127, 140
Yuezhi Zhao, 117
Yunnan, 20, 119; Department of Culture of, 138

Zeng Peiyan, 19
Zhang Haitao, 118
Zhang Haito, 109
Zhangjiang HiTech Park, 24
Zhao Houlin, 61, 70, 142
Zhejiang, 21, 40, 46, 111
Zhejiang Radio and Television Group, 118
Zhengzhou, 31
Zhu Rongji, 56–57
ZTE, 83, 85, 91–92; China-only standard and, 87–88; mobile communications and, 99; production and, 135, 137

YU HONG is an assistant professor in the School of Communication at USC Annenberg. She is the author of *Labor, Class Formation, and China's Informationized Policy of Economic Development*.

THE GEOPOLITICS OF INFORMATION

Digital Depression: Information Technology and Economic Crisis   *Dan Schiller*
Signal Traffic: Critical Studies of Media Infrastructures   *Edited by Lisa Parks and Nicole Starosielski*
Media in New Turkey: The Origins of an Authoritarian Neoliberal State   *Bilge Yesil*
Goodbye iSlave: A Manifesto for Digital Abolition   *Jack Linchuan Qiu*
Networking China: The Digital Transformation of the Chinese Economy   *Yu Hong*

The University of Illinois Press
is a founding member of the
Association of American University Presses.

―――――――――――――――――――

Composed in 10.25/13 Marat Pro
with Trade Gothic Condensed display
by Kirsten Dennison
at the University of Illinois Press
Cover designed by Dustin J. Hubbart
Cover illustration: hxdyl/Shutterstock.com

University of Illinois Press
1325 South Oak Street
Champaign, IL 61820-6903
www.press.uillinois.edu